MANAGING SECURITY OVERSEAS

Protecting Employees and Assets in Volatile Regions

MANAGING
SECURITY
OVERSEAS

Protecting Employees and Assets
in Volatile Regions

SCOTT ALAN AST

CRC Press
Taylor & Francis Group
Boca Raton   London   New York

CRC Press is an imprint of the
Taylor & Francis Group, an **informa** business

Auerbach Publications
Taylor & Francis Group
6000 Broken Sound Parkway NW, Suite 300
Boca Raton, FL 33487-2742

© 2010 by Taylor & Francis Group, LLC
Auerbach is an imprint of Taylor & Francis Group, an Informa business

No claim to original U.S. Government works
Printed in the United States of America on acid-free paper
10 9 8 7 6 5 4 3 2 1

International Standard Book Number-13: 978-1-4398-0467-4 (Hardcover)

Library of Congress Cataloging-in-Publication Data

Ast, Scott Alan.
    Managing security overseas : protecting employees and assets in volatile regions / Scott Alan Ast.
        p. cm.
    "A CRC title."
    Includes bibliographical references and index.
    ISBN 978-1-4398-0467-4 (acid-free paper)
        1. Corporations, American--Foreign countries--Security measures. 2. International business enterprises--Security measures. 3. Corporations, American--Employees--Protection. 4. Americans--Employment--Foreign countries.--Protection. 5. Business travel--Safety measures. I. Title.

HD2785.A88 2009
658.4'73--dc22   2009006646

Visit the Taylor & Francis Web site at
http://www.taylorandfrancis.com

and the Auerbach Web site at
http://www.auerbach-publications.com

CONTENTS

PREFACE

At the time this book was being finalized, three serious international security incidents took place in quick succession. Two of these would impact citizens around the world, and news networks would cover the incidents intensely, with the occurrences of the second incident quickly supplanting the media's insatiable interest in the first, while shifting the world's attention from one country to another in an instant. The third incident did not make world or even local headlines, and not many persons would have even known about it taking place. But, all three occurrences represented the kinds of events for which we in corporate security and crisis management must prepare for. All three represented incidents that either escalated in intensity to a point that required critical decision making involving many departments of major corporations, or happened quickly, like a punch to the solar plexus, leaving us gasping for air while we struggled to determine who was in harm's way and what needed to be done immediately to protect the lives of those we were charged to protect.

On Tuesday, November 25, 2008, thousands of protestors belonging to the People's Alliance for Democracy marched on the Suvarnabhumi and Don Muang airports in Bangkok, Thailand, after months of occupying the grounds surrounding Government House to protest what they claimed was corruption in the current government regime. What began as the blocking of some taxi cabs entering and exiting the airport, led to the cancellation of all flights from the Suvarnabhumi International Airport on November 26 due to thousands of protestors disobeying police orders to not pass barricades. At least 100,000 travelers were left stranded. The situation grew tense as police and the government vowed to seize control and retake the airport, while some protestors advised the media they were prepared to die if attempts were taken to remove them before the government resigned. On Sunday, November 30, reports began to trickle out that explosions had taken place at the prime minister's compound, occupied by protestors since August 2008. Other explosions were reported at an antigovernment television station and on a roadway leading to the occupied domestic airport, Don Muang. Members of the protest group blamed the government for the explosions.

On Wednesday, November 26, 2008, at approximately 10:30 p.m. local time, gunmen armed with AK-47s and grenades began a coordinated and complex attack on several locations within Mumbai, India. Targets included three hotels, a railway station, a Jewish center, a police station, a movie theater, a café, a hospital, and a taxi cab. At least 125 persons were believed to be killed in the attack, with up to 325 injured. Targets were believed to be chosen due to the likelihood that Westerners would be present at five-star hotels, popular restaurants, and night spots, and the availability of many targets at a mass transit station. Westerners were known to have been culled from groups of people rounded up by the attackers, with specific attention given to locating those persons with U.S. and British passports. The frontal attacks and assaults with hostages being taken reminded many of the 1972 Munich Olympics attack.

As the first reports were received by those in U.S. corporate security charged with monitoring world events and such situations, those reports of gunfire taking place in Mumbai, of unknown location and origin, another report was streaming into a corporate security office.

On November 27, in the city of Jos, Nigeria, capital of the Plateau State, ethnic and religious violence broke while votes were being tallied for the Jos North Local Government Area elections. By November 29, reports were filtering out that hundreds of people had been killed and the Nigerian Red Cross estimated that up to 10,000 people had fled the fighting between Christian and Muslim villagers. Raging gun battles had erupted between state security police and people protesting election results as the Plateau State Independent Electoral Commission estimated that the ruling People's Democratic Party won 16 of 17 council areas of the state. There were sub-stantiated reports that the police and military had used lethal force killing approximately 100 civilians. At least 300 Muslim bodies were reported to have been taken to the city of Jos central mosque.

For security professionals with operations and or personnel in these affected cities and regions, it was going to be a very busy weekend. In the United States, it was a long weekend for many celebrating Thanksgiving. There are many such weekends, actually, when you are part of a multinational corporation's security force. I guess one should give thanks for job security.

INTRODUCTION

When I was a young boy, growing up in the Midwest city of Kansas City, Kansas, I dreamed, like most kids, of seeing the world. I had two older brothers who were serving in the armed forces while stationed in Panama and Vietnam. I began to thumbtack world maps to my wall, much to the chagrin of my mom. I listened to the news on television and radio. I bought an old short-wave radio to listen to the British Broadcasting Corporation news and broadcasts from all around the world into early in the morning hours. I read the *New York Times* and *Washington Post*, the *Christian Science Monitor*, and magazines such as *Time* and *Newsweek*. I wanted to go to as many of the countries that I saw on these maps as possible. By listening to and reading the news, I recognized that the world had complex issues, struggles and altercations, social and political unrest, and wars. In school, I was fascinated with history, and wound up earning a BA in political science focusing on international relations. I then earned a master's degree in public administration with international business attracting my attention. One of my brothers served in Vietnam, and a cousin gave his life in service to his country. My middle brother served in the Army, training jungle experts in survival tactics. The world was changing, and while my profession of corporate security some might say makes me more naturally suspicious than most, I remain optimistic that world situations can and will improve. I had no idea when I was starting out that later in my career doing my job in hostile areas would get me shot at with rifles and rockets.

Volatile: adj. 1. Evaporating quickly. 2. a) Unstable; explosive. b) Fickle.

Webster's New World Dictionary

Volatile is an interesting word. The word might be used to describe an unstable world or one's surrounding environment. It might be phrased to illustrate a potentially explosive situation or circumstances. A cynic might consider the world a fickle place, to be sure. The title of this book might lead some to consider that I am paranoid about the world, or that I see only threats and difficulties. On the contrary, during my travels and discussions around the world, I have been constantly reminded and surprised by the good people I have encountered in faraway places. I know that there are many places on this planet where one can travel and feel and be perfectly safe, comfortable, and enjoy the beauties and wonders one might encounter. On the other hand, I also know of and have been to many locations where one's survival and security depend on keeping your wits about you, and in acting in a very careful manner. These are locations where being a Westerner is not a benefit, but can be a risk.

I am referring to volatile situations, circumstances, and locations in this book in order to provide you, the reader, with tools you might utilize in order to make your jobs a little easier. The word *volatile*, some might think, is pejorative in nature. How can a location or country be inherently volatile? I am referring to locations that, due to the propensity of man-made events, such as lawlessness, robberies, theft, kidnap, and extortion. Some locations are prone to natural disasters, such as severe weather, hurricanes, typhoons, earthquakes, tsunamis, volcanoes, and other occurrences, which makes working and residing in such areas a difficult endeavor. In some instances, governments declare their hostilities toward the government of the United States, or Western governments in general. Such pronouncements make it more difficult, and often nearly impossible, for Westerners/expats to successfully travel or work in such regions.

In this book I will attempt to provide you with the benefits of my experience—by way of my mistakes and successes—over 28 years in government and corporate security and crisis management. The experience I am concentrating on is that which has to do with protecting people and assets around the world, specifically in volatile regions.

The preparations and components of the protection of your people and assets might originate from paper plans, well constructed, exercised, and practiced. The structures within which you house your employees, or the offices where they work, might require blast protection—such as setbacks from roadways or access points, or laminates on windows to prevent the effects of shattering and shrapnel. You may be required to delve deeply into the world of physical security. You might be working or traveling in some areas where you will require armed security professionals with you, personal security details (PSDs), bodyguards, or other variations of these. You may require the use of armored vehicles.

I could not have predicted when I first began my security career that I would someday be entrusted with the security and safety for personnel working in Iraq and Afghanistan, Algeria, China, Colombia, Egypt, Indonesia, Israel, Mexico, Pakistan, the former Soviet Union, Venezuela, Vietnam, and dozens of other locations around the world. But having been involved now with extremely successful multinational corporations with broad-ranging foreign-based operations, it has become something I have learned to deal with as a challenge and with the confidence that this experience brings.

I did not have a manual I could turn to explaining the do's and don'ts of protecting people internationally. I learned by the seat of my pants. It was not always easy, but it has been rewarding. I can sit here today as I write this book and let you, the reader, know that during my career I never lost any employees who were operating outside of the United States due to a terrorist event, criminal incident, or natural disaster. I cannot say the same with respect to contract protection personnel working in Afghanistan and Iraq. I was involved with projects that did result in the loss of lives of security contractors who were working in support of reconstruction engineering projects in several locations within Iraq. I tell myself that this could not have been avoided, that working in war zones by its very nature is a roll of the dice, a crapshoot. The law of averages tells us that if you go out on the road day after day in areas where snipers, ambushes, roadside bombs, and vehicle-borne improvised explosive devices (VBIEDs) are commonplace, your luck will run out. I would like to commend here and now those brave men and women contractors who have lost their lives in Afghanistan and Iraq, and especially the men who were part of PSDs operating in these countries for projects with which I was involved.

To be perfectly honest, when I first began dealing with international security and crisis management, it was at the tail end of the 1970s' international terrorists' reign—post-hijackings, as well as past incidents at the Munich Olympics and various Popular Front for the Liberation of Palestine (PFLP) incidents. There were Japanese Red Army terrorist acts around the world, Abu Nidal Organization attacks, and other spectacular incidents. And yet, for the most part, Americans were focused inward, and travel was for fun. Later, when we were turning the corner on crime at home, international terrorism was still a major factor in larger American cities, but most Americans were feeling pretty comfortable at home. The Middle East would remain the Middle East, and tensions there would always be present.

The Americans who had been taken from the Tehran Embassy were released in 1980. The United States would soon be dabbling in El Salvador, Nicaragua, Grenada, Lebanon, and Panama, but again, Americans felt reasonably secure in the knowledge that they could travel the world with relative ease and security. I began to quickly realize, however, that Americans living and working overseas would be faced with the dilemma of carrying out their efforts in environs where everyday life—the things that most of us take for granted, going shopping, taking our children to school, and driving to and from the office—could be a potentially life-threatening endeavor.

Later in my security career, I was part of security briefings that took place in 1988 for a group of pharmaceutical research scientists who would be spending 2½ weeks working in the Soviet Union. Most of the group considered it silly and pointless when a retired CIA case officer advised them of the many ways they might be compromised or how attempts to recruit them might take place. Their biggest concern, it seemed, would be how to keep up with the frequent and relentless vodka toasts that awaited them at get-acquainted business dinners. Security managers were faced with these reactions quite often in the 1980s and early 1990s. What intelligence and security professionals preached at this time was: There is a Cold War; the Soviet Union is volatile toward the United States, and efforts could be made to compromise you or get any information they want/need from you by hook or by crook. What most professionals, engineers, scientists, academics, and others saw was a "cold war." Around the world there were in fact "hot wars" that raged. But, we Americans saw ourselves much as our European cousins, the British, once saw themselves at the height of their empire.

Fast-forward to the conclusion of the first Gulf War, the rise of the Taliban, 9/11, and the multitude of horrors since, and it is increasingly less difficult to gain the attention of corporations to preach the religion of protecting personnel and assets. Not that convincing corporations nowadays that it is in their best interests to more adequately equip and protect their people and assets is a breeze. Unfortunately, there are some who still don't see the need for precaution with respect to traveling or operating overseas.

Quite often, security managers can talk until they are blue in the face about security practices and procedures. They can speculate, prognosticate, and fulminate all day long. And yet, there are those who remain skeptical and reluctant. Perhaps they are looking at the bottom line. Perhaps they have "been there, done that, old boy."

Lucky you! You could be the new security manager who works for a company of engineers and senior management who have been traveling to Pakistan for decades, without one little problem. They may have married foreign nationals, have relatives, in-laws, friends, school chums, colleagues—you name it—in country. How are you going to convince them that this country they love contains some risks that might be potentially hazardous to their health?

Maybe it is because the sharp pencils did not take into account the need for round-the-clock security details—unless you count the night watchman whom the project manager was sure could be located from the local community, for fairly cheap wages. Maybe the watchman can sleep on site, so an extra benefit is received. And, of course, "security is security is security is safety is janitorial is manual labor." How often is security relegated to lower-echelon, to say the least, duties?

As an international security manager, you may be faced with a situation involving a joint venture partner, contractor, subcontractor, or supplier who has operated in this country forever or, better yet, they are from the country you will be operating within. They are local nationals of, say, Algeria. How do you tactfully tell your bosses to tell their new business partners that you need to protect your employees because they are going to visit the partners' country? Maybe the expats are quite familiar with the country, have never had any issues, and don't see what all the fuss is about.

You might be lucky, and something I call the consultant syndrome could set in. It is insidious, like the Stockholm syndrome—that psychological condition in which captives begin to identify with their captors, to the point of choosing sides and even defending them. The project managers, and even senior management, might feign interest and listen intently to the security manager recite the things that the corporation needs to do in order to protect people and assets. But it is not until the corporation retains a consultant to set up shop, to tell them the same things the security manager has been saying (you have been—right?), but in a more succinct, well-packaged way, that they begin to fall under his or her spell and choose sides. Now, if you can work with a consultant who is willing to listen to your ideas as the resident expert within the corporation on all matters security, you can assist in crafting a reasonable solution. Or, and this one I do not wish upon anyone, your corporation has experienced a tragedy, a loss of life, and your senior management is now in tune with your singing. Maybe a near miss, a bomb that went off in a hotel at which your employees were staying, but luckily they were at the office or the job site when the blast occurred, has shaken people up.

You might logically surmise that given your background and experience it would be best for you to visit the location of the project/office or endeavor. You would be correct in thinking so, but is there a project budget for this? Does your budget have the funds? Is there time given project/contract concerns and constraints?

BE READY FOR "THE QUESTION"

> You there, Mr./Ms. Security Manager, thank you for your presentation. But, are you just trying to arrange for a free trip to [name of foreign location] so you can have a good time?

Author's note: Depending on the location, this may be more than a little absurd! Not to be insulting, but given the times, restrictions, and hassle, travel is not all it is cracked up to be.

Honestly, the "you just want to travel" issue has been raised with me several times. You will find out, however, that sometimes it will be necessary to look for yourself.

This book is intended to provide you with the tools (and ammunition) with which to advise your corporations, senior management, and travelers of how to plan for travel to and work in volatile regions.

BE READY FOR "THE STATEMENTS"

> Mr./Ms. Security Manager, what you are telling me is going to cost this project/our company an extreme amount of money. Our margins are very tight. We have not built these types of expenses into our budget.

And:

> No other companies working in this area are doing the types of things from a security perspective that you are advocating.

You are going to have to counter these arguments. You will need to stand your ground. You have a job to do and an obligation as a security manager for your corporation. If you buckle under to comments such as those listed above without successfully beating the bushes to determine what are the determined risks and what countermeasures are required to mitigate these, you will have placed your company in a precarious legal situation.

Because, trust me, when something happens to the expat who was assigned to a particular country where something has happened, or a traveler is on his or her business trip when something unfortunate occurs, or a dependent is injured or worse, you will be sued. It might be a kidnapping, it might be an assault, but your company will be faced with a civil suit.

Consider this tactic: Construct a robust program and lobby hard for your international security program. Keep in mind one very important point. You are working for an organization that, unless it is a nonprofit or nongovernmental organization (NGO), is in business to make money. You are going to find yourself in a very unpopular position should your standard or oft-repeated response to working in volatile regions be: "We can't work under those conditions or circumstances. We can't put employees in that country, it is too risky." If this is your attitude, you are going to be overruled, shut out, or worse. I am not saying you need to bite your tongue and be quiet, skulking back to your office. If you find yourself adamantly opposed to placing employees in a particular region or country, take a deep breath. You are going to need allies and information. You will need to make your case to your manager and hope that he or she backs you up. You will then need to come up with a plan of action. I will tell you that I used to have no problems in making such a broad-stroke statement. But, after successfully protecting employees around the world in some of the most dangerous and volatile regions you can imagine, I now have more of a conciliatory attitude.

You will need advice such as that which I am offering here in order to demonstrate due diligence in protecting people in volatile areas.

AUTHOR BIOGRAPHY

Scott Ast has 28 years of security management and consulting experience in the private and public sectors. His responsibilities have included international security program development and management, project risk assessment, security vulnerability assessment, disaster management/emergency response team, investigations, security awareness, executive protection, security of government installations, and government and law enforcement liaison in foreign and domestic locations from Afghanistan to Venezuela.

Mr. Ast's background has included risk analysis and the implementation of extensive operational security assessments at remote, austere, and hostile reconstruction sites throughout Iraq and Afghanistan and around the world. His travels have taken him to most of the major cities in Iraq in support of the reconstruction of critical infrastructure and electricity. He has extensive expertise in establishing security across a wide variety of critical infrastructure, including water and wastewater treatment facilities, oil and chemical infrastructure, and traditional and nuclear power generation facilities.

Mr. Ast is a board Certified Protection Professional (CPP), Certified Fraud Examiner (CFE), and Certified CPTED Planner (Crime Prevention through Environmental Design). He has assisted the Department of Homeland Security, the Environmental Protection Agency (USEPA), the White House Office of National Drug Control Policy, the U.S. Department of Agriculture, and the RAND Corporation in developing national policy. He has chaired the production of security guidelines and recommendations used as a model by the federal agencies. Mr. Ast has chaired industry national security working groups for the protection of critical infrastructure, and has received recognition from the Federal Bureau of Investigation for this work. He has received a letter of commendation from the U.S. Secret Service, and has presented at Department of Homeland Security, chemical, and security industry national conferences. He is a published author in ASIS's *Security Management* magazine. Mr. Ast earned a BA in political science and a master of public administration from the University of Missouri–Kansas City.

1

Challenges to Security Management in Companies with Global and High-Risk Operations

Security is an illusion. Life is either a daring adventure or it is nothing at all.

—Helen Keller

Congratulations! You are a successful security professional in an organization that has a global footprint. You work for a company with an international/multinational method of doing business. Accordingly, in your role of security manager you have just been advised that your company will build a chemical facility in Colombia, and you now have the responsibility and obligation to ensure that your company's people and assets are adequately protected. Whether you have had international security experience or not, you are about to get an education in the ups and downs, the ins and outs, of dealing with people and projects operating outside of the United States of America or wherever you country of origin might be.

You are faced with major opportunities and gigantic challenges. The opportunities include:

- Ensuring adequate protection for your company's key resources, its people and assets
- Establishing your credibility with senior management, your colleagues, and the entire organization
- Demonstrating your strategic value to the organization

The challenges include:

- Ensuring adequate protection for your company's key resources, its people and assets
- Establishing credibility with senior management, your colleagues, and the entire organization
- Demonstrating your strategic value to the organization

Seriously, the way you handle the challenges presented to you not only can ensure that your company is on the best footing with respect to risk, but also can be beneficial or even critical to your success or longevity with the organization. I have been exactly where you might be right now—new to the job, and new to the area of international security. Maybe you have never been to the country or countries you are now going to become very familiar with, or perhaps you have never even been outside of the United States. Maybe you don't even own a passport.

So, what to do? Well, first, take a deep breath and do not freak out. Two months into a new security manager's position, I was advised that we would be sending employees into Iraq to work as part of Restore Iraqi Infrastructure and Restore Iraqi Electricity. Talk about going from 0 to 60 in 2 seconds flat! You can do this! You can build up your international security credentials and confidence at the same time.

You might want to immediately purchase a really good map of the country. Not always an easy thing to do. I would suggest beginning a Google search for maps of your project location. You will want a hard-copy map, but check these out online to see if they have the detail you want and the cities/locations you need. Finding a really good map, especially one with details down to streets, is difficult if not sometimes impossible. I have known U.S. embassies in foreign countries that did not possess city street maps, even for the capitals or major cities where they were located. Sometimes this is due to the host country's reluctance to place such detail at the fingertips of whomever, or just due to the lack of sophistication with city planning and infrastructure. Even if you have a detailed city map, as you will discover, there are often changes that have been made—little things like the street being completely gone and a high-rise hotel or apartment buildings blocking the way, construction under way, and other such concerns.

You will want to locate adjacent countries, which might be a concern if these are undergoing political or ethnic strife. The surrounding countries can be a concern if any type of hostility tends to shift back and forth across borders. You will want to know if the surrounding countries are easy or difficult to enter in case of the need to evacuate to such locations (more about this in later chapters). Armed with a country map, grab some pushpins and tack this to your wall. Locate a city map, as detailed as possible, and hang it up. Now, when people enter your office they will be impressed that you know where your employees are heading. Knowledge of geography, as you may or may not have realized, is not as common as one would think.

Your next task will be to find out as much about the country as you can. You may have to accomplish this in a fairly quick manner. There are several ways to go about this. You can check the *CIA World Factbook*. This is available online and will provide you with a quick assessment of the country's location, geography, population, government, major imports/exports, political status/tensions, crime, and other pertinent information. You should check with the U.S. Department of State website. You will find crime and safety reports for many countries, along with media reporting of a more current nature. Hopefully, you are already a State Department constituent member of the Overseas Security Advisory Council (OSAC), which will open up more online information and resources. OSAC has many country councils, which are made up of private sector security professionals such as yourself, who are located in these countries and regions. OSAC is open to U.S. corporations only. If you are not a member, apply and join. The benefits of sharing/gathering information among colleagues are invaluable.

Make use of professional organizations, such as the American Society for Industrial Security International (ASIS). One of the first things I do when learning of foreign projects is to use the ASIS member directory, searching by country and even city. Say, for example, my company is planning to open an office in Mumbai, India. I would check out the ASIS directory for India, and I would hopefully find someone who is located in Mumbai or Calcutta. I could contact this person, introduce myself, and begin the task of laying the groundwork for finding out as much as possible. I have done so on many occasions, locating ASIS members in foreign cities. I have yet to find someone reluctant to discuss the security situation with me or to converse about threats or concerns to foreigners. One will need to consider the cultural sensitivities and avoid generalities. For example, you will not want to begin your conversation with a resident of the Republic of Chad by asking him or her just how dangerous or awful the country might be.

Finally, but of equal importance, go to the public library. You will want to look for travel guides and reports on the country of interest, atlases and *National Geographic* magazines, as well as political journals and trade magazines (you might discover competitors who are working in the same country or region). I would look for all manner of newspaper and magazine articles that refer to the country and issues that might be of concern. I would look for records of natural disasters that have taken place. If you are fortunate enough, you may work for an organization that has taken the time to implement its own library resources, with employees educated in library science. I have seen such resources in action and I can't recommend them enough. Not only can they save you time and effort in chasing down articles, books, and magazines, but once you give them the country, the region, and the location, they can comb all of their resources to find more than you ever could.

You will want to ask about things such as road conditions and how companies get from Point A to Point B from a transportation perspective. Will you need four-wheel-drive vehicles? You will need to know the infrastructure and capabilities of road systems. You need to discover all the things your engineers, scientists, academics, and employees will be undertaking in this country.

What is often most important for security managers concerning international organizations is being wired into the decision-making process for international projects, travel, and operations. Being as well informed as possible about international projects or operations, or persons traveling internationally, is half the battle. To some, this might be considered the intelligence required in order for you to make informed judgments and decisions concerning security programs for protection.

How one learns about projects, travel, and operations in foreign locations or volatile areas is a complicated matter. Establishing and maintaining positive relationships with the decision makers and project management personnel is critical. The most advantageous time to gain critical knowledge of overseas operations, travel, and projects is in the planning stage. Once a project is under way, whether it is the construction of a new facility, office, or manufacturing plant, or the travel of employees to countries for meetings or negotiations, it is much more difficult to successfully impact the safety and security of these operations.

One method of becoming forewarned of impending projects, office construction, or employee travel is to have developed good relationships with your various business unit managers. Knowing the risk management personnel, legal department team, human resources, and environmental health and safety employees will be critical to your success. If your company has a crisis management team (if not, it would be a huge feather in your cap to start one!) that has broad representation among business units and corporate functions, their meetings are a great opportunity to determine who is going or working where. Much of the critical planning you will need from a safety and security standpoint can be initiated in such meetings or with this preliminary knowledge.

It is one thing for your employees to travel to a foreign country for meetings, and have these meetings take place only in a hotel. It is a more far-reaching concern if your colleagues will be not only meeting, but also visiting potential business partners, future construction sites, manufacturing locations, or other points. In some cases, merely traveling from the airport to a city or town can be risky. Many criminals prowl the airports and surrounding area and engage in bump-and-rob attacks—where vehicles such as taxis are rear-ended and occupants are robbed when cab drivers stop to investigate.

KEY POINTS

Working in volatile areas necessitates that you equip your personnel and protect your assets from the threats you identify. Let's say you identify that major metropolitan areas in the country you will be visiting are plagued by high levels of street crime, with pickpocketing being the most common occurrence. You would need to provide the traveler, any dependents who might be traveling with him or her, and those expats who might be assigned permanently in-country with this information and some tips for deterring becoming a victim to such criminal acts. Such training might include "street smarts" instruction for not looking the part of a victim: looking up and around and being confident, not displaying expensive jewelry, keeping laptops secured and out of sight rather than dangling from shoulders while strolling around, being aware of your surroundings, and other useful tips.

If your research indicates that the threats come from terrorist acts, such as truck bombings that have targeted Western hotels, one might want to prohibit your employees from using these chains for lodging. You may want to advise travelers that they should attempt to stay on lower floors of the hotels—not the first floor, but under the seventh floor, for example. Many cities that have a robust emergency response capability would be hard-pressed to respond with ladder trucks that could reach any higher. You could also advise travelers to choose rooms located toward the back of the hotel property, away from front entrance drives and roadways.

Locating in these areas can increase the setback and distance from potential for blast sources. Threats of bombings against your offices and facilities might warrant initiating further setbacks at these locations, extending vehicle checkpoints, initiating intense vehicle search techniques, and improving or adding lighting, closed-circuit television, surveillance, and guard tours.

CASE STUDY

As I mentioned from the outset, I was 2 months into a position when I was brought into a meeting and advised that our government group had signed a contract to conduct work in Iraq as part of the U.S. government reconstruction effort. Notice, I said they had signed the contract—not that they were thinking of signing a contract and wanted my input from a safety and security standpoint. The contract was a done deal. Signed, sealed, and delivered. *Fait accompli.* All I had to do was ensure our employees, in this case, engineers, were kept safe and sound in some of the worst locations within Iraq. Oh, yes. The year was 2003, and the security situation in Iraq was dire. The first thing I did? You mean, outside of banging my head against the wall? We were subcontractors on this project; later we would become joint venture partners with another company in Iraq. The primary contractor had the security and safety responsibilities according to the contract, as is usually the case. This did not, however, make me any less responsible for auditing and approving the security measures the primary was implementing on behalf of our employees.

In this particular case, the primary contractor had been working in Iraq for some time. Its security measures had been in place for a few months. Iraq at that time was chaotic at best. The "Green Zone"—a less appropriate name for a location I have yet to find—was going to be our primary location of office space, but we would be venturing out with projects and site visits around the country. The Green Zone was getting peppered daily by rockets and mortars, and the nine-mile stretch of highway from Baghdad International Airport (later called BIAP) would remain for several years the most dangerous stretch of roadway in the world.

Concerning vehicular transport, our project immediately had two choices: take advantage of the protection provided by the United States military and wait for military convoys of troop and supply carriers, armored vehicles and the like, or take chances on our own. Closer inspection revealed that many contractors who took advantage of this "protection" came under frequent attack, just by being part of the convoy while the bad guys attacked the military. Similarly, many contractors decided to merely remain close to the convoys and not actually become embedded with these groups, but were also attacked. No, it quickly became evident that we would require our own means of conveyance, our own armored vehicles and protective forces—"shooters," as the term would be coined. Our employees would wear heavy ballistic jackets and helmets (although initially we were not aware of the drawback of not adding the ceramic plates in the ballistic jacket in order to stop 7.62 caliber rounds—an oversight we quickly corrected).

Static security was an entirely different issue. Due to the continuous overflight of rockets and mortars, with frequent impacts near or inside our perimeters, we constructed a variety of bomb shelters. Some were as simple as inverted concrete culverts under which personnel could take refuge, surrounded by sandbags. Later, due to more frequent incidents, we began to scoop shelters out of the ground, reinforced with concrete, and with steps and lighting leading down to safety. We held unannounced drills designed to create a conditioned response to whistles and other alerts indicating incoming ordnance was imminent or under way. We also gravitated toward ensuring employees wore their ballistic helmets and vests, even when walking from lodging trailers to office trailers, or whenever traveling in the Green Zone—on foot or in vehicles.

2

Travel Tracking and Intelligence Issues
It's 3:00 a.m.—Do You Know Where Your Expats Are?

If you don't know where you're going, any road will take you there . . .

—George Harrison

Knowing where employees are located, especially in case of an emergency, is one of the most important programs or tools a successful security manager can have at his or her fingertips. And yet, as important as it is to have knowledge of what countries, regions, and locales employees are traveling to or are presently traveling within, it is equally important to know where employees are traveling prior to their journey.

In emergency situations, such as the incidents that took place on 9/11 in the United States, or 7/7 in London, it was critical to possess the ability to quickly ascertain the whereabouts of employees who might have been traveling in New York City or Washington, DC, for example, or who were in London when the Underground bombing and mass transit attacks took place. For nonemergency situations, it is equally important to have an idea in advance of where employees, or contractors, might be traveling to before they depart.

Fortunately, technology and procedures can be set in motion that will solve this lack of information and provide you with forewarning. In addition, travelers may now receive critical safety and security information vital to their personal protection by way of emails or text messages on their ubiquitous mobile phones and PDAs. The technology is called "travel tracking" and consists of computer software linked to travel agency reservations platforms.

Here is how it works: Traveling employees continue to contact travel agents for their reservations. Once the electronic tickets are purchased, the travel agency uploads a coded packet of information to the travel tracking/intelligence vendor. The vendor, in turn, returns to the traveler a notice that he or she has been entered into the travel tracking/intelligence database. The traveler is asked to complete an online profile of some additional information and return this to the vendor.

The traveler is now able to access travel intelligence information pertinent to that country and region. They are able to receive email "pushes" of information intended to provide them with safety and security information, ranging from, for example, an outbreak of measles to ethnic clashes, terrorist attacks, coups, evacuation notices, or other useful and timely tidbits. These pushes of information commence once the tickets have been purchased and last for the duration of the trip. For example, on Tuesday, a traveler books and purchases tickets for an upcoming trip to Algeria. His trips lasts until the following Sunday. He receives the first notice on Tuesday, and subsequent emails throughout the week, which cease on Saturday once he is due to arrive at his home/final destination.

There are added benefits for the travelers' responsible manager and the corporate security manager. Depending on who is given access to the tracking database, there is an instantaneous record of the booked travel, in advance of the scheduled trip. This enables the trip to be scrutinized prior to it being made. If an employee books travel to Bogota, Colombia, for example, the security manager can ascertain if there is a valid business reason for going there. The travelers' responsible manager may be contacted to verify if such travel is business essential.

Travel tracking works in case of emergency in the following manner: If a serious incident takes place in London, Mumbai, Bangkok, or Israel, those managers with the database access would go online and could immediately access a link that provides a world map, with a link on each country. Once clicked, this link exposes the itineraries of each traveler in that country at that particular time. Drilling down on this link provides details such as the airline they traveled on, the hotel in which they are staying, even the rental car company—whatever they booked at the time of their reservation. If the world map does not show employees in India, for example, then the security manager can breathe a little easier.

If the travel tracking world map does show a traveler in that country, and especially one booked in a hotel in the city of interest, the security manager could spring into action. Telephonic attempts could be made to contact the traveler to determine if he or she is OK and aware of the emergency situation, and to describe to him or her the best course of action to follow. If the traveler is unable to be located via the information on the itinerary that had been entered onto the travel tracking database, then other means of tracking the traveler could be initiated.

Hopefully, your company has initiated a mandatory "lifeline" program, whereby the traveler, prior to their trip, has designated a lifeline. The lifeline is a person with whom he or she works. This designee is a colleague, not a family member or next of kin, but someone who will know where the person is going while on his or her trip, with whom he or she will be meeting, things he or she might do prior to or during the meeting, and other pertinent facts. The lifeline can be the traveler's manager, who should be in a position to know the purpose of the trip, vendors the traveler might be meeting with, and critical details that might be useful in locating the traveler. The lifeline should not be leery about being brought into an emergency situation, whether it is in the middle of the night or the middle of a holiday weekend. The lifeline should be easily accessible, with home and mobile phone information readily available. Again, this lifeline information would be plugged into the data entry of the travel tracking software platform.

While you are attempting to contact the traveler, and have subsequently alerted the lifeline, you both are now in the search mode. The traveler, if the system is working correctly, should have already initiated attempts to contact the lifeline, knowing that he or she would be worried about the traveler's status if he or she had heard about the serious incident that has taken place. Between the three of you, you now have in place an emergency contact system ready to locate the traveler, determine his or her status, and pass along information as to safety and security concerns. It is important that you relate to the lifeline the information he or she should gather from the traveler, and the information that should be passed along to the traveler.

Travel tracking software programs allow for one additional piece of critical assistance. There is a function that allows for an instantaneous worldwide "broadcast" email message to be sent to all travelers at once,

11

or to one particular traveler at a time. The message can be of the nature: "Check in immediately to corporate security for critical information" or "Initiate stand fast protocol." Of course, *stand fast* is a term the traveler should be briefed on, and is a process in which the traveler should remain where he or she is—instead of venturing out into unsafe road conditions, road blocks, the aftermath of a natural disaster, or other circumstances. You could even send an email with the country or region crisis management plan attached. Regardless of the information to be passed on, you now have another resource to add to telephonic attempts to reach the traveler.

Another method of travel tracking (and one that will cost your company nothing) is managed by the U.S. government. It is the process of performing online travel registration with the Department of State at www.travelregistration.gov. Travelers are asked for information such as their name, date of birth, passport number, destination country, and address where they will be, as well as a contact number. The database asks for their email address in order to send them alerts and notices pertinent to their travel immediately upon registering and during the duration of their trip. Travelers may enter the name and contact information for persons with whom they would want the State Department or local embassies to share information in the case of family or personal emergencies while the traveler is in-country. In the event of emergency or disaster, U.S. embassies send what are called "warden messages" to your email. The information is stored in a secured State Department database. The State Department, via the local U.S. embassy or consulate, will attempt to locate that traveler in the event of a national emergency or if some personal emergency has arisen. In addition, personal emergencies may warrant the location of the traveler, such as a family member contacting the State Department in order to track down the traveler immediately for tragic information, or may be useful in the event that a traveler has gone missing or has not checked in lately. Travelers may also register by contacting the embassies in the countries they are visiting.

Not surprisingly, travel tracking has gone high-tech. The advent of personal Global Positioning Satellite (GPS) travel tracking transponder devices has emerged. These devices are an offshoot of the personal locator beacons used for decades in nautical search and rescue. The automobile version of this technology has been on the road for years. Simpler personal GPS or personal GPS locator devices have also been used to track tractor trailer rigs hauling precious cargo, or have been "seeded" in packages being transported for countertheft stings and deterrence. The technology makes use of the geosynchronous satellites circling the Earth, which "ping" the tracking devices once activated. The devices can be two-way functional in that they can be activated by the traveler when there is an emergency, sending an alert to monitoring services. A signal can be returned by the monitoring service, checking on the status of the traveler. The device can be small enough to be placed into a briefcase, or can be mounted under the dash of vehicles. In case of emergencies, a criminal act or an attempted or in-process abduction, for example, a signal button might be depressed once. If there is a medical emergency, the button might be depressed twice in close succession. The device can be used to track the whereabouts of the traveler as long as it is on his or her person or the traveler remains in the vehicle.

Automation and technology are wonderful things. And yet, through the years, I have known security managers and directors who have not embraced its benefits for a variety of reasons. Some have felt threatened by the possibility that the new technology might be used to replace them or their positions. Say, for example, one purchases the travel tracking software that provides a daily intelligence digest. The intelligence digests of such products can be extremely beneficial and timely. They come in the form of predigested snippets of critical facts and indicators. It is quite easy to cut to the chase and determine that travelers in a particular region or country might be at risk due to natural or man-made calamities. I have used such information on many occasions to warn travelers and project and senior management of everything from approaching typhoons and hurricanes, to coups, violent protests, and demonstrations, to outbreaks of disease. I have regularly submitted this type of daily intelligence to my manager and other key managers and employees. I had one vice president of safety for a major corporation indicate that he thought this was the best information, in the most concise package that he had ever seen. I agreed. Some security professionals I have encountered would have been hesitant to pass along these tidbits for fear of appearing to be only the middleman and, therefore, less useful. I think we have all run into people who have a tendency to hoard information and use it like a savings account. Rather than appear less useful, I would argue that the security professional can look like the hero. He or she has now found this treasure trove of information, which, when combined with other means of information, can guarantee that the corporation is providing the best oversight with the maximum effect of protecting people and assets.

Utilizing technology and resources such as those mentioned here can bolster and supplement a security management program; make it current and timely, responsive and flexible, capable and alert. Unless your organization is fortunate enough to have a full-time analyst capable of combing through the hundreds of publications and online sources (and even if you do) such intelligence summaries and email notices can make all the difference in the world.

KEY POINTS

The important thing to remember concerning travel tracking is how critical it is to have knowledge of where employees are likely to be traveling, and the ability to track them when they are on their trip or assignment. It is critical to know where employees are planning to travel to prior to their departure in order to assess the necessity of the trip, allow you to brief them, and to plan for their security and safety while gone. Selling a travel tracking program to employees and senior management is often more successful if you frame it as a safety program. Good intelligence prior to employee travel, proper briefings of employees, and technology one can turn to in emergency situations can be crucial to success or failure of your crisis management and security plan.

CASE STUDY

The Mumbai, India, train bombings took place on July 11, 2006. The bombs were geared for rush hour, designed to inflict as much damage as possible upon the greatest number of commuters. The bombings happened at 0000 Central Standard Time where I was located. When I discovered what had occurred, I immediately pulled up my iJet online travel tracking via the Internet. Within a matter of minutes, I had located several employees who were either traveling into or out of Mumbai or nearby Pune, India. I was able to locate the itineraries of the travelers, when they had arrived, when they were leaving, and what their lodging arrangements were. I located their lifelines (the predetermined people/colleagues with whom the travelers worked who would have important knowledge of the travelers' work schedule while in-country, planned meetings, and other vital information). I contacted the lifelines and inquired if they had heard from their traveler. Four out of seven lifelines had either contacted the traveler by phone or had been contacted by the traveler, who indicated they were fine. One traveler remained unaccounted for, and attempts to reach him by mobile phone had not succeeded. The mobile phone lines were soon overloaded and inoperable. The traveler was an American citizen who had been born in India. I then utilized the broadcast email function for the iJet software and was able to send an email indicating that we were concerned for the traveler's safety, and for him to please contact his lifeline or corporate security immediately. I was beginning to locate the number for the U.S. embassy in Cairo when the gentleman's lifeline called me to advise that the traveler had just phoned to say he was OK. The traveler had received the email on his Blackberry and phoned the lifeline from a landline since the cellular system was still down. One or two less gray hairs for the corporate security manager!

3

Risk Assessment Methodologies
The 5:00 p.m. Friday Telephone Call—"We've Got a Project Kicking Off Monday in Colombia"

If a man is alive, there is always danger that he may die, though the danger must be allowed to be less in proportion as he is dead-and-alive to begin with. A man sits as many risks as he runs.

—Henry David Thoreau, *Walden*

Assessing risk is a critical means of determining the protection profile required for your organization, and what you need to be concerned about in the area(s) in which you are working. It is different from typical risk assessment in that geopolitical concerns must be addressed, and typically create or add to existing risk more often than other factors. I prefer to break down disasters into two categories that comprise risk: natural and man-made.

Let's take an easy example. Say you are setting up a project in the Andes mountain range. Your office will be built on a high plateau, next to a glacier that is known for weekly, devastating avalanches. Sound too risky? You bet. Hopefully, to refer back to recommendations from a previous chapter, you were advised by the responsible engineer/project manager 6 months before the project planning proposal was due to senior management. If you had been told at that time, you could have advised the project team that this area was prone to avalanches (determined by your checking statistics provided by the Chilean government's Andes skiers information report).

You check out the Andean ski report website for the region you are heading into and discover that the city your office is building an office in is just below a mountain range that had an avalanche about once a week during the height of snow season. Accordingly, you advise the engineers on the project looking to inhabit this office that they may want to pack snowshoes. In all actuality, this would be the type of situation when you would want to notify your company's risk management department of such a concern and reality. If an area in which you are going to be working is prone to tropical storms, hurricanes, or earthquakes, you would want to know about and plan to mitigate such occurrences. More about the steps to mitigating such risks later.

Assessing the possibility of natural disaster is much easier, in most circumstances, than determining the risk of man-made incidents and turmoil. Man-made incidents of concern can include civil unrest, political upheaval, strikes or work stoppages, protests, and of course, crime and terrorism. One can look at crime and terrorism statistics, presented by the U.S. Department of State, at www.osca.gov. Another resource is reports from overseas written by ordinary people. It is called "Tales from a Small Planet" at www.talesmag.com. The website contains volumes of information on all aspects of overseas life. It is lighthearted and fun, but is written with an understanding that by sharing this information, travelers might overcome the challenges of doing so.

Natural disaster is one area of concern that can impact the personal security of your employees. Personal safety and security for expatriates is of utmost concern. The people who work for you in foreign countries are most concerned with their own safety and security and the security of their loved ones. As a security manager, you share their concerns in this area.

Concerning personnel, if you are going to be working in foreign countries, you will have a need to assess the character and motives of any foreign nationals who are working for you—as contractors, subcontractors, vendors, and suppliers. Where you will be working and the assets you require for doing business will need protection; this is a given. You will need to protect your information, patents, and proprietary information, and you will need a secure means of communicating while you are conducting your business.

Your concern, regarding the assessment of risk, is finding a happy medium between what you are attempting to accomplish and what is standing in your way or is a potential minefield. Half the battle in some cases is in understanding what might lie ahead that represents risk. There are threats in this world, to be sure. The threats that we cannot mitigate for or counter we have to consider our vulnerable areas.

Threat requires that adversaries have the intention to cause you harm. They must possess the ability to wreak this harm upon you. They must have the methods, and items, and an understanding of how to operate or implement these things that can harm you. This is risk, and that risk becomes your threat. Your job, Mr. or Ms. Security Manager, is to identify and develop effective countermeasures to obliterate or otherwise deflect or thwart this risk.

Threats exist in many forms, with terrorism being one that instantly comes to mind in this day and age. But there are others you should be aware of in your role as steward of that which protects your company's people and assets. There are those with whom you compete in particular industries and areas of business. Foreign businesses might seek to obtain your proprietary information by stealing or buying it from employees, or compromising these employees. Employees, both your expats and foreign nationals, if fired or disciplined, might become potential conduits of your secrets to other companies or host governments. Maybe foreign competitor companies have the assistance of their intelligence service. Maybe this foreign intelligence service targets you not to benefit one of their own nation's countries, but due to their interest from a defensive or offensive consideration. You might be operating in a country that has a history of violent civil unrest, rioting, ethnic difficulties, separatist movements, or other internal strife. You could be operating in a country or city that is ripe with criminal activity, and this criminal atmosphere might be the result of gangs or organized crime. On the far extreme, wars could break out. You are going to need to protect your personnel and assets by keeping the access away from the bad guys. Think of this as access control.

If there is risk, you will need to consider the places where your employees work. This can be traditional office space, or if their work is done from housing, apartments, compounds, etc. Employees might be at risk while on travel status in hotels, or maybe they will be working from these hotels. One of the most common times to be at risk is while traveling. The various components of travel risk that should be considered are airline, seagoing vessel, rail, and vehicular.

Crime can be broken up into two concerns, internationally speaking. These are divided into the threat to your people and the threat to your assets. The threats to your people from crime range from threats to their well-being, such as murder, kidnap/extortion, rape, and assault, to rob-bery. Threats to your assets include theft, embezzling of funds, extortion (toward the business), product tampering, and vandalism. The threats are the same one might face when a foreign national working for a U.S. corpo-ration comes to this country. He or she can face threats to his or her person in Chicago, Kansas City, or Los Angeles. This is one factor that is often lost on security managers who are responsible for employees traveling safely outside of the United States. Travelers coming into the United States can feel the same angst about entering our sunny shores. They might hear about the U.S. "gun culture," about serious crime issues facing large urban areas. Given the size of the United States and our population, and depend-ing on where these foreign employees of your company might be traveling to, they could be more prone to becoming victims of some nasty event here than anyone else you might be sending overseas. It is important to keep this in mind and not be so biased as to lose track of this concept.

But, let's say that you contact the regional security officer (RSO) in the U.S. embassy located in the city to which your personnel will be traveling, meeting, and working. The RSO informs you that crime surrounding the hotel you mention has been rampant, with muggings taking place within a few blocks of the hotel. You would want to inform your employees to forgo pedestrian activities and stick to cabs. Next, you discover from the RSO that express kidnappings (those that are sometimes characterized by someone being snatched and driven around to automatic teller machines (ATMs) and forced to withdraw money until their cards are maxed out, whereupon the victim is tossed out—unbeaten and unharmed if they are lucky) have taken place using criminals working in concert with some cab drivers. Now, you must advise your employees not to use the ubiquitous green and white city cabs, and opt instead for hotel-arranged livery services.

Terrorism concerns remain an issue of which security managers should be acutely aware. The State Department publishes annually its global terrorism report. The report is actually mandated to be presented to the U.S. Congress in compliance with Title 22 of the United States Code Section 2656f(a). The report catalogs events and groups associated with terrorism that are deemed to be "of major significance." The report itself is quite detailed and is packed with information about terrorism trends and all manners of issues relating to terrorism. Another resource is the National Consortium for the Study of Terrorism and Responses to Terrorism (START), whose website is www.start.umd.edu. START allows the user to construct online detailed incident trends by country and region. Keep in mind that whatever information you discover relating to terrorist incidents must be weighed against your efforts and projects in the country within which you will be placing employees. Just because a terrorist act takes place in a country, doesn't mean you should assume your employees will be falling over themselves to seek out you and your advice. I have rarely seen employees presented with information concerning previous, or even fairly current, terrorist acts influenced by them to the point of forgoing travel to a country.

Another source of critical information is speaking with project personnel or other employees who have been to the country in order to gauge their experiences or concerns. This is a very important aspect of corporate risk analysis concerning expatriates working in other countries. I have found that if you have a country you are concerned about with respect to crime, and you work for a company that has a history of working in this country, you had better discuss the experiences of those personnel who have worked there, in particular the senior or project management. If these personnel have extensive or even limited exposure to the country, they will have impressions, good or bad. Having been to this location, they have experienced firsthand the issues, or nonissues, as the case may be. If you, the security manager, have not been to this country, you are going to have a more difficult time. Prepare yourself—no, steel yourself—against the comment of "Well, you haven't been there, so what do you really know about the situation there . . . etc.?" What I often have wanted to tell persons in response to these situations is: "Well, I have not been to the surface of the sun or the moon, but I can tell you one is extremely hot, and you will burn up before you reach it, and the other is not made of cheese, but has no atmosphere, so you had better bring one with you." But, of course, practicing decorum, I do not.

I want to hear from employees who have been to countries that I have not. I like to get their impressions of everything—their arrivals at the airport, transportation, road conditions, lodging, and many other aspects of their visit. Many employees have shared very detailed and quite useful information with me concerning their visits to foreign countries—whether they knew I had been there or they were aware that I had not. If your company has an established safety program, such as construction site or chemical/manufacturing safety, you might want to have a safety person with whom the employees may have worked take part in conversations or briefings in such circumstances. If the safety person is associated with that particular office or project, bonus points! So much of security management is utilizing people skills. If you can meet with the safety person in advance and share with him or her your role/concerns/responsibilities for this particular project or office, you will be well on your way to having an ally in your quest for acceptance/information sharing.

Another means of determining risk, and an important firsthand or current impression of what is going on in your country of concern, is to do a little old-fashioned "benchmarking." I really like this method of information and intelligence gathering with respect to risk. It is important for several very important reasons. First of all, by doing this correctly, you might be establishing working relationships with colleagues who might provide you with lifesaving (and I am not kidding about this) assistance some time down the road.

Sometimes you might be approached by a risk manager, or someone within your corporation responsible for insurance policies, who calls you up to ask: "I'd like to send you a form from our insurance company that states we are taking adequate steps to protect our employees in Darfur, Algeria, Iraq, and Afghanistan. Would you attest to this?" Hopefully this is not a surprise to you. It is an indication, however, of how seriously those with a fiduciary responsibility for protecting (or insuring) employees take risk. If you are going to send employees into a war zone, for example, Iraq or Afghanistan, you are going to have to purchase a rider, over and above the existing policy coverage.

A document that might assist you in determining risk is one that assesses the types of security and emergency preparedness programs present at the job site, project, or office. It is intended to give you an idea how much is present or lacking, and it will show you where you are lacking or proficient.

Simply put, you will need to provide standard procedures for office and project security analysis in moderate- and high-risk areas. Security analysis for overseas (or outside the United States) and domestic risk areas is necessary to ensure that proper precautions and preplanning are accomplished. Your success in preplanning will ensure that security programs, procedures, or practices are in place to provide a secure environment for your company's professionals. For many areas, security plans and evacuation plans (Form 3.1) may be developed in coordination with your company corporate security and program management, and that of joint venture companies, partners, contractors, and subcontractors (Form 3.1). In some high-risk areas, for example, security precautions may include personal security details (PSDs) of armed security operatives, to cite an extreme. Security analysis involves successful implementation of assessments, practices, and procedures in order to protect the well-being of personnel, property, the community, and clients. Once a security analysis is

FORM 3.1   PROJECT/OFFICE SECURITY AND EVACUATION PLAN

COMPANY project/office name: _____

COMPANY project/office manager name: _____

Project manager contact information: _____

Landline phone number(s): _____

Cellular phone number(s): _____

Email address(es): _____

Location: _____

Country: _____

State/province: _____

City: _____

Address/zip/postal code: _____

GPS coordinates: _____

Location on digital map (include map copy): _____

Building owner/client owner: _____

State/province: _____

City: _____

Address/zip/postal code: _____

Contact name: _____

Contact phone number(s): _____

Client company/agency name: _____

Client/agency location: _____

Country: _____

State/province: _____

City: _____

Address/zip/postal code: _____

Client/agency contact name(s): _____

Client/agency contact telephone number(s): _____

Landline number(s): _____

Cellular number(s): _____

Email address(es): _____

Project/office lifeline completed/updated?

    ☐ Yes   ☐ No   ☐ In process

COMPANY professional(s) responsible for lifeline maintenance:
Name: _____
Contact information: _____

_____
Telephone number(s): _____
Email address(es): _____

Lifeline information submitted to:
Name _____
Date _____

Office/project security systems (check all that apply):
Federal/national police or military stationed? ☐ Yes ☐ No
   In what capacity?
      ☐ Checking vehicles/personnel IDs
      ☐ Lobby or entrance posted
      ☐ Checking vehicle entrances/vehicles
Private security guards
    ☐ Armed   ☐ Unarmed
    ☐ Mobile guards (foot patrols)
    ☐ Mobile guards (vehicle patrols)
    ☐ Private security guards present 24/7
    ☐ Other shifts (please describe):

Office/project-controlled entry
    ☐ Lobby entrance   ☐ Office entrance   ☐ Vehicle entrance/checkpoints
    Staffed by
      ☐ Private security officers
      ☐ Military/police
      ☐ Combination of private/military/police
      ☐ Entries/entrances/gates not staffed

    ☐ Access control cards utilized
    ☐ Photo ID badges utilized
    ☐ Keypad code
    ☐ Locks/keys

Office/project alarm systems (check all that apply):

☐ Burglar/office alarm   ☐ Perimeter/fence alarm

Other security provisions/manner of security operations (please describe):

Has client or agency provided a security plan?   ☐ Yes   ☐ No
Has client provided a copy of security plan?   ☐ Yes   ☐ No
Have COMPANY professionals been briefed and understand security plan?
   ☐ Yes   ☐ No
Please provide COMPANY corporate security with a copy of the plan or information related to the security planning, or contact information for client/agency in order to discuss such planning.

Please provide COMPANY corporate security with a description of any incidents of crime, including theft of property from the office, job site, etc. AND any incidents of a serious nature—attack upon persons, extortion/kidnap threat or acts, terrorist acts or terrorist threats.

Has client/agency provided a security evacuation plan?
   ☐ Yes   ☐ No
Does client/agency security representative regularly liaise with COMPANY project manager?
   ☐ Yes   ☐ No
   Name of COMPANY professional who is contacted by client/agency security representative: _____
Office building owner/client person(s) responsible for security:
   ☐ No such person
Name: _____
Contact information: _____
Address: _____
Telephone number(s): _____
Email address(es): _____
COMPANY professionals lodging consists of:
   ☐ Client-provided compound/housing
   ☐ Hotel
   ☐ Professional-acquired apartment/home

Lodging is:
- ☐ On site of project/office
- ☐ Approximate distance from office/project

Lodging security in place?   ☐ Yes   ☐ No

Lodging security consists of:
- ☐ Private security guards   ☐ Armed   ☐ Unarmed
- ☐ Military   ☐ Police   ☐ Armed   ☐ Unarmed

Lodging security:
- ☐ Burglar alarm system
- ☐ Vehicle-controlled checkpoints
- ☐ Lobby-controlled checkpoints

Manner of lodging security operation (please describe):

Transportation:
- ☐ Client/agency-provided transportation
- ☐ Client/agency provides vehicle and driver
- ☐ Client/agency provides vehicle but no driver
- ☐ COMPANY professionals responsible for transportation
- ☐ COMPANY professionals self-drive

COMPANY professionals have driving security awareness
- ☐ Yes   ☐ No

Office/project professionals registered with appropriate embassies?
- ☐ Yes (which ones?):
- ☐ No
- ☐ In process

Receiving embassy emergency and other email/telephonic notices?
- ☐ Yes   ☐ No

Office/project has an evacuation plan in place (provide copy)?
- ☐ Yes   ☐ No

Office/project requires an evacuation plan?
- ☐ Yes   ☐ No

COMPANY professionals have been briefed on evacuation plan?
- ☐ Yes   ☐ No

COMPANY professional who has briefed professionals on the plan:
Name: _____
Contact information: _____
Telephone number(s): _____
Email address(es): _____
Office/project would like a site visit for a detailed security assessment?
 ☐ Yes ☐ No

---

conducted, a security briefing will be provided for project/office management. The philosophy behind these instructions is based on the objective of your company to provide a secure work environment.

You will want to show your employees that your company corporate security department has developed vulnerability analyses, and benchmarking. In addition, liaisons within the industry, government, and law enforcement, both domestically and internationally, will provide proactive risk assessment and mitigation for both office and project locations in moderate- and high-risk areas (Form 3.2). These programs should provide guidance for company managers and professionals as they perform their day-to-day activities. It is then the responsibility of each division to ensure that corporate security is contacted prior to work being conducted in moderate- or high-risk areas. The definition of *moderate to high risk* can include factors such as significant crime rates, political unrest/instability, and terrorism. Advise your internal partners, business units, and divisions that domestic (if concerned with U.S. or international locations) crime rates may be obtained by corporate security, as well as country risk of terrorism and instability. Corporate security can also post country alerts and ratings on your corporate, security, or safety website, and provide a recommendation as to the level of security required to operate in a secure manner, which will be useful to budgeting, proposals, and procurement. Risk analysis and mitigation programs may be modified to meet a specific division, client, or project need with the assistance of corporate security.

Your security analysis should be designed to identify and manage/mitigate risk in project and office locations operating in areas of high risk to professionals and assets. Your program will provide an administrative structure within which business units, departments, and project

FORM 3.2   QUESTIONS FOR A POTENTIAL JOINT VENTURE PARTNER ON AN OVERSEAS PROJECT, OR TO BE COMPLETED BY YOUR CLIENT

YOUR COMPANY project/office name: _____

YOUR COMPANY project/office manager name: _____

Project manager contact information: _____

_____

Landline phone number(s): _____

Cellular phone number(s): _____

Email address(es): _____

Location: _____

Country: _____

State/province: _____

City: _____

Address/zip/postal code: _____

GPS coordinates: _____

Location on digital map (include map copy): _____

Building owner/client owner: _____

State/province: _____

City: _____

Address/zip/postal code: _____

Contact name: _____

Contact phone number(s): _____

Client company/agency name: _____

Client/agency location: _____

Country: _____

State/province: _____

City: _____

Address/zip/postal code: _____

Client/agency contact name(s): _____

Client/agency contact telephone number(s): _____

Landline number(s): _____

Cellular number(s): _____

Email address(es): _____

Project/office lifeline completed/updated?

   □ Yes   □ No   □ In process

YOUR COMPANY professional(s) responsible for lifeline maintenance:

Name: _____

Contact information: _____

_____

Telephone number(s): _____

Email address(es): _____

Lifeline information submitted to:

   Name: _____

   Date: _____

Office/project security systems (check all that apply):

Federal/national police or military stationed?

   □ Yes   □ No

   In what capacity?

      □ Checking vehicles/personnel IDs

      □ Lobby or entrance posted

      □ Checking vehicle entrances/vehicles

Private security guards

   □ Armed   □ Unarmed

   □ Mobile guards (foot patrols)

   □ Mobile guards (vehicle patrols)

   □ Private security guards present 24/7

   □ Other shifts (please describe):

Office/project-controlled entry

   □ Lobby entrance

   □ Office entrance

   □ Vehicle entrance/checkpoints

   Staffed by

      □ Private security officers

      □ Military/police

      □ Combination of private/military/police

      □ Entries/entrances/gates not staffed

☐ Access control cards utilized
☐ Photo ID badges utilized
☐ Keypad code
☐ Locks/keys
☐ Office/project alarm systems (check all that apply):
 ☐ Burglar/office alarm
 ☐ Perimeter/fence alarm
Other security provisions/manner of security operations (please describe):

Has client or agency provided a security plan?
 ☐ Yes ☐ No
Has client provided a copy of security plan?
 ☐ Yes ☐ No
Have YOUR COMPANY professionals been briefed and understand security plan?
 ☐ Yes ☐ No
Please provide YOUR COMPANY corporate security with a copy of the plan or information related to the security planning, or contact information for client/agency in order to discuss such planning.

Please provide YOUR COMPANY corporate security with a description of any incidents of crime, including theft of property from the office, job site, etc. AND any incidents of a serious nature—attack upon persons, extortion/kidnap threat or acts, terrorist acts or threats.

Has client/agency provided a security evacuation plan?
 ☐ Yes ☐ No
Does client/agency security representative regularly liaise with YOUR COMPANY project manager?
 ☐ Yes ☐ No
Name of YOUR COMPANY professional who is contacted by client/agency security representative: _____
Office building owner/client person(s) responsible for security:
 ☐ No such person
Name: _____
Contact information: _____
_____
Phone number: _____
Email: _____

YOUR COMPANY professional lodging consists of:
- ☐ Client-provided compound/housing
- ☐ Hotel
- ☐ Professional-acquired apartment/home

Lodging is:

- ☐ On site of project/office
- ☐ Approximate distance from office/project

Lodging security in place?
☐ Yes ☐ No

Lodging security consists of:

- ☐ Private security guards ☐ Armed ☐ Unarmed
- ☐ Military ☐ Police ☐ Armed ☐ Unarmed

Lodging security:

- ☐ Burglar alarm system
- ☐ Vehicle-controlled checkpoints
- ☐ Lobby-controlled checkpoints

Manner of lodging security operation (please describe):

Transportation:
- ☐ Client/agency-provided transportation
- ☐ Client/agency provides vehicle and driver
- ☐ Client/agency provides vehicle but no driver
- ☐ YOUR COMPANY professionals responsible for transportation
- ☐ YOUR COMPANY professionals self-drive

YOUR COMPANY professionals have driving security awareness?
☐ Yes ☐ No

Office/project professionals registered with appropriate embassies?
- ☐ Yes (which ones):
- ☐ No
- ☐ In process

Receiving embassy emergency and other email/telephonic notices?
☐ Yes ☐ No

Office/project has an evacuation plan in place (provide copy)?
☐ Yes ☐ No

Office/project requires an evacuation plan?
☐ Yes ☐ No

YOUR COMPANY professionals have been briefed on evacuation plan?
☐ Yes ☐ No

YOUR COMPANY professional who has briefed professionals on the plan

Name: _____

Contact information: _____

_____

Telephone number(s): _____

Email address(es): _____

Office/project would like a site visit for a detailed security assessment?
☐ Yes ☐ No

managers may initiate the process of risk analysis, assessment, and mitigation. The program should provide for consistency in the approach to security in high-risk areas. You might consider listing high-risk areas on a world risk map.

BEGINNING A SECURITY ASSESSMENT

In starting to develop a security assessment, here are some questions and considerations to get you started.

Sample the professionals for their concerns: What do they worry about with regards to security? What have they experienced that causes them concern? What suggestions do they have to better secure the parking lots, entrances, work space, etc.?

Getting started:

- Is the office space secured?
- Is the space secured with proximity card readers or standard locks?
- Do the office space doors remain open during business hours?
- Is there a need to have the doors open during business hours?
- Are there other entrance/exit doors leading into the office space?

- Are these doors secured during business hours, or are they kept unlocked for convenience, access to restrooms, break-rooms, etc.?
- Would it be possible to keep the doors secured and utilize access control, such as proximity card readers, intercom/phone with door release?
- Does the office have a policy of security cabling laptops?
- Are professionals asked/advised to take laptops home each evening?
- Are professionals encouraged to keep personal belongings (wallets, purses, etc.) locked in desks while away from their desks/offices?
- Is there a receptionist?
- If there is a receptionist, is the desk always covered or are there periods when the desk is unoccupied when someone might enter the space unnoticed?
- Is there a "door chime" or some means to alert a receptionist who might step away from the desk for a minute, or to notify professionals in the space that someone has entered?
- Where do professionals park?
- Is the parking covered or uncovered?
- Is the parking lot well lit?
- Are there parking lot or parking garage emergency call stations or phones?
- Who monitors the phones and are they monitored 24/7?
- Are there intercoms at building entrances professionals can use to request assistance?
- Who monitors the intercoms and are they monitored 24/7?
- Do professionals use stairwells or elevators to access office space?
- Is there a building security officer?
- If there is building security, do they patrol YOUR COMPANY space during the day shift or after normal business hours?
- Are security officers available for providing escorts for professionals to their vehicles or into the building?
- Do professionals enter/exit the facility in view of security officers?

- Are there CCTV cameras in office space, parking lots, hall-ways, or other areas?
- Is there 24-hour security that monitors CCTV?
- Are there phone numbers professionals can call for building security?
- Do professionals have these numbers?
- If no security is present, can professionals contact building maintenance for assistance. If so, are they 24/7?
- Does the cleaning crew service the office space during business hours or after YOUR COMPANY professionals have left?
- Is the cleaning crew instructed to keep doors secured while servicing YOUR COMPANY space so as not to allow unauthorized persons into the space?
- Would it be possible for the cleaning crew to perform their duties during business hours?
- Does building management advise YOUR COMPANY of incidents/crimes that have taken place in the buildings, parking lots, or surrounding area?
- Are the restrooms in YOUR COMPANY space, or located outside in hallways?
- If the restrooms are publicly accessible, are the doors kept locked and persons required to use a key for entry?
- Do the restroom doors lock behind the person entering?

Submit results of assessment to YOUR COMPANY corporate security for assistance.

Contact local law enforcement for a site/office security inspection.

Additionally, you should have regular meetings with building management to discuss security status of the area, the building, and your concerns/requests. If anything suspicious occurs, contact building management security, maintenance, or administrative offices. Call 911 in emergency situations or if no security is present. Report suspicious activity to security, maintenance, or building management, or contact police. Report crimes to police, building management, and YOUR COMPANY corporate security.

If you have any security issues you require assistance with, contact YOUR COMPANY corporate security.

RISK ANALYSIS AND SECURITY PROGRAMS

Keep in mind that risk factors include, but are not limited to:

- Insurgency, civil/tribal/factional strife, or state of war
- Multiple serious incidents of hostilities upon expats/corporations/industries, of both a criminal and a terrorist nature (improvised explosive devices (IEDs), vehicle-borne improvised explosive devices (VBIEDs), bombings, murder, kidnapping, arson, rioting, or other events)
- Multiple incidents of terrorist threats upon expats/corporations/industries
- Unexploded ordinance (UXO), such as land mines, artillery, etc.
- Significant crime rates and incidents of violent crime, to include murder, rape, armed robbery, armed criminal assault, and arson

Depending upon the location, conditions, resources, and risk, security programs might contain:

- Armed security escorts with armored vehicles/armed static security
- Unarmed security escorts with unarmored vehicles/unarmed static security
- Physical security to include protective perimeters and barriers, alarm systems, access control, and other measures
- Security evacuation or sheltering needs in the event of insurgency
- Predeployment security briefing conducted by YOUR COMPANY corporate security

Your program should be written in a site-specific format and developed for each individual project. Advise your company that for initiation of the security analysis for overseas risk areas, they should contact YOUR COMPANY corporate security manager.

In order for such a program to be effective, each division management should review this instruction and integrate the policies and procedures that govern the work in their division. To ensure thorough understanding of the requirements and effective

implementation, each division shall implement structured communications programs, including notifications, reviews of implementing policies and procedures, and training relative to the resulting
policies and procedures.

You should advise the managers that countries of risk will be
posted on YOUR COMPANY security or safety website. Department,
division, manager, project manager, or appropriate individual will
determine if projects/offices/travel is to take place in high/moder-
ate-risk areas.

Department or division manager, project manager, or appropriate
individual will contact YOUR COMPANY corporate security well in
advance of projects/offices/travel in/to high/moderate-risk areas.

YOUR COMPANY corporate security will complete a risk analy-
sis/assessment and discuss this with the appropriate professional.
When necessary, corporate security will develop security and evacuation management plans, liaisons, and other project essentials.

KEY POINTS

Assessing risk in hostile areas is probably the most important and difficult
task that any security manager can be handed. Assessing risk is a challenging and time-consuming proposition. To be successful, the security
manager should rely on and expect prior notification of corporate projects and initiatives. Through careful crafting of relationships with decision makers within your organization, and the right internal resources
from which you can draw upon their expertise, your efforts can be more
seamless and successful. Careful consideration of the risks that you can
identify, and those that you can anticipate, is critical to success. This, plus
the ability to adapt to unforeseen circumstances and developments that
keep risk a moving target.

CASE STUDY

I was once contacted and advised that my company was going to work in
an African country. The contract for the company services was close to
being signed, negotiations had been held, engineering studies had been

conducted, and employees were being contacted regarding their ability and willingness to commit to a 2-year project located in a desolate country, in what one person termed a "difficult area." Difficult it was. I asked the usual questions, after determining an exact location using project maps and GPS coordinates. Would the client be providing security? What emergency response/evacuation capabilities would be provided? Would there be government assistance? Was the project a government or private-funded project? I discovered that the employees who had been planning the project had not seen the need for site security, outside of a front-gate guard, using a locally hired tribesman. I found out that petty crime was relatively as to be expected, with what was not nailed down being subject to disappearance. Serious crime was rare, a good indication. But, I had heard a little bit about the country in previous years, and a little more research provided some very crucial information. What I found was not a serious risk of kidnapping or extortion. The country was not a hot bed of terrorist activity. It had a troubled past and UN peacekeepers (United Nations reports provided a major part of my risk analysis) were present in some areas. What was most troublesome, and led to subsequent follow-up phone calls by me to colleagues who had worked in the area, and the retrieval of more press and government reports, was the proliferation of land mines. Almost 140 kilometers of land was believed to be at risk for land mines. Roughly 5,000 casualties had been attributed to land mines. I asked the obvious question, and what I was told was shocking. There had been no planning or budgeting for UXO and land mine removal. None. As it happens, the area where the project was to be located was known to be an area where the locals, and any hapless visitors, never drove off the road for fear of land mines. The main project employees had not even been to the proposed site, probably a very fortunate thing, in hindsight. The project was nixed, dead in the water, from that point forward.

EXAMPLE OF A COUNTRY RISK ASSESSMENT ONE MIGHT CONDUCT IN CHINA

Compared with many other countries, China is considered one of the safest in the world for personal security. But petty crime has increased in recent years, especially in and around the major cities.

However, serious crime against foreigners is relatively rare. Petty crimes such as pickpocketing and purse snatching occur somewhat

---

frequently, especially in crowded areas such as stations, markets, shopping areas, sightseeing destinations, etc. So, it is wise to be cautious with your personal possessions in public place. Below are some precautions to avoid potential problems:

- Do not show off your money in public.
- Keep enough money for your immediate needs in your pocket, and hide the rest on your body or leave your backup supply in a safety deposit box at your hotel.
- Always keep valuables in a safety deposit box at your hotel instead of leaving them in your room.
- Remove any jewelry that may draw a thief's attention before you go out for a stroll.
- Never wear a bag or purse on your street-side shoulder in order to avoid becoming a target of the "snatch and ride."
- Never carry your passport/visa, credit cards, traveler's checks, or other travel documents in your shoulder bag or bum bag.
- Ensure that you are aware of the values of different local banknotes to avoid being deceived.
- Be particularly cautious about your possessions in crowded areas, such as local festivals, markets, tourist sites, railways, bus stations, and on trains and buses.
- Respect the custom of the local ethnic groups.
- Do not quarrel with anyone during your trip.
- Any disputes should be reported to your local guides for resolution.
- Avoid traveling in any areas or sites that are not open to foreigners.
- Do not voice publicly any opinions contrary to China's laws and code of ethics and morals.

The threat level is considered low for crime and medium for terrorism. The U.S. embassy is not aware of any specific, implied, or general threats that would impact or be directed against American citizens and interests in China. Should a threat develop, Chinese security services are committed to advise the embassy of pertinent information and provide necessary security services coverage.

Terrorism is rare in China, although a small number of bombings have occurred in areas throughout China. Recent bombings have largely been criminal activity, frequently the result of commercial disputes. Last year there were more than 80,000 incidents of social unrest according to the Chinese government. The vast majority of these local incidents related to disputes over land seizures, social issues, or environmental problems. While some incidents have grown to larger scales and involved some violence, these demonstrations have not been directed against foreigners. In April 2005 anti-Japanese demonstrations resulted in property damage and some reports of violence being directed against foreigners of Asian appearance.

Foreigners are often approached in tourist areas by individuals seeking to exchange U.S. dollars or to sell pirated or fake products, such as CDs, DVDs, etc. These transactions often result in foreigners being arrested along with the criminals. Incidents of crime continue to increase, primarily due to the influx of rural populations into the city (with the lifting of social controls on the urban population now allowing these persons to visit/move to cities), disparity income between rural and urban, corruption of law enforcement, and poor training of law enforcement. Compared to other large cities, crime rates in Beijing are low. Petty theft is common in crowded locations, such as marketplaces, stores, and tourist locations. Keep your wallet in your front pocket, and keep a photocopy of your passport handy, which is sufficient for identification while venturing around. Limit credit card use to reputable establishments and tear up receipts before discarding.

U.S. businesspersons engaged in sensitive projects have reportedly returned to hotel rooms to find their laptops or computers downloaded by technically efficient Chinese intelligence services. The majority of U.S. personnel do not come under surveillance by Chinese intelligence, but those who are engaged in negotiations or possess vital proprietary information, and multinational personnel should play it safe by using discretion in all forms of communications. Sensitive paper or electronic documents should be kept to a minimum and not left unattended.

Security personnel may at times place foreign visitors under surveillance. Hotel rooms, telephones, and fax machines may be monitored, and personal possessions in hotel rooms, including computers, may be searched without the consent or knowledge of the traveler. Taking photographs of anything that could be perceived as being of military or security interest may result in problems with authorities. Foreign government officials, journalists, and businesspeople with access to advanced proprietary technology are particularly likely to be under surveillance.

REGISTRATION/EMBASSY LOCATION

Americans living or traveling in China are encouraged to register with the nearest U.S. embassy or consulate through the State Department's travel registration website so that they can obtain updated information on travel and security within China. Americans without Internet access may register directly with the nearest U.S. embassy or consulate. By registering, American citizens make it easier for the embassy or consulate to contact them in case of emergency.

BEIJING—The U.S. embassy is located at Number 2, Xiu Shui Dong Jie, Chaoyang District, Beijing; the American Citizen Services section can be reached at (86)(10) 6532-3431 (8:30-12:00 a.m. and 2:00-4:00 p.m., Monday-Friday), after hours, (86)(10) 6532-1910. For detailed information please visit the embassy's website at http://beijing.usembassy-china.org.cn. The embassy consular district includes the following provinces/regions of China: Beijing, Tianjin, Shandong, Shanxi, Inner Mongolia, Ningxia, Shaanxi, Qinghai, Xinjiang, Hebei, Henan, Hubei, Hunan, and Jiangxi.

CHENGDU—The U.S. consulate general in Chengdu is located at Number 4, Lingshiguan Road, Section 4, Renmin Nanlu, Chengdu 610041; telephone (86)(28) 8558-3992, 8555-3119; after hours, (86)(28) 1370 8001 422; and email consularchengdu@state.gov. This consular district includes the following provinces/regions of China: Guizhou, Sichuan Xizang (Tibet), and Yunnan, as well as the municipality of Chongqing.

GUANGZHOU—The main office of the U.S. consulate general in Guangzhou is located at Number 1, South Shamian Street, Shamian Island 200S1, Guangzhou 510133. The consular section, including the American Citizens Services unit, is now located at 5th Floor, Tianyu Garden (II phase), 136-146 Lin He Zhong Lu, Tianhe District; telephone (86)(20) 8518-7605; after hours, (86)(20) 8121-6077; and email GuangzhouACS@state. gov. This consular district includes the following provinces/ regions of China: Guangdong, Guangxi, Hainan, and Fujian.

SHANGHAI—The consular section of the U.S. consulate general in Shanghai is located in the Westgate Mall, 8th Floor, 1038 Nanjing Xi Lu, Shanghai 200031; telephone (86) (21) 3217-4650, ext. 2102, 2013, or 2134; after hours, (86)(21) 6433-3936; email shanghaiacs@state.gov. This consular district includes the following provinces/regions of China: Shanghai, Anhui, Jiangsu, and Zhejiang.

SHENYANG—The U.S. Consulate General in Shenyang is located at No. 52, 14th Wei Road, Heping District, Shenyang 110003; telephone (86)(24) 2322-2374; email ShenyangACS@ state.gov. This consular district includes the following provinces/regions of China: Liaoning, Heilongjiang, and Jilin.

A diverse country description and additional information are available at http://travel.state.gov/travel/cis_pa_tw/cis/cis_1089.htm.

SECURITY PLAN PHASE

Shortly after a threat assessment is developed and delivered to the client, a security plan should be developed, using the threat assessment as a stepping off point. This procedure is illustrated in the following document.

Following agreement between the assessor and the facility/ location being assessed, the security planning phase will commence ahead of deployment. This will involve:

- Meeting with corporate managers in the (country or countries) to gain a full understanding of their operational plan and requirements
- Detailed reconnaissance of the accommodations and likely work sites

- Liaison with police, security, and intelligence agencies in (country)
- Liaison with other security teams in (country)
- Development of the plan, which will comprise:
  - Physical enhancements, if required, to selected residential and office accommodations. This may include a range of technical measures, such as CCTV, entry phone systems, intruder detection systems, and emergency communications. (Small, portable equipment is readily available and easily installed.)
  - The development of a movement security plan for the safest achievable movement of staff around the various residential, office, and other locations.
  - The production of security briefings and procedures for staff.
  - Emergency procedures to be carried out in the event of an incident.
- Communications plan to ensure that all corporate staff can be contacted at all times. This will include emergency contact numbers, backup systems such as satellite phones, and emergency radio system frequencies/channels.

4

Protecting People Who Don't Believe They Need to Be Protected
"I Would Prefer to Go Low Profile"

The general who wins the battle makes many calculations in his temple before the battle is fought. The general who loses makes but few calculations beforehand.

—Sun Tzu

"I would prefer to go low profile" is a refrain I have heard many times. "Low profile" is a basic premise that goes something like this: your principals (those whom require protection), whether they are to be protected while being driven through a volatile area, or provided with protection while operating at a job site or office building, should be protected in such a manner so as not to draw attention to themselves or the operation. The theory is that by providing what some might consider adequate and appropriate security, such as armed security details, armored vehicles, perimeter fortifications, and other measures, you are actually attracting the attention of the "bad guys."

Low-profile advocates, for some reason tend to be British security professionals, probably going back to their status as a once far-flung global empire with experience in many locations most people couldn't even locate on a map. The theory is quite prevalent in countries such as Iraq or Afghanistan, but also part of security practice in Central and South America, some African countries, and elsewhere. The practical application involves operating in personal security details (PSDs) without guns bristling and being waved around, and the use of nondistinct vehicles, rather than the typical large, armor-plated sport utility vehicles. The theory behind this use of beaten-up, less flashy vehicles is that these are more apt to "blend in"— another term often used in conjunction with "low profile."

I have debated this philosophy with those practitioners who swear by it. They tell me that it has kept their clients and themselves from harm in volatile areas, including Iraq and Afghanistan. My main argument has been (and maybe this is a Midwest U.S. perspective) that when I am working in the field, I would rather not have to drive all the way back to the house to get my screwdriver. I have to be prepared with tools I need—or think I might need. And when I was in Iraq, I am quite sure that the local population knew I was not from Iraq or the Middle East. With my blonde-brown hair, green eyes, and light skin, I am fairly certain they pegged me for a Westerner—from the second I stepped off the airplane.

Whether you cover yourself with a dashiki, wear dark sunglasses, stocking caps, hooded sweatshirts, or clown shoes, they are going to know you, and know you quickly. Don't kid yourself about this. The bad guys will find out rather quickly, either through subterfuge—such as knowing of your plans, travel routes, or other details provided by co-conspirators, hotel employees, or office workers—or by other means. Your vehicle might "look the part," but your detail (you do have an armed detail—don't you?) might brandish a weapon at an inopportune time. Or, an old man or young boy standing at a street corner might notice two sturdy men seated in a front seat with blazing eyes scanning all points for any movement. One or two men might be seated in the back seat. One man looks slightly scared, the other one is just as determined as the two in the front seat. Oh, and here is the dead giveaway: there is another vehicle following behind this one. And, oh my gosh, is that an earpiece for a radio I see? Hmm.

If you want to cover your faces and drive around in crappy vehicles (and let's hope you have at least some armor in that crappy vehicle—and a very nice engine capable of getting the hell out of Dodge when you need to), you can even blare local music from a cassette or CD player. I once heard a corporate legend of someone who said he was able to "blend in" and remove himself to safety by donning a dashiki to "look the part" and driving into the desert. Now come on! You show me a Caucasian U.S. business man or woman, who is not native born to that country, who can blend in in any Middle Eastern country and not be recognized as a Westerner (albeit one who is acting mighty suspiciously trying to blend in); and I will show you someone who is sticking out like a sore thumb and is most likely giving the locals a really enjoyable time watching. As they say, you can put lipstick on a pig, but it's still a pig.

Having said this, I do feel that lowering your profile is an effective and proven method of keeping out of harm's way. Those who have been born to a particular country or region, or are of the same nationality and speak the language fluently, can manage. However, even such a traveler who has overlooked just how Western he or she has become can slip into careless mistakes. Something as simple as clothing can keep you safe. Really. For example, if you are traveling into a country that is known to have bad feelings or outright hostility toward the United States and Americans, it would not be wise to wear your brand new t-shirt with the American flag emblazoned on the front and back. Similarly, wearing a New York Yankees baseball cap or even corporate logo polo shirts, can be dead giveaways. Sports team jackets and jerseys can call attention to one's self in the same manner. Basically, I would avoid logo apparel of all kinds, even if not printed in English. You might be offending someone or alerting another to the fact that you at least have enough money to purchase logo-ed apparel that the average, or below average person, might not.

Jewelry is great if you are heading to that gala event, but it has little use when traveling to an underdeveloped country. For one thing, who are you trying to impress? You are likely already wowing the local nationals just by having a nice pair of shoes, a nice shirt and belt, a watch of any sort, and the fact that you traveled to their country (probably business or first class) with a ticket that might cost more than their earnings in a year. Don't overdo it; be less conspicuous. Here is where I am agreeing with the low-profile crowd. You like Gucci or Channel? Fabulous! But, leave the bags in the trunk of the Rolls while parked at the airport. Ostentatious clothing, handbags, jewelry—it all makes you stand out like a target. Less is better. Consider that you are here to work, or vacation, for that matter. And you, being the Westerner, don't want to be looked upon as a nice piece of opportune cash, loot, or booty for the bad guys.

To me, low profile is less tangible than what most people consider. Low profile consists of not broadcasting where you might be from, whether overtly through corporate names, or by your actions and words, when traveling. It means having an attitude that is not "in your face"—being the loud, boisterous American who regales those surrounding him or her with euphemisms, anecdotes, and backslapping "Hey, look at me, I'm an

45

American!" mannerisms. These frequently take place in Western gathering places and watering holes. But they can also be displayed in hotel lobbies, airports, and other public places. You see it in those bars/clubs/restaurants that draw foreigners and expats because the ice is cold, the band is good, the waitstaff is cute, the food is good, etc.

Be ready for the typical nature of a lot of expatriates to "let their hair down." Show me an engineering and construction crew that will not want to go out and tie one on as soon as they have the opportunity and I will be amazed. The fact is that going out to dinner in some locations can be hazardous to your health. And, I am not only speaking of the threat from food poisoning, although this could lead to a serious situation involving intestinal distress. Such a scenario once required emergency medical treatment to alleviate severe food poisoning. Getting drunk and disorderly in a volatile region is not recommended. I have observed employees get into fights over the smallest perceived infractions, resulting in broken bones and damaged egos. What you might quite often be presented with is the need to have man camps or compounds, which will allow folks to party to their hearts' content. No need to worry about drinking and driving—one can stumble back to their cottage, apartment, or trailer.

Call me old-fashioned, but I prefer the principle of "deterrence" over "low profile." Deterrence in volatile situations would mean that you have a big club, in the way of a bodyguard or personal security detail. Low-profile advocates would say, "If you have a club, they will just get a bigger club." Maybe. But, when it comes to being confronted with a club, I would still rather have a club, no matter what size. I might survive and I could live to run away and grab a bigger club. Deterrence means that when the bad guys surveil you, having picked you out even though you were traveling low profile, they realize that you have protection. They may not know exactly what types of armament you are carrying in the vehicle. They could determine that it is armored, has bullet-resistant windows, run-flat tires, or other safety features.

I have often heard the argument that by having protection, the bad guys will get the impression "Hey, this must be an important American in the vehicle!" I don't buy this argument either. I simply don't see the empirical evidence that supports this theory of persons being chosen as a target because they were driving around in an armored vehicle, or who had a bodyguard as a means of personal protection. Once, when dealing with such protests from seasoned project veterans who had worked in a particular city for which I had many concerns, they argued that by my insisting they use a protective detail I was increasing their chances of something happening. So, my manager asked me to scour my sources to see if I could find one incident or report, any piece of information that proved this theory. I could not find any. If you ask any five carjackers whose vehicle they pick to hijack, are they going to tell you "I picked the vehicle that appeared to have someone sitting in the SUV with two guys in it who I was pretty sure were armed"?

What do you tell the spouse, sister, mother, father, or brother of a victim when they are kidnapped, murdered, or beaten and left by the side of the road when you did not provide them with a security person or detail in a country in which all the information and intelligence should have led you to consider this occurrence as a possibility? Do you say, "We felt that by providing them with a security detail we would have just drawn attention to them"? I personally do not want to have that conversation with a widow. I don't want my corporation to be sued to compound the misery of having an injured or, worse, dead employee.

KEY POINTS

In my opinion, if you are going to be working in an area where armed conflicts have taken place, where kidnappings and other attacks upon Westerners or Western businesses and interests occur, the concept of low profile, in the context of personal protection details I have described above, is not for you. Rather than go with an option that has a risk of someone getting into a situation where they do not have the resources to fight their way out, if necessary. On the other hand, the idea of not drawing attention to yourself as an American while on overseas travel is a worthwhile and smart tactic.

CASE STUDY

I was once part of a team of security professionals working in Iraq off and on from 2003 through 2006. During that time, I spent a lot of time in Iraq, including at the Coalition Provisional Authority (CPA) in Baghdad. The CPA is now the U.S. embassy in Iraq. During this time frame, however, it was a meeting ground and crossroads for military and civilian personnel dealing with the occupation and reconstruction of the country. One hot, dusty day, of which there were an endless amount, I met four Americans who were coming in for a hot lunch in the chow hall, formerly one of

Saddam Hussein's larger conference rooms. One of the Americans was an executive with a major U.S. corporation. The other three were his protection detail. They were retired military—Marine recon and an Army ranger. I could have told you the minute I saw them walk into the building they were Americans, by their style of dress, demeanor, and actions. Before they spoke I could have assured you three were ex-military and the one guy was their principal, or the one whom they were protecting. We started sharing our stories about the type of work we were doing and how we were doing it. When it came to security, I found out that they worked and lodged outside of the Green Zone, the protected area where many Western contractors based themselves due to the relative safety provided there. They were working in the Red Zone, downtown Baghdad and the surrounding area, which was not protected by Coalition Forces. They were traveling back and forth, going low profile. Instead of the ubiquitous General Motors or Ford SUVs, they were traveling in an older European model vehicle, one predominantly seen on the chaotic streets of Baghdad. The vehicle was slightly beaten up, hardly what would be expected of Americans and their bright, shiny new SUVs, rushing and rampaging through the city streets on most days. The vehicle had a reliable engine and was mechanically sound, but had no armor protection, just the vehicle steel shell of the original manufacturer. The three retired military guys of course had weapons, and there was personal protective equipment (PPE) such as ballistic vests and helmets for them and the principal. But without the extra firepower provided by additional team members, the three admitted that their best option, if attacked, would be to get out of the area as fast as they could. Not always an easy task, as I had seen along the clogged and jammed city streets all over Baghdad. When I asked if the three of them felt they had blended in by covering their heads with the traditional keffiyeh worn by Iraqis, they stated they didn't think so. Did they feel when they drove around that Iraqis thought them not to be Westerners or Americans? Did they believe that there was no "buzz" around the neighborhood about who the "new neighbors" were living in the villa across the way? They indicated they really didn't know. About this time, their Iraqi interpreter chimed in. He told us that he was certain each time they drove around, most everyone knew they were a vehicle full of Westerners. He stated the neighbors constantly asked him why the Americans covered their heads in the Arab manner. The interpreter told me that he felt in danger every time they drove into the Green Zone, and every time they left. Anyone, he said, could follow them easily and pick them out with no trouble. The three Americans then told me they had realized they were being surveilled a day or two ago, and they were dropping the low profile for a more robust method of protection. "Good for you," I answered.

KIDNAPPING SURVIVAL TIPS

What if the unthinkable happens and you are kidnapped? Most kidnappers today consider themselves businessmen. They are not interested in harming their victims; they want to conduct a business transaction and be paid, at which time they will release their victim. Kidnappers have found that it is not profitable to harm the individual, and since money is the goal, methods have changed. Victims may still be roughed up and verbally abused.

Emotions are high when the victim is captured. Chances of escape are low since victims are surprised and overwhelmed, outnumbered. Your best chance of survival is not to resist. Follow the directions given to you. You will be placed in a vehicle, possibly with a gun to your head. You may be struck just to prove who is in control. You will receive verbal abuse and possibly death threats. Keep your head about you and do not resist. The key in this situation is to survive.

You will be taken to a predetermined location. Once the initial onslaught is over, you can expect reasonable treatment. The living conditions may not be the best, but they will be tolerable. The average number of days spent in captivity is thirty. Keep yourself physically and mentally alert by doing exercises and playing mental games. Time is a survival weapon even though it seems like everything is taking forever. Do not make threats or vow revenge when you are released. Remain passive, not necessarily submissive. Be cooperative, not argumentative, hostile, or competitive.

While you are in captivity your company and your family will be working to have you released. Negotiations will be going on with the kidnappers and representatives of the company/family. Offers will be traded back and forth until an agreement is made. To keep up your morale, always remember that people are working tirelessly for your release.

To follow are a few checklists with pointers on personal security.

SOME KIDNAPPING AVOIDANCE AND SAFETY TIPS

Kidnappings occur most frequently in the home or in a vehicle. Therefore, protective measures suggested below emphasize these areas.

- Keep your doors locked even while in the home. Keep alarm systems armed on exterior doors.
- Utilize sturdy door construction and locks, and have a peephole in your door.
- No stranger should be admitted into the home unless prearranged.
- Do not allow door-to-door salespeople into the home.
- Do not participate in general surveys.
- Do not give your name or phone number in response to a wrong number call.
- Be suspicious of anyone representing himself of herself as a phone company employee.
- If utility repairmen appear at your door, obtain their name and ask to see an ID, contact the main utility office, and verify the person's reason for being present.
- Avoid establishing a regular routine such as mail or newspaper pickup, jogging/walking, or other activities.
- Avoid using the same vehicle routes to work or when taking children to school or other activities.
- Look inside your vehicle before getting in.
- Keep vehicle doors locked and windows rolled up.
- Be skeptical of calls advising of a family member's injury.
- Create a special secure room where family members can retreat if an intruder is attempting to gain entry.
- Obtain a complete fingerprint card through your local police agency for each family member.

A Quick Checklist on What to Do If Kidnapped

- Cooperate fully with abductors.
- Try to remember details such as vehicles used, routes taken, noises, time to destination, etc.
- Do not provoke the abductors.
- If medical attention is needed, ask for it.
- Speak as calmly as possible to the abductors.

- Eat meals without complaint.
- If an escape decision is made, have a plan and consider consequences before you act.

SOME CARJACKING SAFETY AND SURVIVAL TIPS

Statistically speaking, your chances of survival if a carjacking victim are low; however, preventative actions can reduce your risk. Below is some information regarding this type of crime.

Areas Used by Carjackers

- Intersections controlled by lights or stop signs
- Garages and parking lots for mass transportation, malls, and stores
- Self-service gas stations and car washes
- ATMs
- Residential parking areas
- Highway exit and entry ramps

Reduce Your Risk

- Approach your car with keys in hand.
- Look inside before getting in.
- Have a cell phone and preprogram emergency numbers.
- Be cautious of asking people for directions.
- Keep doors locked and windows rolled up.
- When coming to a stop, leave room in front of your vehicle for maneuvering around other vehicles.
- When possible, drive in the center lane.
- Park in well-lit areas.
- Do not stop and assist strangers whose vehicles have broken down; call for help.
- Avoid parking next to dumpsters, wooded areas, and large trucks.

If It Happens to You

- If threatened, do not argue. Give up your car.
- Get away from the area as soon as possible.
- Try to remember a description of the carjacker.
- Report to the police as soon as possible.

STAGING SECURITY IN A THEATER OF WAR: PERSONNEL SENT TO REBUILD IRAQ'S INFRASTRUCTURE SHOULD BE TRAINED THOROUGHLY ON THE PHYSICAL AND MENTAL CHALLENGES THEY WILL FACE*

Iraq is a country of extreme beauty, but it also presents extreme challenges, both natural and manmade. Thus, arriving in Baghdad can be a physical and psychological shock and personnel should be prepared. It starts with how the plane lands. As a defensive maneuver, approaching planes typically corkscrew down to a landing strip that appears to be directly below where the planes began their descent. The drop can be harrowing as well as nauseating, and stepping off the plane with a full airsickness bag in hand is not the best way to start an assignment.

As the operational security manager for Black & Veatch, an engineering and construction firm in Overland Park, Kansas, I visited Iraq several times, most recently in May of 2004, to provide security inspections and oversee the security operations of my employer, which has been contributing to programs called Restore Iraqi Electricity and Restore Iraqi Infrastructure. My responsibilities included training our engineering and construction personnel, who volunteered to deploy to Iraq, for the challenges of the mission. I have had the chance to see firsthand what worked best in terms of the pre-mission training and what needed improvement. While elections have occurred since that time, the violence has not abated. Consequently, the lessons learned are still valid for anyone headed to Iraq in the future.

Don't sugarcoat. There's no point in misleading employees about the risks they will face. Iraq is a theater of war, and while operating in parts of Pakistan, Algeria, or other hotspots might provide some insight, Iraq is unique.

I have witnessed veterans of projects in some of the most difficult and dangerous areas in the world pass up going to Iraq or return shortly after arriving. Companies must be honest about the risks in

---

* This is an article I wrote in 2005 (*Security Management*, April 1, 2005) that provides useful tips for expats traveling to a hostile area, in this case, Iraq. Reprinted with permission from *Security Management* and ASIS International.

Iraq and give workers who aren't cut out for that level of risk a chance to opt out. Not doing so will only create problems down the road.

Prepare. Those who will go must be physically and mentally prepared. For example, personnel must don personal protective equipment consisting of 30 or so pounds of Kevlar flak jackets and helmets. They will have to wear this equipment often, and I prepare staff for this burden by having them wear the equipment around their homes.

I also try to prepare them for the fear, shock, and possible trauma that come from being in a war zone. I explain that they will see and hear explosions and gunfire. They might encounter improvised explosive devices, vehicle-borne improvised explosive devices or vehicle-concealed improvised explosive devices.

Tracers will light up the sky, the ground will tremble, and smoke will suddenly plume. We spent hours of training preparing workers to avoid or prepare for these threats before they set out for Iraq.

Another issue is the threat of kidnapping in Iraq. Trainers must discuss the facts and risks clearly and openly. Trainees should be taught when and how to look for a means of escape. Thomas Hammill, the Kellogg, Brown and Root truck driver who was kidnapped and escaped (twice) in Iraq, proved that escape is possible.

Briefings and training should cover a variety of other topics as well. The scope of that training is too vast to outline here, but some of the salient information that should be included in the training is raised throughout this article.

Attitude is also important. Each time I traveled to Iraq, I did a quick "gut check" to make sure that I had the right mind-set. So that I would not be distracted by unresolved issues at home, I set my priorities and affairs in order prior to departing.

Beware loose lips. Kansas City to Baghdad is a long, exhausting flight, and personnel deployed to Iraq from the United States could well be desperate for chit-chat with a fellow passenger, if only to calm their nerves. That's fine, but caution is in order.

Beware the ubiquitous "What do you do for a living?" question. It seems innocent enough, but answering it truthfully might violate a cardinal rule of operational security (OPSEC).

Last April, I was standing in line at an airline ticket counter on my way to Iraq, via Amsterdam and Kuwait, when a man posed such a question to me. While waiting on my reply, the man stated that he was a student at a Middle Eastern university. Had I said "I am a Department of Defense contractor, working on security issues connected with restoring Iraqi electricity/infrastructure, and we will be based in Basra," where might the conversation have led?

Not everyone is a terrorist or collaborator, of course, but someone—a person in line, an employee behind the counter, the cleaning person pushing the mop nearby—might find the information useful. In this kind of case, there is no such thing as being too cautious.

Practicing OPSEC can be as simple as my reply: "I'm just on vacation." If I am pressed on my nationality, I often offer up "I'm Canadian," and the interest tends to wane. That simple ruse can avoid potential conflict.

I was in a Muslim nation on the first night of cruise missile and bombing attacks of Operation Iraqi Freedom, for example. As the large-screen televisions (rolled into the lobby especially for this event) blared, viewers who assumed I was American questioned my country's reasons for the attack.

I'm proud to be a United States citizen, but acknowledging my nationality right then might have unnecessarily jeopardized my mission. I became Canadian for the rest of the trip, and the cab drivers and hotel guests left me alone.

I fly U.S. airlines when possible, but whether I am on a U.S. or foreign-owned carrier, I do not review materials or documents relating to business while en route, and I do not discuss, read, or review business matters with anyone accompanying me, be they a colleague or total stranger.

I am continually conscious of "shoulder surfing." I advise workers going to Iraq not to even bother taking out a document if they don't want to see it in the newspaper the next day. I also encourage them not to work at all on the trip. They will need all their strength once they touch down.

Expect extremes. Some basic advice is in order: Don't eat a heavy meal prior to the flight, and avoid alcohol. An airsickness pill such as Dramamine might be a good idea as well.

If possible, personnel should always arrive in the bright light of day. Both air and land travel is riskier at night because darkness conceals possible threats. The intense heat—temperatures can exceed 120 degrees Fahrenheit—saps the life of anyone who is not well prepared. To give my trainees a sense of what to expect, I tell them to imagine placing their face directly in front of a hair dryer that has been left on "high" for about 10 minutes. Such is the furnace of Iraq.

Water intake is crucial. I advise our personnel to begin drinking lots of water in advance of their trip and to maintain or increase this level of intake while they are in-country. If they wait until arrival to up their water intake, it's too late. It takes a few days for a body to acclimate to increased water intake; until then the body quickly expels it.

During my first visit to Iraq, I had been walking around for a few hours when I realized that my flak jacket was white from the salt escaping from my pores. This underscored the importance of continual hydration.

Timing isn't everything. Newcomers to Iraq are often seen checking their wristwatch when a "whoomp" is heard or felt. Someone has spread the information (no doubt to calm the uninitiated) that the military deals with unexploded ordnance on the hour and half hour. In fact, that type of information is dangerous.

Personnel who believe it is okay to act casually during an attack that one thinks is just the U.S. military disposing of explosives are putting themselves and their coworkers at risk. Even if the information were true (at one time it may have been possible to consult your watch for ordnance-disposal time assurances), insurgents are clever enough to catch expatriates unawares by timing their attacks to correspond to the military's destruction of ordnance.

Plan for transport. Travel in Iraq is never routine. The route to and from Baghdad's airport to the International Zone—the "safe" zone of the city, often called the Green Zone—is one of the most dangerous stretches in Iraq, and great caution, concern, and preparedness must be exercised while traversing this area. But all travel requires some measure of point-to-point protection.

Many companies choose to use private personal security detachment (PSD) convoys for transportation security as opposed to riding with the U.S. military convoys. That's because military convoys tend to be more noticeable and attractive targets. They are also not likely to be available on the contractor's schedule.

Also, a private car traveling in a military convoy is likely to be the most vulnerable link in the chain. Government contractors can find out about PSD providers from the government and other contractors. They should have teams in place well before any personnel are sent to Iraq.

At the airport, our personnel join a PSD, which accompanies them to their destination and elsewhere during their stay in Iraq. The PSDs we use consist of highly trained former military special-forces personnel. Most are former U.S. forces, but others are from countries in the U.S. coalition in Iraq. Other PSDs also use Iraqis and other foreign nationals as part of the details.

The best PSDs "call out" information to each vehicle as they travel, such as "Three men, 3 o'clock" or "Two on the roof, 9 o'clock." This approach lets forces in each vehicle assess potential threats themselves and train weapons on a target if necessary.

That's vital because vigilance should not be left to the PSDs alone. It takes everyone on board to serve as the eyes and ears of the group.

I trained my staff to be always alert and on the lookout for suspicious activities, objects, or people, such as fast-approaching vehicles, people on rooftops, and debris in the road.

It pays to be "consistently inconsistent" in Iraq, never traveling at the same times and on the same routes if possible. I also encourage our professionals to practice the "buddy system" with colleagues. That is, when they are up and around, traveling in PSDs or in other settings, they should check up on each other.

I ask them to inquire as to how their colleague is feeling that day. They should ask, "Are you 100 percent?" If they say no, and describe having a headache, being tired, or otherwise not being in peak condition, they need to be observed to determine what the issue is. Maybe they have been bitten by an insect or an animal, are dangerously dehydrated, have appendicitis, or suffer from an infection.

I would be remiss if I didn't give due credit to the PSDs with which I traveled. The crews I worked with and observed provided outstanding service and protection as I made my way through

Hillah, Fallujah, Najaf, Diwaniyah, Tikrit, and other destinations such as Bayji and Mosul.

Beyond providing physical security, they conducted reconnaissance of planned routes and were constantly reassessing risks and tailoring their protective posture. Their bravery, determination, and grit warrant special mention.

Have emergency plans. I have always operated on the "Six P Principle," which is shorthand for "Proper Planning Prevents Pretty Poor Performance." Relying on the U.S. government or military is not always an option, so internal readiness, coupled with mutual assistance and contingency arrangements with others, is mandatory.

It is critical to have self-explanatory emergency action plans in Iraq and for workers to be well-acquainted with them so that all players will know their roles and be ready to act after being shaken out of bed by a missile, mortar, or small-arms-fire attack.

Each worker should be given a list of actions to take immediately after an emergency. These can be presented on index cards, but they must also be ingrained in everyone's minds. For example, as part of the plan, our personnel know what to do if their PSD team is incapacitated or they are kidnapped.

Medical assistance. Emergency medical assistance is frequently needed. Medical treatment is handled by trained professionals at the job site, camp, or compound. The more serious the injury, the more it may require emergency medical transportation or an airlift to the closest U.S. military medical facility outside of Iraq.

Personnel should be trained in telltale signs of medical conditions, such as rashes, headaches, and listlessness. They should also know basic first aid and how to quickly summon medical attention.

Evacuations. Work-site evacuations must be expected. One critical factor is ensuring that personnel know the locations of all blast shelters and bunkers, when to take cover, how to take cover, and what to do next. It is also important to know what types of structures are safe to use as shelters.

Some shelters consist of squared sections of concrete that might someday end up being used to construct sewers, with more elaborate versions being dug at an angle into the ground with poured concrete steps and incandescent lighting.

An important precaution before entering any shelter is to check for desert pests such as scorpions and camel spiders. This is especially true in the hottest part of the day; they love the shade.

Poor attention to evacuation procedures left me with an extremely sore jaw in one case. When a Katyusha rocket whizzed over our camp early one cool morning, two workers in a panic sped face first into each other. After the impact, one of them continued running, crashing his forehead into my jaw. I grabbed both men by the collar and shoved them into the closest shelter, which was less than 15 feet away.

The rocket detonated in a blinding flash, and the concussion of the blast disoriented us for a few moments. A trailer was destroyed in this incident, but thankfully no one was injured. Not everyone can keep their wits about them in such situations, but having a working knowledge of the bunkers closest to your present location, as well as what to do in all other emergencies, will help.

Communication. My company uses what it calls the "Lifeline" program, whereby any time a professional is outside of the United States, we provide him or her with around-the-clock emergency contact information. The numbers are used to reach our security and safety managers and their own management team.

Personnel may also provide this information to relatives or friends. In the case of Iraq, I have received many worried telephone calls after media reports of attacks or explosions from persons attempting to determine the safety of someone they care for who was in Mosul, Bayji, or Baghdad at the time. The value of having a quick resource for determining the well-being of a loved one is incalculable. Fortunately, our staff has been unharmed in these incidents.

Physical security. Even nonsecurity personnel should at least be familiar with the basics of effective physical security in the Iraq environment. They should understand what security purposes are served by equipment and personnel. These include the role of barriers, staffing, and protection from projectiles. They should also understand the proper use of security lighting.

Barriers. Barriers, such as Jersey and Hesco (collapsible wire-mesh containers with a heavy-duty plastic liner, filled with sand, dirt or gravel, as described by the Army News Service), are an important piece of a layered defense system. Hesco barriers, single rows or double-stacked, are quickly installed economical protection that provide peace of mind.

In addition, preformed, tall concrete walls can be stood on end and fused together to form barriers. Topping these and existing walls with concertina wire and adding observation towers provides for solid reinforcement, protection, and response. Concrete barriers forming vehicle entry points and reinforced guardhouses provide protection for checkpoints.

Manpower. Observation towers and vehicle entry posts must be staffed with properly trained, equipped, vetted, and supervised security officers who guard specific posts. Additional backup and mobile security guards should operate in tandem to form a proper security force. Concerns include training and drills, standard operating procedure, weapons proficiency, and rules of engagement, to name a few.

Projectile protection. Interior layers of defense include sandbags or Hesco barriers surrounding mobile units/trailers serving as offices or living quarters. Wherever possible, units should be constructed without windows to limit the potential for glass projectiles resulting from blasts.

Personnel should keep work areas away from windows, and if there is window glass, it should be taped over or laminated for protection from flying fragments after a blast.

Steel plating is often inserted into mobile unit walls, roofs, and flooring to provide additional protection from projectiles. In those cases, staff need not be as concerned with being near a wall. Stacking sandbags along any structure provides additional peace of mind.

Lighting. As opposed to a security setting in a stable society, lighting in Iraq is less a deterrent than a risk. Personnel should be informed that lighting actually provides targets for insurgents' small-arms fire, mortars, or rockets. And too much lighting allows insurgents to observe the numbers of protective personnel, their equipment, and level of expertise.

Night-vision equipment is useful for those tasked with watching for signs of movement outside of the perimeter. There are, however, times when lights must be used. Emergency lighting and generators are indispensable, and spotlights, whether portable for vehicles or mounted in observation towers, are handy as well.

In a theater of war, of course, personnel must continually update risk analysis and reevaluate the security posture. Countermeasures must constantly be refined to correspond to threat levels and enemy tactics. Thus, personnel should expect constant readjustment of security measures.

Building the Iraqi infrastructure is a humbling, exhausting, yet exhilarating experience. Contractors who wish to serve in that capacity probably won't have military training or the full resources of the U.S. military behind them, however, and it is incumbent on firms to properly train personnel for that environment and review ongoing security strategies to maintain their effectiveness. Doing so will go a long way towards ensuring that their workers, though constantly in harm's way, are not actually hurt.

5

Security, Crisis Management, and Evacuation Planning
The 2:00 a.m. Friday Telephone Call— "The Missiles Are Flying All around Us!"

Let our advance worrying become advance thinking and planning.

—Winston Churchill

Security and crisis management are mutually dependent upon each other, in my opinion. Each is an important program for protecting people and assets around the world. I honestly believe that you can't have an effective security program without a crisis or emergency management program to back it up. You must plan for and implement an effective security management program, but whether you are dealing with a man-made or natural disaster, your crisis management must be robust and inclusive.

Crisis management is like muscle conditioning. In order for your muscles to work at their optimum level, the proper plans must be in place and should be exercised. Crisis management planning and emergency response works best when it rolls out like falling off a log, like a practiced and efficient procedure. Of course, many things can and do go wrong during emergencies, but with proper planning and well-exercised procedures and plans, you can work through these and even anticipate the bad things that can occur.

Let me mention one thing from the outset. The most important thing to consider concerning your crisis management plan is having and constructing your plan in such a way that it is sufficient to stand on its own and operate without the direct supervision or oversight of your corporate functions. This is the dilemma: you must have in place a program that is operable in a situation where your personnel/offices/projects could very likely be cut off completely from the mother ship, through either a process of communications failure, which frequently occurs, or the multitude of problems that arise. Think about some huge natural or man-made disasters.

Consider the Underground and transit bombings in London on July 7, 2005. On July 7, many employees knew they might not make it into the office, and some thought they should turn around and go home, or continue on to the office and arrive late. In July and August 2006, how many employees working in Israel knew what to expect when Hezbollah began lobbing rockets into that country? Once the bombings took place, many companies with operations in London began calling their personnel to make sure everyone was OK. Colleagues located in London began trying to contact employees on cell phones. Before too long, the mobile phone system was overloaded and crashed. Email was still available, but people were still attempting to contact personnel at home on landlines, or continually trying the mobile phones.

Or for that matter, how many employees had a clue what to do or how to react to the bombings directed at the trains in Mumbai, India, or Madrid, Spain? What if you not only had employees working in these countries and locations, local national employees, but also had travelers from the United States, employees who might have been in harm's way?

The fact is, when a crisis or natural disaster takes place halfway across the world, you will most likely be asleep. Unless you have a 24-hour operations center, and someone in-country or elsewhere is cognizant enough to place a call to that center, you will probably not hear about the incident until you turn on the TV news or hear it on a car radio. Woe to those who find out about such incidents when they walk into the office! Been there, done that.

In such situations your first priority is to track down all of your local nationals and expats in-country and determine they are safe, where they are located, and what they need from you or the corporation. But, you, Corporate Security Manager, can't help them if the phone lines are jammed.

Your job site, office, and business locations should have an emergency action plan. Your expat employees should be asked to develop their own plans, especially when taking dependents overseas. You can help them develop a personal emergency action plan that will allow for collection of the important papers and other items they will require. They should be discussing among their family members what they would do should there be a natural or man-made disaster, or should family members become somehow separated. They should provide family and friends with their emergency contact numbers. Use the lifeline program as mentioned previously. This would be someone within your company who would know where the employee is located and the best means to contact him or her in an emergency. Official documents and original papers, such as wills, insurance papers, marriage and birth certificates, and naturalization certificates, should be kept back home. Certified copies can be brought with the employee. Keep in mind you will be developing this into a formalized program of an emergency action plan to be maintained by the office or project manager.

AN EXAMPLE OF A PERSONAL EMERGENCY ACTION PLAN

Know your exact location of lodging, offices, and job sites. Maps and GPS grid coordinates are important for two reasons. These might direct assistance to your location if necessary, but can also indicate routes for evacuation, if the situation warrants.

Keep a listing and knowledge of "safe houses" (not just a spy term) or locations of safety you can go to in case of emergencies, and if it is deemed safe to venture out on the streets. Safe houses can be the obvious locations, such as police stations, fire stations, and other locations, if these are deemed to not be affected by the emergency situation. These can also be the houses of other trusted expats or local nationals. Determine the first location you would go to in an emergency situation and what means you would use for transport.

Know your best options for transportation, and the contact information for such means of transportation:

- Airport/airlines. Keep flight information printed out and at the ready.
- Train stations/train lines. Keep train schedules printed out and at the ready.
- Car rental agencies and livery and chauffeur services.
- Bus terminal schedules.
- Underground/subway times and routes.
- Boat/ferry/port authority/cruise line schedules.

In addition to your lifeline (that company employee who knows your project/office and other pertinent information and with whom you have shared 24/7 contact numbers) contact information, it is recommended that you know the following numbers and locations:

- 911 emergency call equivalents for the country you are in
- Embassy/consulate information, including regional security officer contact information
- Police station/fire department listings and locations
- Hospital/ambulance listings and contact information
- Locations of post offices
- Government visa/Customs offices locations and contact information
- Red Cross contact information if in-country, or international contact information
- Translator services or local nationals who could translate phone calls and other information

Forms of communications (adequate communications will vary based upon country conditions):

- Telephone
- Cellular phone/text messaging
- Satellite phone
- Email/Internet
- Post office/Federal Express, etc.

Keep a first aid kit at the ready; you can call it your "evacuation kit" or "go bag."

- Money, such as local currency and U.S. dollars.
- Is first aid kit fully stocked?
- Are there emergency cash, traveler's checks, and credit cards on hand in case of bank closings, lack of ATMs, etc.?
- How many days do you estimate you can sustain yourself on these supplies?

Concerning emergency and crisis management planning, I would strongly recommend you not tackle these issues and planning procedures/processes alone, or with just your security team. You will not get the project done, and it will burn you out in the process. Instead, in order to have the broadest applications and successes for such a program, create a disaster recovery task force. The task force should include corporate functions such as security and safety professionals, human resources, information technology (IT), risk management, legal, operations (maintenance, receptionists, food services), and the corporation divisions and business units, such as retail, manufacturing, engineering, and consulting, comprising broad and all-inclusive representation of the company.

An office/project emergency action plan should be developed with the end users in mind. It should include organizational terminology, names, titles, and contact information. The plan should indicate which resources will be required for successful outcomes. Information that will be required should be listed for the various types of emergencies. I am a believer in checklists to be utilized in emergency situations.

Concerning an emergency action plan, paper copies must be made available to all employees at a given location or facility. One method of ensuring all persons are acquainted with and have access to the plan is by posting the plan on the company intranet. Managers should ensure that all employees have been trained on the plan, one method being during new-hire processing or when being assigned to the overseas project. If a project, facility, or site has multiple locations, care must be taken to ensure that each location has a version of the emergency action plan that is specific to that place. The manual is only as good as the information contained within; therefore, an audit of the manual must be made mandatory to ensure all information is current and pertinent.

Concerning medical emergencies in foreign locations and hostile areas, you will need to consider if there are numbers similar to 911 in the United States for reporting medical emergencies. Security and safety managers should determine the capabilities of local emergency medical resources, and if these are not available, an internal medical capability is required. In extreme circumstances, you may be forced to hire your own medical personnel, doctors, nurses, or trained emergency medical professionals, and to supply a clinic or medical unit at your project site or facility. If the nearest trauma centers or basic qualified medical facilities are a great distance from your location(s), emergency medical evacuations might be required.

International SOS offers multifunctional emergency evacuations and diverse capabilities for corporations. Not only are they able to provide for emergency medical evacuations, such as the one I mentioned above involving trauma or severe medical emergency requiring immediate evacuation of employees, but they will also provide security evacuations in situations involving civil unrest, coups, and other security meltdowns. In addition, International SOS will provide a survey of nearby medical capabilities, visiting local doctors, clinics, hospitals, dentists, and other health care locations. The organization can provide you and your project with recommendations for which doctors speak English and have been rated competent and capable, and assist you with emergency action plans for dealing with medical emergencies involving your employees. In hostile areas, a well-crafted medical emergency action plan can be critical to success and survival.

Fire emergencies in foreign locales can offer their share of unique challenges. In many foreign cities I have been to, high-rise buildings may not have building fire alarms. Or, when fire alarms sound, it is a roll of the dice whether or not the fire department will respond. When fire crews in foreign cities respond, they may or may not be capably equipped with the latest in lifesaving equipment, including ladder trucks and other response tools. Security and safety managers should do their homework with respect to the capabilities of the fire responders in project and office locations. When necessary, local employees may need to be trained in fire response. Local concerns will include the absence or insufficiency of fire escapes, fire alarms, a sprinkler system, fire extinguishers, and other such emergency building systems. Of special concern, if you are working in remote locations where fire response is not an option, will be your forming a fire crew that can handle these issues for you when they arise. Lodging arrangements for expatriates should be a concern, especially when many apartment and high-rise buildings may not have adequate fire escapes, or design flaws such as iron bars across windows that may not be removed in emergencies.

Natural disasters, such as earthquakes, as previously mentioned, are concerns that must be addressed, given the location of your employees and the nature of the region or country. You will need not only to ensure that employees are trained to protect themselves during such events, but also to plan for response activities when you know that local government resources may be ill-equipped and incapable of offering assistance.

In hostile regions and countries, one necessary aspect of emergency action plans is that which responds to bomb threats, threats of extortion, and criminal vandalism. As with fire response planning, local capabilities to respond to bomb threats might be limited at best. You should consider the training of a local employee capability for the purpose of keeping your expats and local nationals aware of the methods for conducting proper searches for suspicious packages. As with any such occurrence, the best way to ensure that you are not susceptible to actual bombings is to include as part of your preparation and planning such things as proper access control, facility and building setbacks, training for handling unusual mail and parcels, and other important characteristics of mitigation. Again, depending on the location you are operating within, the local law enforcement or military may not be up to the task of proper response, or would be some distance away to warrant you do things on your own. As with any such situation, if you think you have found the real thing, an actual suspected explosive device or truly suspicious package, leave it to the experts. If local law enforcement cannot handle the situation, or are not present, have them contact the military. If this does not work, there are private companies that deal with unexploded ordinance. Evacuate per your emergency action plan, and keep everyone away.

Prevention of and response to workplace violence will be a concern in hostile locations just as it is in the United States—even more so. As has been mentioned earlier, prevention of bad things happening depends a lot on deterrence, detection, delay, and proper planning. Workplace violence in a foreign location that happens to be a hostile area can take many forms. It can range from the routine intramural/interracial/interethnic squabble on a job site, to armed invasions of expat homes. Prevention can range from site security officers at job sites to panic or safe rooms at expat residences. Training in workplace violence response is critical not only for security officers and personnel, but for line management and other employees. Noticing behaviors of individuals that might be warning signs, whether in contractors or full-time employees, is of great importance. Following the logic of medical and fire response, if your local first responders are not capable of providing you with the right support when such occurrences take place, then you will be forced to ensure you can handle the situations with your own employees.

Safety concerns are going to include prevention of and treatment for bloodborne pathogen exposure, as well as safety programs that for the most part should mirror those you have in place in the United States.

Emergency numbers, call lists, calling trees, whatever you want to call them, are vitally important in emergency and other situations. Landlines may work fine during normal circumstances, but during emergencies, natural disasters, terrorist acts, and other occurrences, these may fail or be taken down immediately. Mobile phone systems may fail as well or be very limited. Satellite phones should be considered an option after being tested for operability. Satellite phones continue to improve in quality and can be a vital source of communications. I have had great success in volatile regions using these. Your emergency numbers should include any for ambulance and first responders, including fire, police, and any local poison control, if available.

Numbers and arrangements for medical treatment should be vetted in advance. List the numbers for preferred nonemergency medical treatment, and the hours of operation for the clinics. Have a backup location and numbers for this location. Addresses and maps will be very beneficial. Of course, you will want to seek English-speaking doctors and clinics if possible, or have a translator readily available.

You will want to have the numbers listed for your emergency team in-country: residence, mobile, and backups for each. If you are using satellite numbers, and I would highly recommend you do, list these also. List office staff and backups for them, local nationals included. Indicate numbers for appropriate embassies: United States, Great Britain, and others. If you have developed acquaintances, you should have after-hours contact information for regional security officers and other embassy or consulate staff. List the contact information for your headquarters emergency action staff, corporate security, safety, risk management, and others. (Form 5.1 is for listing contact information for primary and secondary critical team members for both the local management team and corporate headquarters; some additional components of an emergency action plan are contained in Appendix A of this book).

Fire is an area of concern that might be exacerbated given the location and types of resources available. As with most safety programs, general fire awareness and safety are only successful when part of a well-communicated and exercised plan. Work areas should be kept free of debris and clutter, items that might be combustible but also an obstruction in case of emergency. Smoking areas should be areas of concern, with proper extinguishment of cigarette butts. Someone should be in charge of fire extinguishers and ensuring these are filled and are located in conspicuous areas. Employees should be instructed as to the locations of the extinguishers. Fire hoses should be inspected and employees should be trained in the use of these, as with extinguishers. Fire exits should be well marked and kept free of obstructions that might cause slips and falls. Evacuation drills should be conducted, with floor or area marshals sweeping the area to ensure everyone has cleared out.

Concerning bomb threats, information received by employees should be taken down and passed along to their manager and security personnel. Employees need to remain as calm as possible and collect information as indicated on a provided form. If the threat is received by telephone, the perpetrator should be stalled or kept on the phone. The longer the caller is on the phone, the more data you can obtain and the greater the potential you will hear background noises or other useful information. Evacuations, if warranted, should be orderly and handled much like fire evacuations. Windows and doors should be opened in order to cut down on pressure waves and possibly minimize destruction. As with fire evacuations, employees should know where and how to assemble and how to be accounted for. Only the employee in charge can order employees to reenter buildings after evacuations are made. Bomb searches are not an easy proposition; however, it is possible to train employees in how to carry these out. Of course, if you have security personnel with a background in these areas, these employees can be utilized.

The following is offered as an example of the protocol for reporting emergencies to corporate emergency and crisis management teams, and illustrates some of the functions of the subsections of such a team

CHECKLIST FOR REPORTING EMERGENCIES TO THE CORPORATE CRISIS MANAGEMENT TEAM

In the highly volatile situations that require a report to the corporate crisis management team, it is essential that the initial message provide as much information as possible. The message should:

- Describe the type of emergency (terrorist attack, state of war, civil unrest, anti-American demonstrations, anticompany demonstrations, natural disaster, other).
- Report who declared the emergency: host government, ambassador or his representative, project manager or his deputy, other.
- Report who received the notification: general manager, officer manager, secretary or receptionist, other American employee, local national employee, other.
- Report how the notification was conveyed: telephone, messenger, public broadcasting, private sources, personal observation, other.
- Report when the emergency was declared: time/date groups in local time using 24-hour clock (e.g., 1500 hours/20 May 09).

- Report where the emergency has been declared: countrywide, certain states or provinces or regions, designated cities, other.
- Report why the emergency was declared: immediate danger to life, immediate threat to property, precautionary measure to protect life or property, other.
- Report what measures have been taken by host government in face of the emergency that might influence evacuation or other actions: airports closed to civilian traffic, roadblocks on major arteries, commercial communications out, curfew in effect, public gatherings prohibited, other.
- Report what actions have been taken by embassies in the area: ordered immediate evacuation, placed personnel on "alert" status only, recalled personnel in outlying areas, destroyed documents, ordered their citizens to collection or evacuation points, other.
- Report what action appropriate embassies and the U.S. embassy recommend: await instructions, remain indoors, assemble at collection points, destroy equipment and records, other.
- Report in detail what actions you have already taken.

CORPORATE MANAGEMENT TEAM

COMPANY corporate management team consists of preselected corporate personnel together with the incident response team to safeguard employees and property. This corporate crisis management team (CCMT) will utilize:

- Corporate crisis management plan
- Local management team guidelines
- Incident response team guidelines
- Training sessions, at least biannually, to maintain a high level of proficiency and awareness
- Awareness training, regarding personal safety overseas, for key executives

INCIDENT RESPONSE TEAM

The incident response team (IRT) consists of the company's global corporate security team with the background and experience to assist the local management in resolving major incidents at the convenience of the corporate crisis management team. They are responsible for providing regional/country data, formulating plans as part of the CCMT, deploying within 4 hours of notification, and assisting/supporting the local management.

Local team managers should include:

- Senior operations representative in area of incident
- Financial representative
- Local legal representative
- Human resources/administrative/payroll representative

Corporate team members should include:

- Corporate crisis management team coordinator
- Corporate crisis management team chairman
- Corporate crisis management team deputy chairman
- Executive vice president
- Comptroller or chief financial officer
- Vice president of human resources
- Senior corporate legal counsel
- Director of communications

Note that once the corporate crisis management team coordinator's alternate is called, the entire team should be notified.

**FORM 5.1   CONTACT FORM FOR CORPORATE
CRISIS MANAGEMENT TEAM (CCMT)
MEMBERS AND LOCAL MANAGEMENT**

Primary: _____

Home no.: _____   Office no.: _____

Cell no.: _____   Email address: _____

Alternate: _____

Home no.: _____   Office no.: _____

Cell no.: _____   Email address: _____

The following is offered as an example of the protocol for reporting emergencies to corporate emergency and crisis management teams, and illustrates some of the functions of the subsections of such a team.

EMERGENCY NOTIFICATION PROCEDURES

If anyone becomes aware of a crisis situation, or any emergency situation involving or affecting COMPANY personnel, immediately call:

1. The local management; if unsuccessful:
2. The corporate crisis management team; if unsuccessful:
3. The IRT at:
   - Normal appropriate U.S., UK, or country embassy or consulate during business hours:
   - After-hours/holiday number:
   - Special 24-hour number:
     (The special 24-hour telephone number should be used only for emergencies. Please limit distribution of this number.)

If unsuccessful, contact the regional security officer at the appropriate U.S., UK, or country embassy or consulate.

If unsuccessful, contact a friendly foreign embassy.

Do not contact local authorities unless directed to do so. The only exception to this should be in a life-threatening situation where emergency police/fire response is absolutely necessary to save lives and property.

PROCESSES

Local Management Team (Local Management)

The exact duties of a company local management team will be coordinated with the corporate crisis management team in the event of a crisis incident. However, they generally include the following.

Upon being advised of a crisis situation, the local management will meet as soon as possible, after immediately notifying the corporate crisis management team. Once the corporate crisis management team is notified, the following should be accomplished:

- Select a secure base. Select secure premises to be used by the local management.

- Communicate rising tensions to the crisis management team for analysis. Establish and maintain a reliable source of communications with the corporate crisis management team. A secure telephone line must be kept exclusively for communications with the corporate crisis management team, manned 24 hours a day. Additionally, establish alternate means of communications with the corporate crisis management team in the event primary communication is lost.
- Initiate a 24-hour incident log to record all relevant details.
- Stay in touch with local events, contacts, and State Department personnel (U.S. embassy, etc.).
- Account for all personnel.
- Establish a tracking procedure to locate all personnel at all hours.
- Ensure any personnel involved are briefed on the need for strict security.
- Instruct personnel to maintain a low profile.
- Make tentative travel arrangements (open airline ticket reservations, etc.) for employees and dependents. Arrange alternative modes of transportation out of the country in the event the initial plan is impeded.
- Ensure that all personnel have compiled important personal documents (passports, records, and other travel documents), in the event that an evacuation becomes necessary.
- If time allows, make arrangements for the storage of personal belongings, luggage, and portable household items. A warehouse or some other designated place should be used where the items can be recovered at a later date.
- Ensure that personnel know the best way to the airport, including alternate routes.
- Instruct personnel to pack one suitcase with a maximum of 66 pounds per person.
- If time allows, prepare the office—identify documents to be removed and to be destroyed. Consider disposition of outstanding contracts, accounts, etc. Inventory, pack, and store all office equipment and supplies.
- Keep the corporate management team informed!
- Continue to evaluate events as they occur.

- Liaison with corporate crisis management team. Provide accurate, timely, objective and unbiased information to the corporate crisis management team to ensure effective coordination between all the participants.
- Ensure the security of all employees by taking appropriate steps to protect personnel from possible aggressors.
- Protect sensitive information from unauthorized access.

Team Functions—Public Relations

As directed by the corporate crisis management team, and through the medium of an authorized spokesman, control media statements, their contents, and timing.

Establish contact with friendly journalists who may be prepared to assist in inserting helpful articles in the media. No media comment should be made unless authorized by the corporate crisis management team; all media inquiries should be referred to the authorized spokesperson.

With corporate crisis management team direction, prepare a press statement, as a contingency, to handle possible media inquiries.

Initiate detailed examination of legal implications, to include:

- COMPANY liability
- Consumers and client contracts

Team Functions—Administration

- Organize general facilities, transport, accommodation, equipment, and medical assistance required to sustain the local management (and family) throughout a protracted uprising.
- Advise the corporate crisis management team on the possible liability of COMPANY in connection with the medical and legal consequences following the injury or arrest of personnel.
- Consider the implications of liaison with other interested companies, clients, unions, etc.
- Consider communicating with other foreign companies in the area to share intelligence and resources.

- Prepare a position paper for corporate crisis management team, setting out:
  - Nature of the threat
  - Actions taken to date
  - Police input and requests
  - Legal exposure
  - Local authority interests
  - Public relations policy
  - Liaison policy
  - Communications details
  - Commercial implications
- Preferred objective and course of action

Team Functions—Corporate Management Team (CCMT)

Upon receipt of notice that a serious incident has occurred, the initial corporate crisis management team response will include:

- The corporate crisis management team coordinator (corporate security manager) will immediately start notifications.
- Alert the corporate crisis management team chairman, and ascertain meeting time/location.
- Notify all corporate crisis management team members of incident and meeting time/location.
- Alert other senior management, or environmental resource personnel, as directed.
- Activate a 24-hour, secure command center to receive, evaluate, and pass on information to the corporate crisis management team.
- Contact appropriate local management (if not originally contacted by the local management).
- Maintain 24-hour incident log.
- Establish secure telephone or cyber link with incident location to acknowledge message.
- Ensure appropriate local management is convening and taking action until corporate crisis management team can provide guidance.
- Alert IRT, as directed by corporate crisis management team.

The corporate crisis management team's general responsibilities upon convening include:

1. Legal concerns: Responsible for advice and information on all legal aspects during and subsequent to an incident, to include:
   - Liability to a suit brought by shareholders
   - Liability to a suit brought by the public or other person affected by the incident
   - Liability due to injury or prosecution of individuals responsible for implementing corporate policy
   - The local law on passing information to law enforcement agencies
   - The contents of documentary records, the extent of permitted access to these, and their ultimate disposal

2. Financial concerns: Responsible for advice and information on all financial aspects during and subsequent to an incident, to include:
   - Deciding the origin of the emergency funds, whether to be drawn against COMPANY or a subsidiary company account, or use of the bank "special arrangement"
   - Arrangements for the discreet withdrawal of cash from the bank
   - The procedure to be used in accounting for money, while at the same time protecting information relating to its intended use
   - The transport arrangements for emergency funds, including the crossing of international boundaries
   - Knowledge of currency exchange regulations
   - The possibility for offsetting sums paid in emergency actions against a corporate or subsidiary company tax liability

3. Human resources concerns: Responsible for advice and information on all corporate relations/human resources aspects during and subsequent to an incident, to include:
   - The advisability of replacing personnel during a prolonged disturbance/uprising

- Liaison, welfare, and briefing of the families of personnel stranded by a disturbance/uprising
- Employee morale
- Effect of the incident upon local labor relations
- Terms of service for COMPANY executives serving in high-risk areas
- Reception and treatment of returning personnel following a disturbance/uprising
- If appropriate, provision of medical or other information relevant to the victim's health

4. Public relations concerns: Responsible for advice and information on all public relations aspects during and subsequent to an incident, to include:
   - The appointment of authorized spokesperson(s) at the COMPANY corporate headquarters and other location(s) affected
   - Control of the content, timing, and method of issue of all statements to the media
   - Media liaison
   - Liaison with public affairs representatives of other involved agencies or companies
   - Control of media access to the family of stranded personnel and other participants
   - Internal public relations within COMPANY
   - Provision of advice to professionals and family following the resolution of the incident

5. Security response: Responsible for advice and information on all security aspects during and subsequent to an incident, to include:
   - Security of communications
   - Security of meeting rooms used by the corporate crisis management team
   - Security of documentary records
   - Security of the concerned relatives of personnel involved in the disturbance/uprising
   - Security of the local management and staff

- Liaison and coordination with appropriate law enforcement agencies
- As appropriate, security of plant, office, or product affected
- Correct handling of all exhibits (letters, etc.) that may be required to assist police investigations or as evidence

6. International considerations: Responsible for advice and information on all international aspects during and subsequent to an incident, to include:
   - Implications of incident in relations with the host government
   - Implications of joint venture involvement in management of an incident
   - Likelihood of commercial sanctions
   - Effect of the negotiation policy on the current and longer-term trading position of COMPANY within the country of operation
   - Degree of necessity for partial or total evacuation of personnel from the country or operation on a temporary or permanent basis

Team Functions—Incident Response Team

The incident response team (IRT) consists of the company's global corporate security team with the background and experience to assist the local management in resolving major incidents at the convenience of the corporate crisis management team. They are responsible for providing regional/country data, formulating plans as part of the corporate crisis management team, deploying within 4 hours of notification, assisting/supporting the local management while in-country, and acting as the liaison for all kidnap/ransom (K&R) initiatives.

The incident response team will:

- Monitor the crisis situation
- Provide an in-country, firsthand analysis of the crisis
- Advise the corporate crisis management team and local management on appropriate actions
- Assist in the gathering of crisis area intelligence

- Serve as liaison between government officials, hostile groups, aggressors, protestors, embassy personnel, and evacuation elements
- Assist in coordinating the safety and security issues during the crisis
- Provide physical protection for the senior company executives

---

POSTCRISIS EVALUATION

In the aftermath of the crisis, the executive team will evaluate all facets of the crisis—those managed successfully, as well as those that require improvement.

An evaluation form is valuable to assist in gathering information to be analyzed. These forms can later be collected and shared with the local management team and the crisis management team.

The crisis management team will meet shortly after the crisis to compare notes and make recommendations to strengthen the existing procedures. Later, new pages and recommendations can be distributed to appropriate managers for inclusion in their copies of the crisis management plan.

GLOBAL OFFICES

It's important to ensure that the global offices have communications systems.

The establishment and maintenance of communications are critical to rapid and safe implementation of the plan. The local management operations leader will have overall responsibility for establishing communications system/procedures, and ensuring that the available equipment is operational. The local management should have a variety of communications equipment available. CB-type radios are frequently installed in vehicles and homes; portable satellite telephones have proven to be reliable in *in extremis* communications; single sideband (SSB) radios may be used in the offices and by employee ham radio operators. Local telephones will probably be available, although their performance may not be dependable, especially for communications with the appropriate U.S., UK, or country embassy or consulate. Verify the country's legal requirements for using any radio to ensure compliance with local laws.

There are several different types of communications networks that should be established:

- **Local company to the corporate crisis management team:** This link may be difficult to maintain because of its dependence on telephone service, which may be easily disrupted. Portable satellite telephones, electronic mail, or fax may be more dependable. The local management leader should be given the authority from the corporate crisis management team to unilaterally decide to implement the emergency evacuation plan. The tenuousness of the communications link with the corporate crisis management team demands that the local management team leader be able to act without directives from the corporate crisis management team, if necessary. The local management operations leader should determine if communications with other COMPANY global offices in the geographical area is possible through a type of long-range communications. If this link can be established, plans should be made for the neighboring global offices to relay messages to the corporate crisis management team.

- **Local office to the appropriate U.S., UK, or country embassy or consulate:** Regardless of citizenship, the appropriate U.S., UK, or country embassy or consulate will usually support all expatriates of a U.S. company. The appropriate U.S., UK, or country embassy or consulate maintains a close watch on political/military events in the country and has plans for the evacuation of expatriates. The establishment of a reliable communications channel with the embassy is thus of great assistance to the local company emergency evacuation plan. The principal communications link with the appropriate U.S., UK, or country embassy or consulate will probably be telephone. The individuals responsible for evacuation planning in the embassy should be identified and a list of their telephone numbers stored with other emergency documents. If there are disturbances in the phone system, the operations officer should arrange for COMPANY to become part of the emergency radio network of the embassy. The final option is for face-to-face meetings with the embassy security officer. This could be hazardous if there are demonstrations in the vicinity of the embassy, and the team leader must make a decision concerning this option based on their assessment of the situation.

- **Intracompany communications:** Communications are necessary to announce the decision to begin evacuation and to coordinate its implementation. CB radios, SSB (single sideband), and satellite/cellular telephones may all be used to establish a link between the global offices and other locations. All systems should be periodically tested to determine which provides the greatest quality and dependability. In times of instability, the link should be monitored on a 24-hour basis.
- **Company offices to individual homes:** The means of communication between COMPANY offices and individual homes can be via CB radios, portable radios kept in individual homes, or cellular/satellite telephones.

Each global office must have in place:

- Contact list of all local management members
- Contact list of all CCMT members
- Contact numbers of the IRT, including the 24-hour emergency number
- Contact list of all in-country personnel
- Contact list of appropriate U.S., UK, or country embassy or consulate support personnel
- Secure and reliable communications with the corporate headquarters (CCMT), to include an alternate means if common source fails
- Contact list of transportation resources out of the country, to include alternative modes if common methods are not available (i.e., aircraft, boat, vehicles)
- A list of alternate airports in the area, including small airfields (their capabilities and contact information)
- Up-to-date personnel information sheets (such as next of kin and other emergency notification information) on all in-country personnel, expatriate personnel, and their dependents
- Any risk analysis and vulnerability assessment reports/results of the in-country facility or facilities
- Established emergency evacuation plan
- A safe haven, stocked with emergency supplies/provisions (periodically check the freshness and quantity of supplies)
- Emergency funds available (cash)

- A layout of your facility/facilities, including surrounding area, provided to the CCMT and IRT
- A procedure for accounting for personnel when a crisis develops or an evacuation becomes necessary
- An incident reporting procedure

CORPORATE CRISIS MANAGEMENT TEAM SPECIAL INCIDENT REPORT

Information will be passed by the fastest means to the corporate crisis management team. Using local time and date, the following should be logged:

- Date of incident
- Time of incident
- Location of incident
- Nature of incident
- Narrative (who, what, where, when, why)
- Notifications (to date)
  - Within company
  - Outside agencies
- Is there media/public exposure?
- Special concerns/needs?
- Name of person reporting incident: reporter's office number/home number

A Special Arrangements Fact Sheet is suggested based on the most common requirements of the customer and COMPANY's bank. If necessary, the fact sheet can be modified to satisfy a customer's particular requirements. However, the procedures should remain as simple and flexible as possible, while maintaining the desired degree of control, since they will be implemented under abnormal conditions.

A photograph and signature fact sheet must be provided for every special arrangement agreement.

Representative—Data covering those individuals, listed on the Special Arrangements Fact Sheet, authorized to request the release of funds and receive funds from COMPANY.

FORM 5.2   CASH MANAGEMENT PLAN

The global offices must establish a means for rapid receipt of emergency funds with COMPANY. Here is a cash management plan form with information that should be included:

The five persons authorized to initiate a request for funds are (include appropriate contact information):

1. _____
2. _____
3. _____
4. _____
5. _____

The three agents authorized to physically receive these funds are (include appropriate contact information):

1. _____
2. _____
3. _____

The specific procedure to follow is that one of the five management representatives, listed above, will call one of the COMPANY (Bank) representatives listed below (include appropriate contact information):

1. _____
2. _____

Recognizing the time constraints that can be imposed, funds may be transported to a metropolitan area airport for pickup and receipt by an authorized COMPANY representative or agent.

Typical currency details: weight/cubic size/amount/denomination/ pounds/ounces/inches/centimeters.

In the event that COMPANY must make arrangements for International Deliveries, the U.S. Customs Department will require you to fill out form 1790: "Currency Reporting."

Custom contacts:

INTERNATIONAL TRAVEL SECURITY MANAGEMENT

The corporate crisis management team must have a personal information sheet that includes the following information prior to an employee departing for an area of civil unrest:

1. Name: first, middle, last, nickname
2. Physical description: height, weight, color of eyes, color of hair, identifying scars, marks, and tattoos
3. Permanent home address and telephone
4. In-country work site address and telephone number
5. Marital status
6. Detailed biographic data on spouse and children: full names, physical description, school attended, school schedule, detailed medical information, emergency contact information
7. Medical information: allergies, medications, chronic conditions, shot records, name and contact instructions for family doctor and dentist
8. Official documents: copies of passport and visa, as well as date and place of issue and expiration date of each
9. Income tax forms
10. Languages spoken
11. Special skills
12. Personal vehicle: description, license number, vehicle identification number (on engine block)
13. Photograph
14. Arrival date in the country
15. In-country itinerary
16. Fight information or other travel arrangements

The traveling employee should have the following with him or her:

1. Open-ended airline tickets
2. A copy of his or her passport and visa separate from the originals
3. An extra set of passport photos
4. Map and directions to the nearest friendly embassy

5. Map and directions to nearest appropriate U.S., UK, or country embassy or consulate
6. Map and directions to a predetermined safe haven

The traveling employee should have on his person at all times:

1. Passport and visa
2. Emergency contact numbers
3. Local management telephone numbers (with dialing instructions)
4. Nearest appropriate U.S., UK, or country embassy or consulate telephone numbers (with dialing instructions)
5. Corporate crisis management team telephone number (with dialing instructions)
6. Emergency 24-hour IRT telephone number (with dialing instructions)
7. Transportation contact numbers
8. Hotel/lodging contact numbers
9. Local police telephone number
10. Local medical emergency telephone numbers
11. Local currency

You should begin your security, emergency, and evacuation plan with the project name, office name, and location of the project/office. You will be providing procedures and guidelines for employees to undertake when faced with different emergencies. The plan, and the method with which it is undertaken, concerns life safety and is of utmost importance. Emergency situations you might be faced with include medical emergencies and the possible need to evacuate, country and regional civil unrest, security evacuation, terrorism, criminal acts directed at your project/office/company, and natural disasters. Your plan should be crafted to fit into various situational uses, such as in an office environment, manufacturing plants, construction sites, expatriate lodging, and other locations and circumstances involving your employees.

In hostile areas, your plan might range from everyday security and safety procedures to how employees get from lodging to the job site/office and back home safely. Your evacuation might take place from lodging or from the office/job site, and could be to an adjoining safe haven country. Your security, safety, and emergency/evacuation plan should be geared toward providing your site managers, senior management, security and safety management, and all employees with guidance for actions in the event of the emergencies you have outlined. It should take into consideration, and place great emphasis upon, the fact that you are dealing with expat employees and local national employees, that you might have multiple sites and locations, and that you will be dealing with contractors, subcontractors, vendors, and others at your facilities.

Your plan should envision application to expat employees, as mentioned, but also consider temporary assignment and those who are on a business travel assignment. You will need to appoint local responsibility for the completion and maintenance of the plan and program, and I would recommend it be the office manager or senior project manager who gets the nod. Local staff who will need to assist include any local safety and security personnel, crisis management team members, human resources, finance, and key departments and functions. As mentioned previously, it will be critical for the success of the program that you know the location of your expat employees and local national employees as accurately and in as timely a manner as possible. Your security plan might include security officers who are posted at expat lodging, offices, or job sites, or might be involved in transporting employees between all of the above. Security will most likely be subcontracted and may include locally hired guards if qualified candidates exist. Training for the officers should be under the direction of the corporate security manager, carried out and overseen by corporate regional or site security managers or qualified subcontractor staff. Use of a site security manager makes for an easier method for security program success.

Regarding evacuations, use of a company such as International SOS may provide medical evacuation and repatriation of remains, and can offer personal assistance, including lost document help, provision of emergency cash, and embassy/consular information. International SOS has international call centers staffed 24 hours a day, 365 days a year.

An additional example of an emergency and security management plan developed for a volatile area can be found in Appendix A.

KEY POINTS

Security and crisis management are key aspects of a life safety program intended to protect people and assets around the world. These two components of protecting people are especially important when considering the safety of expatriates in foreign locations. In volatile regions your plans need to consider each aspect that you would normally have in place for a domestically based security and crisis management program, with one very important difference. In foreign and potentially volatile regions, one critical component of your program will be that of the evacuation of employees should the situation warrant. Your employee protection programs and procedures must be constructed in a way that they can operate independently of your U.S.-based headquarters. Due to distance and possible loss of communications, and the potential for failure of local support infrastructure, your security and crisis management plans must remain robust, be exercised regularly, and be totally supported by your headquarters organization.

CASE STUDY

In the summer of 2006, a Southeast Asia project was experiencing ongoing unrest and protests from nearby residents in villages. Protests had caused the shutdown of the ill-fated project a few years earlier. And now, international environmental and other activist groups were becoming involved. An unpopular government had further inflamed the local populace by failing to meet with local leaders and continuing to ignore the villagers' requests. By this time, there were expatriate employees working at the job site every day. The expats lived and worked in a nearby compound, surrounded by the same villagers who were upset over continued construction of the facility. There had been good relations with the villagers surrounding the lodging compound where the expats lived. The villagers next to the facility under construction, however, were less sympathetic. They saw only daily progress being made on a facility that environmental groups were continually telling them would pollute their villages and cause the health of their people to diminish. Smaller protests began to be fueled by larger groups and outside agitators. The protest effort began to garner international attention, and the project expats were getting worried. The project had a security and crisis management plan in place, which had been exercised when the expats first moved back into the country. It was a good thing, since on one particular Saturday morning, and without warning, hundreds of protestors descended upon the front gates of the facility. The project manager had a copy of the crisis management plan, and while the front gate and control center security operations began deploying additional security resources around the facility, the project manager began delegating portions of the crisis management plan to his staff. By the time a few telephone calls had been made, the front gate was an out-of-control riot situation. The crowd was unstoppable and overran the front gate. The staff continued to put into motion the plan that had been crafted and honed for months. Calls went out to local police, which in turn contacted the military. The police responded and began to set up, but not before some equipment was destroyed and a small fire was set near a storage area. As the military responded, the project manager received word that a helicopter was at the ready and could be at the site in 15 minutes to evacuate the expats should the need arise. The project manager kept the phone line open as the military began to gain control of the situation. The crowd relented, having released their tension on the construction equipment and by lighting a fire. The chopper crew was advised the situation was under control and the groups were retreating to the village. The crew was told to stand by, as the next few days would be critical.

6

Crisis Management
Do's and Don'ts
Pushing the Crisis Button

A good plan violently executed now is better than a perfect plan next week.

—General George S. Patton

Often a crisis jumps from 0 to 60 in a flash, such as in a bombing situation like those discussed in the previous chapter. In the Madrid and Mumbai bombings, by the time news of the bombings reached Western news markets, the event was in the recovery, or the response, phase. The situation in Israel in 2006, on the other hand, escalated over weeks and months, with Hezbollah rockets beginning to trickle into Israel, later becoming more common as the days passed. Israel during this period was a slow boil. As the rockets' frequency and accuracy became more intense, those of us involved in emergency planning stateside began to worry for the safety of the project team. We held conference calls with the project team and met internally. I contacted the Overseas Security Advisory Council (OSAC) to see what they were hearing, and what additional information they could provide. We decided to pull employees back to Tel Aviv to ride it out in a hotel. One day after pulling the employees, two rockets landed and detonated at the project site front gate and within the perimeter. No one was harmed.

A bombing, a rocket attack, a vehicle-borne improvised explosive device, a suicide bomber—all fit the description of what I consider immediate crisis response operations. One has to remain on guard that follow-up attacks do not take place in the same city, region, or country. But, for the most part, your main function and the function of the crisis planning is to ensure that your personnel and assets survive the attack, and to offer any assistance that might be required to personnel on the ground and in-country. You have now stepped into a protection mode while the country's internal resources, government, first responders, and military may be preoccupied or unable to assist you. You will be dealing with employees who are frightened and are looking to you for advice and suggestions.

In classical crisis response parlance, planning and preparation are geared toward ensuring you can not only respond to but adapt during a crisis. Let me cite an example. Years ago, one of my employers had expats in a country experiencing violent internal political upheaval and change of government. The situation was initially a slow boil, with politicians fighting it out in the press, and charges and countercharges flying about. Then, without too much warning, the military moved in, with radical elements supporting them, and ousted the government party—a coup. Instantly, foreigners, especially Americans/Westerners, were persona non grata and were seen as opportunities to be shaken down for money, or worse. At first, the expats remained where they were—they "hunkered down" and sheltered in place.

On another occasion in a different country, expats had hunkered down ("stand fast" is the common correct term) until they felt they could do so no longer. They gathered what they could and what they felt they needed, and decided to drive for the coast. Employees, dependents, and pets ventured out only to find roadways swarming with bandits and various political and factional groups manning checkpoints along the way. The travel did proceed, with groups splitting up and venturing on their own, a true "every man for yourself" scenario. Amazingly, and only after paying many roadside "tolls" and being stopped many times by armed groups along the way, the groups reached the safety of coastal towns where they obtained charter boat accommodations to another country. Had these groups had a plan in place and competent corporate security managers at home or in-country to guide them, they could have been advised of "trip wires" and had a strategy to move preparation along incrementally toward a safe evacuation, if warranted. Trip wires are what I like to call "indicator lights," such as those on the dash of your car.

In order for you to have successfully planned for the risk in hostile regions, a necessary component for designing indicator lights is determining your security risk. As mentioned earlier, such risks can include natural disasters known to occur in the region, and the likelihood or history of civil disorder and political unrest. Potential political situations, coups, outside influences, breakaway republics, ethnic tensions—all factor in. If terrorism has taken place in-country, or is a factor that appears to be looming on the horizon, take this into consideration. Another concern for your trip wire planning would be the risk presented by health concerns, be they dengue fever, bird flu, you name it. If the air or water in a project or office city becomes extremely polluted or leaks of radioactive material occur affecting the environment, these will require monitoring and could possibly create a trip wire scenario. In some cases, failure, degradation, or cessation of services of transportation, such as airlines, rail, train, subways, and other modes of public transportation, or failure of utilities like power and water, or stoppage of fuel supplies, may be precursors to eventual further collapse of internal country support mechanisms.

Additional situations might be considered indicator lights for your attention and require implementation of a tiered approach to your response plan. These could possibly escalate into serious situations, such as frequent or ongoing protests and demonstrations. Opposition leaders, antigovernment groups, and media groups might begin spreading anti-American articles, speeches, and publications. Terrorist groups may be making threats against U.S. or Western interests in the country. These threats may be followed up by or preceded by actual terrorist attacks directed toward American or Western concerns. With respect to the local resources such as electrical utilities, drinking water, supplies of fuel, and other essentials, shortages, rationing, and scarcity should begin to raise the alarm bell.

If reports are considered believable and credible about approaching hurricanes, typhoons, severe flooding, snowfall, forest fires, and further impending natural disasters, your approach should be similar to that for man-made scenarios. After what happened on December 26, 2004, in the Indian Ocean, most people take tsunami warnings seriously. Those operating in Indonesia take heed when notices of impending volcanic eruptions are reported. Any natural disaster that is anticipated or results in extreme loss of life will necessitate the implementation of your tiered trip wire system.

As mentioned, having your plan written, reviewed, and exercised is critical. I have often used a checklist in order to prepare for a threat of civil unrest, labor stoppage, general strike, or limited/nonviolent protects. Appendixes B and C include sample plans for a general strike/protest and for bomb threats, respectively.

PANDEMIC PLANNING

I have actually found debate in many organizations about the necessity of having a pandemic plan in place, and whether or not critical resources, such as time, money, and supplies, should be devoted to this as a bona fide risk. The fact is that influenza pandemics with novel viruses are recurring events. The events are unpredictable and result in serious health effects to large proportions of the population, with significant disruption to the social, economic, and security concerns of the community.

I have seen enough data to convince me that having a pandemic plan is not the equivalent of the Y2K debacle—remember? How many of us gave up our New Year's Eve in 2000 because the data world was going to crash. No, a pandemic plan is not the twenty-first century equivalent of that mistake. It is something I would urge everyone to have in place and ready to roll out. If you never use it, it would be an exercise in emergency planning that will benefit you in the long run.

If you are working in volatile areas, the impact of a pandemic may be more severe. Due to the lack or limited ability of community or even national health services, the local populations of the countries you are working in may be greatly, quickly, and severely affected.

It is due to the notices and press reports of avian influenza virus H5N1, and the belief by many experts that this virus can mutate into a novel virus, then making the jump to humans across the world, that the World Health Organization (WHO) has convinced me that the discussion among security professionals and their corporations should not be how likely is such an event to occur, but to actually plan for one to take place. The WHO has encouraged countries, states, cities, and organizations to prepare for such an event. How governments, businesses, corporations, and citizens prepare for a global pandemic is critical due to the projected impact of such an event, which includes:

- Employees calling in sick, too sick to work due to their own illness, or due to caring for a friend or family member. Is it estimated that up to 25% of the workforce will be affected initially, and that many of them will die, further impacting the workforce. Reduced numbers of employees slows throughput and output, and production suffers. The number of employees who will be willing to travel anywhere on commercial carriers to overseas or national projects will suffer. In order to protect employees, corporations will begin telling employees they cannot travel, or travel will be severely restricted. *Business critical* will be the term used to explain this curtailment of travel. The goods and services companies provide will be less consumed, less purchased, and less in demand due to growing economic and societal health issues. Emergency responders will be fewer in demand, and our infrastructure support employees will be diminished. Hospitals, clinics, and doctors office employees will be impacted, as will public utility workers. One can lay out the scenarios that might lead to situations in the general public where shortages of deliveries to grocery stores, staff to stock the groceries, even production workers to produce the foodstuffs, will cause angst in the general public. What spark would be required to set off a panic or violence among the populace?

- According to scientists, avian influenza has spread throughout Asia, Europe, and parts of Africa. Many believe the virus is changing and reshaping in its genetic structure. Many wonder if the availability of vaccines could keep up, or if the correct vaccines could even be produced.

- Corporate security managers and those within corporations, such as safety and human resources employees, who track and are responsible for the threats, risk, and response to such events, must be aware where outbreaks or occurrences have taken place. Business intelligence sources such as iJet and the WHO website can greatly improve your vision of risk. A proper planning program, procedures, and training are required by your organization's employees in emergency planning roles. If you have an emergency action plan team or committee, disaster response and recovery. These internal working groups of cross-functional disciplines are necessary to provide the depth and correct skills for effective response. The emergency response plans of the offices, facilities, and projects around the world need to have sections dedicated to this effort.

- Your plan should have backup for your backups, or alternates, due to the nature of this problem and the likelihood of many people becoming affected. So, all the staffing requirements of your planning should be deep with qualified staff, who are capable and trained in all aspects of the plan. Your planning and response documentation is intended to provide a platform from which you can continue to operate your business and still respond effectively. It will be procedural in nature. The plan will instruct those who are part of your emergency and crisis teams in the methods and procedures required. The plan will provide for deployment and initializing of your teams. The term *business continuity* could not be more important or critical to this type of planning process. Communications, as always, will be critical, from the point of calling trees and a list of employees and their backups, to how you advise employees of what your company is doing, and what they need to do. A large portion of the document should be educational in the sense that it can provide employees with important health information, prevention, and treatment support. And finally, as with any such documentation, people will need the response plan down on paper, as they say. A process that has been tabletopped, discussed, and rehashed.

- There are phases to a pandemic of flu, and your program should mesh with the recommendations and specifics provided by the World Health Organization. I would urge you to have your plan endorsed and supported by the highest levels of the organization. Senior management is the only group that can drive this effort given their initial push. As with any such program, you will need to enlist the support of the business units within your company, the corporate departments that provide support, and seek to include the best medical information of a current nature. The pandemic plan or program should be a part of your overarching emergency preparedness and crisis management program. As such, mention of a pandemic as a possible occurrence to which you will need to devote time and resources is essential to success.

- Your plan should begin as any emergency response document, with the onset of an outbreak of a domestic or global influenza. Your company and employees around the world need to have a uniform set of guidelines for response. Your plan and response should mirror the advice of the WHO. Company planning may include the purchasing and storage of antiviral treatment medications if the project or office is remote enough that medical resources may be lacking or at a great distance. In such situations, dependents may be in need of immediate need of the prophylactic resources of the antivirals. If the project, office, or facility has engaged the services of an appropriate medical clinic or medical personnel, such as project doctors, these services must be stocked with the antiviral and antibiotic medicines. It will be necessary to assess the local medical resources to see that these are adequate and have the ability to handle a pandemic or influenza situation. Resources such as a medical review by International SOS will enable corporate management on the ground to have expert opinions as to the emergency capabilities of local medical facilities and staff.

- Security managers should realize that due to the nature of pandemics, it may not be possible to immediately bring employees out of a particular country based upon the host nation's health policies—such as preventing people traveling outside the country if they might have been exposed to a highly contagious virus. WHO requirements may also mandate border and travel closures and restrictions. The same conditions and preclusions would apply to dependents. Local national employees would find themselves in a position where government and WHO rules would apply. The services of International SOS could be called on when an employee is going to need medical services that are beyond the capabilities of local medical services and professionals. International SOS would know the closest qualified medical resources, and the legalities and current restrictions or lack thereof for travel. It may become corporate policy that employees are allowed to transport their dependents or leave projects and offices on their own if conditions warrant or allow. It may become necessary to provide employees with countries where they could or could not relocate to, depending upon local health conditions, such as if that country is affected by the same viral outbreak.

- In communicating with your planning team and employees, it should be clearly stated that while the continuation of business, the preservation of operations, and the delivery of products and services are important, the most important aspect will be the protection of employees and any dependents who might also be affected by a pandemic. Your corporation should communicate that it will work as hard as possible to reduce the risk of spreading an influenza and will prevent an outbreak whenever possible. Such an effort will be part of the corporate policies of your company. The policies, again, should be supported vociferously from the top down. The policy statement should be part and parcel of your emergency and crisis response plan for a pandemic.

95

INITIAL RESPONSE AND MITIGATION, RECOVERY

Once an outbreak or report of a serious incidence of influenza is received, the crisis management team (which will most likely be located in the country or location of the outbreak) should be required to delve into the issue and determine whether or not the emergency operations center should be convened and staffed. It may be necessary to immediately determine the need for an alternative location, if the current location of the emergency operations center might be at risk or compromised by the outbreak.

Whether or not the emergency operations center is opened and staffed, the crisis management team must be advised of any incidence of the influenza or outbreak affecting any international office or facility. The crisis management team would be looked upon to provide the advice necessary to on-the-ground management and determine which type of assistance in personnel or materials would be required. As with any such crisis, an outbreak of this nature might be a long-running incident, so plan accordingly for staffing and backup of normal duties for those staffing the crisis management center. If the location of the crisis management team is within an affected pandemic area, care should be taken, including the use of video or other standard phone teleconferencing, to reduce risk of spreading the virus. Each member shall have assigned duties as outlined in your hard copy of the crisis management plan.

As with any crisis management plan, it will be critical to designate and break down key employee positions and responsibilities in order to determine, outline, and provide resources for someone backfilling the position if key employees are infected. This may be termed analyzing the impact upon your business.

If the WHO announces a change to the global phase of a pandemic, your company should enact an emergency declaration. Such announcements will typically be made by the chief medical officers of the countries affected: the surgeon general in the United States, or ministers of health in other nations. The WHO will have advised or will be advising these countries on the response steps to initiate. This might be your first indication of trouble.

It is also likely in the United States that the Department of Health and Human Services and the Centers for Disease Control will issue guidelines and recommendations. Your yardstick and the international organization that should be followed, however, is the WHO.

If the WHO indicates that an epidemic or the pandemic has reached phase 4, the company should activate its crisis management team and emergency operations center. The team shall determine the level of the crisis, and how this crisis will affect company employees and operations. Immediate steps should be taken to reduce, in whatever ways are immediate and possible, the impact upon the business. Your crisis management team and senior management will be faced with serious issues, decisions, and responses to be implemented.

With the level of decision making necessary in order to adequately protect the company people, assets, and business, your approval must come from the president/CEO and board of directors. You will be declaring a disaster situation, requiring the implementation of quick decision making and expenditure of great amounts of time and possibly money. The levels of emergency situations and an explanation of each are:

Level 1 pandemic/epidemic situation: In this level there is no immediate threat to life or property, but the situation can grow in breadth and magnitude. Your crisis management team will most likely be located in the country, city, or region of outbreak, and will in turn be notifying and working with your emergency operations center. The emergency operations center will be monitoring and communicating frequently with the crisis management team and all areas of the company that might be affected. Preparation should be made for the activation of the emergency operations center, whether the emergency operations center will remain where initially planned or be relocated, the need for the possibility of evacuation, and other developments. In a level 1 situation of a pandemic or epidemic, there can be an outbreak locally, but your company has had no employees or very few employees who have been affected. There is no immediate impact to your business operations, facilities, and offices within the country, region, or areas that are reported to have had incidents.

Level 2 pandemic/epidemic situation: During this phase, it may become necessary to move, relocate, or evacuate employees located in the country, region, or affected area. Your crisis management team may then deem the situation a disaster, requiring the standing up of your company emergency operations center. The emergency operations center will continue to monitor the situation closely at this point, with the knowledge that the current level might further escalate into a level 3 occurrence. Level 2 may be declared by emergency officials operating in regions around the countries, by city emergency officials, or those in state

97

and federal governments, and may affect your local projects and facilities due to a local outbreak or occurrence. The situation may prompt the closure of your operations by official acts and orders of local governments. During this phase, many employees and their dependents may be affected by the virus.

Level 3 situation: This may be identified as a situation where your offices or facilities may have been or will require evacuation. Your company resources will be taxed to the point where you might require assistance of local first responders, government agencies, or third-party vendors. Local authorities or governments, or regional national entities may declare an emergency situation. Your emergency operations center should now deem the situation a disaster, and appropriate recovery and response steps should ensue. The situation of pandemic or epidemic will have affected serious numbers of the employee workforce and the world.

At this stage, the WHO will announce or would be ready to declare the probable occurrence of a pandemic, which is global in nature, or an epidemic, which would refer to a local occurrence.

Level 4 situation: At this level the WHO announces an impending pandemic (global outbreak) or epidemic (local outbreak). The crisis management and emergency operations center team should consider this a situation requiring the immediate and ongoing staffing of both of these support mechanisms.

Your corporate senior leadership should of course be involved with decisions made on a magnitude concerning the operations of your company in the midst of a pandemic or epidemic. But this information will be relayed to senior leadership via the crisis management team and emergency operations center. The crisis management team on the ground in the location(s) affected will be called on for continuous updates in order to justify decisions and additional steps to be taken. Daily meetings and updates will be required. The teams, as mentioned previously, will need to remain fresh with backups and shift work of staffing. The jobs of those employees on the teams will need to be backfilled during this time frame. Prioritization and formalizing of duties and recording of all decisions and steps taken will be required. Going forward, a strategy to tackle local issues from a local perspective will be most beneficial in the long run. Corporate resources are always available should local management and local crisis management teams be overwhelmed.

One very important aspect of your response plan to pandemic or epidemic will be communicating your plans and the expectations of your company to your employees. For example, employees should be directed to advise their managers if they are ill, and to not to report to work while they are ill. Local health departments and the WHO can provide your company with information you can package into training programs of basic hand washing and hygienic techniques for the workplace. Managers should be kept up to speed on corporate response to issues so that they can pass along this information to the workforce. Consider publishing all appropriate information on the corporate website or special links to health and emergency response information. If media requests are received, these should be routed to the corporate communications professionals for comment.

Hygienic information will include advising employees of the installation by the company of hand sanitizers in rest rooms, and instructions ranging from proper cleaning of rest rooms to sanitizing telephone handsets after another person has used these. The levels of absenteeism should be tracked and charted. Monitor levels of sickness absence. Assign employees to be tasked with maintaining contact with local state and federal health officials, government ministries, and other appropriate liaisons.

Pertaining to the national and local government agencies, pandemic and epidemic can be a very effective argument for maintaining good relationships. Not only will you be kept up to date on the latest health intelligence and response information, but you could also ensure proper response and treatment options are open to your employees should the need arise. Wherever possible, the active support of government health services (such as clinics, offices, warehouses, technical and even financial assistance) should be provided.

As mentioned previously, the implementation of crisis management and business continuity plans needs to be mandated, but also directed by the highest levels within the organization. Corporate division senior management needs to ensure that the proper contingency plans are enacted. Such planning will include authorizing overtime and shift work, closing down or shutting down segments, production lines, or some projects, or reducing workforce size. It may be necessary to make do with the staff that is capable of working, and cut out all other work that is not critical to the company. Obviously, travel needs to be curtailed or halted. Meetings involving the general public should be stopped for fear of the virus being passed. Videoteleconference and teleconference would be adequate alternatives.

One critical internal member of your crisis management decision-making and response team will be your travel department, whether they are employees or contractors to your company. These travel agents can issue travel advice and ensure there is compliance with your corporate policy, such as restricting travel to various regions. As covered in a previous chapter, a travel tracking software and management program would allow for security managers to be advised of anyone who has booked travel to regions or countries that might become affected after tickets have been issued. These employees could be contacted to cancel such travel. Updated travel policies and restrictions should be kept current on internal corporate websites. Travelers should always be advised to check and maintain current vaccinations for safe travel. If travel is deemed business critical to areas that might be of concern, proper authorization at senior management levels must be undertaken.

Proper staffing for your emergency operations center will be just as critical as the proper response effort. Care will need to be taken if the emergency operations center would be within an area that is affected by the pandemic or epidemic. Teleconferencing of the emergency operations center should be considered an option. The emergency operations center leader should be given the authority to request additional resources and personnel as required.

In order to respond adequately to a pandemic or epidemic, the corporation should determine on a department-by-department basis those critical functions, employees, materials, equipment, and supplies required to do the job and do it in a safe manner. A business impact analysis is an excellent way to start this process. Part of a realistic assessment would be how would your operations continue should between 25 and 50% of your workforce be ill, as some estimates would project. What if they remained off work for up to 4 months?

There will be certain departments, locations, facilities, and assets that would be essential to continuance. These must be identified. The priorities of your company might shift given a loss of productive capabilities, and what would these new priorities be? If your business products are critical to the government for national security or infrastructure purposes, will the government step in to shore you up in order to continue? Finance departments will need to be focused on time-driven reporting and payment considerations. Orderly shutdown practices and procedures need to be developed. The proper personnel required to safely and efficiently operate the corporation must be identified, and these employees must have alternates to back them up. Breaking employees into teams and otherwise maximizing your experience is another option. If critical outside temporary staffing may be trained and brought in, would this be useful?

Supervisors should be trained on how to spot, react to, and report employees who appear to be or have called in sick.

Some key considerations concerning those companies that supply your operations with supplies, materials, and services is that, during a pandemic or epidemic, you will need to contact them and ensure the flows of these goods in coordination with your operational priorities. Your suppliers and vendors may be forced to provide less to you due to their own circumstances. You will need to plan for these eventualities. Once your products or services are ready, there may be less demand for them, again due to the circumstances of customers or end users. Your operations will need to analyze the needs for support of your production, including how you will transport critical employees, communications necessities, food and water supplies if employees must "hunker down" at one facility, and other demands. Similar concerns will include deciding if employees will telecommute and work from home, requiring they be supplied with the proper computer and communications equipment and connectivity, or whether your operations could in fact be located physically at some alternate location. Concerning information technology, the company's needs for backing up and storage of critical data will not cease due to a pandemic or epidemic, and the same people will require access to data in order to do their jobs. Your human resources and benefits employees may want to consider the staffing and special provision of mental health services to allow employees to cope with stress. Security managers should work closely with those in occupational health and safety, who will be expert in dealing with the prevention and treatment response in pandemic and epidemic situations.

Corporate communications and other departments will be necessary to provide ongoing updates as to WHO updates and issuance of warnings and other critical data. They can help you craft the manner of how this should be passed on to employees. Your communications employees should be critical members of both crisis management teams and emergency operations center staffing.

Concerning foreign governments and pandemic or epidemic notifications, they will follow the lead of the WHO. In the United States, the Centers for Disease Control and Prevention (CDC) will follow the protocols set forth by the WHO. Other sources for U.S. recommendations and response include the U.S. Department of Health and Human Services and the state departments of health and human services. Your local crisis management teams should be responsible for communicating with host government health agencies, under the guidance and support of the emergency operations center.

If your crisis management team is advised that a pandemic or epidemic outbreak has taken place, your facility should begin to place written notices at every point your employees are entering buildings and facilities advising everyone that they should not enter if they have or suspect they are feeling symptoms associated with influenza. Make use of bulletin boards and points of prominence (including rest rooms) to post information concerning how employees can work to reduce chances of transmission.

If multilingual resources are necessary, this needs to be taken into consideration. Tips on hand washing, covering one's mouth when sneezing, and use of hand sanitizers (made available) should be covered and demonstrated if necessary. Those charged with responsibility of responding to emergency situations involving pandemic or epidemic should be equipped with appropriate personal protective equipment, such as microfilter masks, as recommended by the WHO. Supplies should also include recommended cleanup kits and materials. Minimize entry/exit points into the facility where possible/practical. The actual number of entry points should be limited to reduce the chances of persons slipping in without noticing the posted materials, and in order to adequately comply with these standards. Hand sanitizers should be placed at entry points, and special trays or kits for sanitizing footwear should be made available.

Another means of controlling the spread of influenza is referred to as social distancing. This is the practice of basically limiting exposure of people with other people, thereby decreasing their chances of contracting the virus. Most people will view this as the practice of avoiding a baseball game, concert, even visiting the mall, but social distancing is also applicable in the workplace. Some of the ways to limit contact and exposure between employees have been mentioned, such as holding conference calls for meetings, even to the extent that employees in the same building or facility hold a virtual telephone meeting/conference. When meetings face-to-face are required, the larger the space, and the more employees are spaced apart, the better. Some experts recommend about 3 feet between participants.

Employees eating together, such as in company cafeterias or lunchrooms, will prove difficult, unless employees are able to eat alone in their own space. If this is not possible, lunch breaks can be timed so as to reduce the numbers by setting firm times. The same would apply for break rooms, where collecting in groups should be discouraged. As with business travel, if meetings, training, and speaking engagements outside of the workplace are not required, these should be canceled or postponed. Make use of flex scheduling to reduce the number of employees on site at any given time. Telecommuting, if at all possible, will assist you in these efforts, and will provide employees with more comfort, and the ability to check on loved ones or friends from their homes and lodging.

Strict communications should be made to employees, and the proper method of communicating by employees to their managers should be in place. If employees are feeling sick, they should not be at work. Ensure this is communicated clearly and multilingually. Employees who get sick at work should report this right away and should be sent home with proper instructions and resources/references where to go for help. If any employees had worked immediately around other employees who call in or go home sick, you should pass along how they should be mindful of feeling any symptoms, and with the information of where to get treated if necessary.

DESCRIPTIONS OF PHASES AND RESPONSE (PER WHO GUIDELINES)

The first two phases can be referred to as the interpandemic period.

Phase 1: No new influenza virus subtypes have been detected in humans. Such a subtype may be present in animals that has caused an infection in humans; however, the risk of infection or disease in humans is considered to be low.

Company response: Monitor the situation, with understanding that the CDC and WHO will be doing the same, while working toward the development of new treatments/vaccines.

Phase 2: An animal influenza subtype is present and animal-to-animal contagion is experienced. No such subtypes have been reported in humans.

Company response: Monitor the situation, checking on CDC and WHO updates.

The next four phases can be referred to as the pandemic period:

Phase 3: There are human infections resulting from a new subtype, but the occurrence of human-to-human transmission is not reported, or is only on rare occasions with very close contact.

Company response: Begin a close review of pandemic/epidemic response plans. Work up various communications to be issued to employees as warranted.

Phase 4: Human-to-human spread has been reported, but this is occurring in centralized, localized clusters, which leads experts to believe the virus is not as contagious at this point.

Company response: All crisis management and emergency operations team members should be made aware of the escalation. Continue to monitor WHO information and compliance with recommendations. Redouble effort to have communications ready for employees if it becomes necessary.

Phase 5: Human-to-human spread of virus is growing in numbers, but is still centralized and localized. There is some evidence that the virus is adapting to be easier spread between humans, but has not achieved this level of success (whereupon it would be deemed a substantial pandemic risk).

Company response: Continue monitoring the situation and readying communications plan.

Phase 6: Virus has adapted to the general population, and there are confirmed reports of an ongoing transmission of it.

Company response: Serious thought and discussion should be given to standing up the crisis management teams. If the decision is made, immediately implement crisis management plans to ensure proper response and recovery in countries and regions that have been impacted.

Some suggested response protocols are:

- Your corporate team of crisis management and response should consist of your crisis management team, and your overarching management center would be the emergency operations center. Supporting the entire mechanism are the local crisis management teams, with the various members in support functions. All functions and processes should be clearly spelled out in your crisis management plan. The crisis management team is designed to assist in immediate response to on-site emergencies. This team provides whatever support is necessary and ensures that these situations are managed effectively and efficiently. If the situation is deemed to be severe enough, the crisis management team would ask that the corporate emergency operations center be convened and stood up. The emergency operations center is dually charged with evaluating the response to emergency situations and events, assessing what additional resources are required or what steps need to be taken. It provides the vehicle or conduit for communicating the needs of the crisis management team to the rest of the company. Major decisions affecting the policies, direction, and operations of the corporation are made via the emergency operations center, with the support and involvement of senior management. Successful operation of the emergency operations center will require continuous and effective communications with all business divisions, and senior management contained within each segment. Emergency operations centers require continuous staffing, and must be staffed as quickly as possible. In the event that first-line members are unable to participate or continue, back-ups and alternates must be ready and equipped to step in. Clearly spelled out roles, leadership, and functions must be in writing, and drilled in advance with tabletop exercises. One note of caution: There can only be one emergency operations center leader.

- Your divisions or business units should have identified recovery teams of specialists designated to attend to the functions required to get the operations back on track. These teams will have backups and alternates to each primary member. Their functions include assessing any additional needs for recovery, which would then be relayed to the senior management of each division, and then on to the emergency operations center. Think of the emergency operations center as the mother ship, providing resources that can be airdropped to whomever is in need.

KEY POINTS

Crises can happen at any time. Some crises develop over time, often those of the man-made variety. Natural disasters such as hurricanes can have some prior warning, allowing preplanning. But earthquakes, for example, may occur in a split second and last only a few seconds. In order for projects to successfully protect people and assets, crisis management plans must have the ability to adapt to changing circumstances. As crises develop, it is important to gauge the severity of the events, and know when to begin your process of emergency and crisis response. One important tool for dealing with crises, especially those that involve potential for evacuation of employees, is a stepped approach, tiered, or using indicator lights of events that take place and can assist the security manager in determining a severe situation is going from bad to worse, or from worse to better. Getting employees back into countries is just as important and critical to operations, and can be just as difficult to determine.

CASE STUDY

In one Middle Eastern country, expat employees were working at a site that had experienced no problems whatsoever with the local populace, or had any issues of any kind. Over one summer in 2006, a terrorist group began peppering various cities with rockets of various sizes and accuracy from across a border. Rockets were landing to the north, and had not quite reached the range of the project site. For the most part, the targets appeared to be to the north and toward the west. As the tense situation continued to get worse, the project manager and corporate security began to converse about indicators that could necessitate removing employees from the project to an area of safety. At the time, that area of safety was the country's capital. One day, reports were received that a rocket had reached deep into the south of the country, well south of the project location. It had detonated and caused damage, but no loss of life. This was confirmation of what had been reported in the news and by private sources. The terrorist group had bragged about having access to better, more technologically sound rocketry, and they were proving their boasts were not idle talk. The daily conference calls had been continuing until this latest incident. It was decided on a Wednesday that if the rocket's range increased, we would pull the plug and evacuate the employees to a safe area. When the report was confirmed of the impact farther to the south, the employees were pulled out and evacuated to safety on a Saturday morning. On Sunday morning, two rockets hit the job site, one impacting at the front gate, the other inside the facility grounds. Damage was minor, and there were no injuries. As the weeks progressed, the rockets diminished. The situation was closely monitored, and as both international pressure and military steps were taken by the country's government, employees were filtered back to the job site. The project manager arrived first, followed shortly after by additional employees, until, once the situation was obviously under control, all employees returned.

7

Protecting People and Assets around the World
From Green Acres to the Green Zone

May St. Patrick guard you wherever you go, and guide you in whatever you do and may his loving protection be a blessing to you always.

—Irish blessing

Protection of people and assets around the world in many ways is like protecting them in Nashville, Dubuque, New York City, or San Francisco. And, in many ways, it is as dissimilar as operating in Paris, as opposed to functioning in the Sahara Desert.

In some countries, for example, the concept of security management and private security guards, for example, is rather unorganized or is not that well established. In other countries, such as Germany, the United Kingdom (where some credit modern policing and security to have originated), and Spain, security is a well-respected occupation and profession. You may be required to protect personnel, buildings, property, and materials in areas where armed security personnel are required, such as in Iraq or Afghanistan.

Protection, as I have already discussed, includes crisis management preparation and response, but here I am primarily speaking of the physical security aspects of protecting personnel and assets. Protection deals with preventing the bad thing happening. It can also be concerned with detection of bad things before they take place. Here I am speaking of detecting and thwarting volatile surveillance.

Protection may be termed mitigation or countermeasures. As previously mentioned in Chapter 3, risk is what remains after you have identified the threat and applied your countermeasures. The remaining risk is the type of consideration that leads some companies, for example, to choose not to bid on contracts in Iraq and Afghanistan, and led one of my employers to submit bids and proposals. I have discussed how your concerns in an international setting from a protection standpoint, would be, respectively, protecting your people and protecting your assets. We live in an information age; assets now include information.

A word or two about information technology and security: there are those who insist that the merging of information technology security and physical security is an inevitable and logical progression. I disagree wholeheartedly with this assumption. The term that is used is *convergence*, and to me it represents a clever term but very bad idea. There are security professionals and IT security professionals. I have 28 years in the business of physical security, consulting, and investigations. My clients and employers range from the U.S. government to Fortune 1000 and Fortune 500 corporations. I hold certifications in protection (Certified Protection Professional—CPP) and fraud examination (Certified Fraud Examiner—CFE). I have been trained in and am an advocate of Crime Prevention Through Environmental Design (CPTED). When it comes to physical security, professionals like me and the tens of thousands of us who are members of the American Society for Industrial Security International (ASIS) and other professional security organizations do not require "schooling" in physical security. I often am struck with the idea, even outright statements, made to the effect of: How hard can physical security be? Surely, an IT professional can construct the physical security around, say, the computer room, or other critical areas? Is this snobbery or foolishness? As with our legal system, anyone who represents themselves in court has a fool for a client. I have observed mechanical engineers, structural engineers, electrical engineers, even chemical engineers often stray into the area of physical security. And I will say this: If physical security were as easy as filling out a checklist, ticking the boxes, then all of these groups and all of the IT professionals could just have at it, and I will retire to the Caribbean, per my personal game plan. It is, however, much more than that. Maybe the world of the Certified Information Systems Security Professional (CISSP), a security certification for IT professionals, which I respect and admire, is all about checklists and audits and subjective data collection. I sense that it is not. I have many friends and relatives who work in IT, and I have gotten along well with IT professionals when it comes to corporate and government security. But, when push comes to shove, and IT security starts to push out the physical security, well, let me just paraphrase the Rolling Stones when I say, "Hey, you—get off of my cloud!"

So, what do I do when it comes to protecting information in a foreign, possibly volatile region? I involve IT professionals from the outset. But, when it comes to physical security associated with protecting information, I have a governance and oversight attitude.

Those who know physical security will recall the concepts of deterring threats, detecting threats, and delaying threats—the "three D's," as they have been referred to. Some add the fourth D—"deny." Some adherents add the word "respond," so we could call the concept: deter, detect, delay, deny, and respond. As I have mentioned in this text, I feel that any security professional worth his or her salt had better prepare for the response phase, which can be categorized as crisis management followed by response.

Some would consider the aspects of deter or deterrence to include physical barriers, chain-link fencing, concertina wire, steel mesh, crash gates, setbacks, locks and fence alarms, microwave detection, ground sensors, security officers/armed personnel, guard dogs, observation towers, closed-circuit television (CCTV), photo identification badges, access control systems such as card swipe and proximity card, and security patrols and vehicle or package inspections. Security policies and procedures, such as visitor clearance and escort policies, along with security awareness training, can also deter would-be bad guys.

Some of these same systems and materials are of course useful for the second D: detection. The first thing that jumps to mind might be alarm systems. Alarms can range from simple burglar alarms for residences or offices, to ground sensors, volumetric and microwave detection, and fence vibration detection, to CCTV and video motion detection. In the United States, debates have raged, some fostered by law enforcement professionals and experts, that improperly installed alarms, such as home alarm systems installed on homes with cheap locks, doors, and door frames, can actually be less preventative and successful than a strong door and door frame, reinforced windows, and sensible exterior design. I agree with this concept, since no alarm system will prevent a cheap door from being kicked in. Keep in mind that when you need and want an alarm system, you need to make sure the physical structure warrants the addition of an alarm system. In some countries and situations, such as extremely volatile areas, you are going to want to use a security officer—and one that is frequently armed—for detection and deterrence. And, you will need enough of them, in opportune areas for observation, in order to do the job. If you are fortunate enough to have electronic alarm systems or CCTV as backup, OK. I think you will find that those who often fill these types of positions in security, ex-military and law enforcement, will be more used to the low-tech principle of keeping their eyes and ears open and being ready to respond. I like guard dogs because their hearing and smell are so keen. They can sense things long before we can, and no one wants to mess with a guard dog. There are guard dogs and bomb sniffing dogs. I like them both, with bomb sniffing dogs being important for checkpoint vehicle and package inspections, but the two types of dogs are distinct. Guard dogs and security officers are instrumental in protection measures such as checking, rechecking, and being "systematically unsystematic," that is, not setting routines for patrol routes, times. Armed guards, well armed, well trained, and well disciplined, can be one of your most, if not the most, important arrow in the quiver of protection.

In hostile regions, just as in less risky locations, delaying an attack is critical to success. If you are utilizing only chain-link fencing in a volatile region, count on it to be cut, dug under, or climbed over. Placing barbed wire or even concertina or razor wire on top can lure you into a false sense of security. Criminals can be thought of as objects of physics. They are going to choose the path of least resistance. Your conceptual guideline considering delaying the attack could be to slow them down—perhaps placing concertina wire on the ground inside the chain-link fence, not only on top. It could consist of installing solid-core doors, steel doors, with reinforced steel frames, using high-security deadbolts or padlocks. You might consider constructing a variation on the medieval castle concept of "castle keep," which would rely on layers of protection, from outer walls, guard or observation towers, followed by concentric rings of more walls, sturdy locks and doors, blast-protected windows, and other measures. Delaying an attack might be your security personnel responding with weapons fire.

Which brings me to response. Here in the United States, we more commonly rely on law enforcement to do the heavy lifting. That is, when an armed response is required, we dial 911. We can rely on professional response to our locations. The response may vary in time, however. In some circumstances, where you might feel it necessary to utilize armed security officers, with the typical rule of thumb being that the risk (liability) of armed officers and the use of deadly force is less than the threat (robbery, physical assault) to employees at the premises, entering and exiting the workplace, or conducting business. In many countries you will be working in you will find it difficult, if not impossible, to legally arm U.S. citizens. And, in most cases, I would discourage you from doing so, unless these employees are trained and have a background in protection (ex-military, law enforcement), and only if you can operate legally, such as within and on the premises of a corporate compound in Saudi Arabia or other locations. You will need to determine, once you are in a foreign country, the qualifications of the security officers and armed guards whom you might wish to employ. I have found speaking with regional security officers to be useful; while they are unable to recommend specific companies, they can tell you which companies are being used in-country by Western corporations and entities. Going by recommendation and checking out the security officer companies is going to be an important part of your process.

Awareness might be the most important factor in your security management program. Without it, I would suggest, deter, detect, delay, and respond are doomed to failure. Unless you create for your company a multilayered program of awareness, which ranges from the awareness of where all your employees are located around the world (travel intelligence, as mentioned before), to having created within your employees a knowledge of how to do the right things to avoid risk as much as possible and react in the correct manner, your efforts will be in vain. I would rank awareness ahead of all else. Awareness = the ability to deter, detect, delay, and respond. I have often taken questions, comments, or inquiries from employees brought up before or after security awareness seminars, to create new presentations, and at the minimum, I always go out of my way to answer their questions. Your employees and senior management will appreciate the efforts you put into websites, online and in-person training sessions, presentations, and ongoing efforts to keep your employees and assets safer around the world.

SOME GENERAL OFFICE SECURITY AND SAFETY TIPS

The office environment should be a place where you can conduct business free from fear of criminal activity. There are a number of chances of being victimized in your work environment.

SAFETY IN THE WORKPLACE

A visitor's ability to gain access to your building or your office area should be deterred by the use of entry systems. There are many types

---

of entry systems, with the most common being an access card system. Employees are issued an ID card with a magnetic or buried coil or chip that is used to gain entry. The place of entry should be outside the work area and should be staffed with a security officer or receptionist. Should a visitor try to enter without authorization, he or she would be detected and apprehended by security officers. It should be noted that additional means of access control include biometric devices such as hand geometry readers and retinal (eye) scanners.

Other security procedures could include cameras at the entrance that would be monitored by the front-desk security officer or receptionist. This system can be set up to allow the individual monitoring the camera to press a button and immediately lock all doors if necessary.

To further enhance security, the executive offices should be separate from the other offices. One of the executive offices should be set up as a "safe room" and include the same specifications as a safe room in the home: a solid wood door, reinforced door frame, deadbolt and slide-lock bolt locks, etc. Doors constructed in this manner would delay entry and allow time for law enforcement and security to arrive in an incident. The room could also be used in the case of a serious workplace violence situation where lives may be in danger.

The parking area should be well lit, and surveillance cameras should be strategically placed so that all or most of the parking area is monitored. The executive parking area should be separate from the employee parking, and a key access system should be used for entry. Executive names and designations should not be used on their parking spaces.

Information security is a problem with most companies operating outside or inside the United States. Many employees are not aware that discarded information in the trash or sensitive documents left on desks may be targets for those seeking such information. Any proprietary information should be shredded before being discarded. Employee telephone directories and client directories should also be shredded before being discarded. At the end of the workday, desks should be cleared of any sensitive or proprietary information or directories. A clean desktop policy should be initiated.

It is recommended that all employees be instructed in conflict resolution and recognizing potential problems before they turn into overt actions, thus providing employees with the ability to "talk down" irate or ill-tempered individuals. Workplace violence is on the rise, according to statistics.

LAPTOPS

Because of the portability and resale value of laptops, these useful tools have become one of the most popular targets of theft. Not only does the laptop present an item of value that would need to be replaced, but the information stored on the hard drive may be extremely valuable or irreplaceable. Your laptop may contain information that is valuable to a competitor. The risk of theft is always present whether you are at work, home, or traveling. To reduce this threat, the recommendation is to follow these security measures:

- Treat your laptop like personal property.
- When available, use lockable docking stations or security cables when you anticipate frequent laptop use during business hours.
- Locked cabinets/desks should be used for overnight storage and other times when your laptop will be idle for long periods.
- Unsecured laptops should never be left on your desk.
- Maintain a record of your laptop serial number.
- Immediately report lost or stolen laptops to YOUR COMPANY'S IT department.

When Traveling

- Never check your laptop as luggage.
- When going through security x-ray procedures, maintain visual contact with your laptop. Hold on to your laptop until you are the next person in line to pass through the metal detector. Should security want to observe its operation, you should perform the function, not security personnel.
- Never leave a laptop in a vehicle unattended.
- Laptops should not be used nor documents read in public where they can be "shoulder surfed," or seen from behind you. You can see how this could easily occur without your knowledge while you are on an airplane.

- At your hotel utilize a room safe, if one is available, for laptop storage when the room is unattended.
- If a hotel room safe is not available, utilize a portable lock or cable, or consider using the hotel's luggage storage or safe facilities to secure your laptop when your room is unattended.
- Keep the laptop make, model, and serial number in a separate location.
- Do not store your laptop in airline overhead compartments.
- Do not keep sensitive or proprietary information on the hard drive.
- Store disks containing sensitive or proprietary information in the hotel safe.

CELLULAR PHONES

Cellular phones present several security issues. There is the threat of phones being stolen and being fraudulently used by thieves. Cell phones are vulnerable to eavesdroppers and identification number cloning. Recommendations for cellular telephone security include:

- Never discuss confidential information on your cell phone. Many transmissions can be intercepted by a simple radio frequency receiver.
- To diminish casual eavesdropping risks, obtain digital conversation capability.
- Carefully review your monthly bills to spot unauthorized calls that may have been placed as a result of a cloned identification number.
- Immediately notify your provider of any unauthorized calls appearing on your monthly statement.
- Use the lock code feature to prevent unauthorized phone usage.
- When not in use, protect your cell phone by storing in a locked cabinet or drawer.
- Immediately report any phone thefts to YOUR COMPANY management.

SOME EXTORTION PREVENTION AND RESPONSE TIPS

Extortion is threatening harm or injury to a person or damage to property to obtain something of value. In many cases, an extortionist will attempt to con the victim into believing a kidnapping has occurred when it actually has not. Ransom may be demanded for the safe return of nonexistent hostages. The extortionist will attempt to sever communications between the victim and the person supposedly held hostage. Measures to disrupt an extortion attempt include:

- Maintain a cellular phone in your residence for uninterrupted communications.
- Be suspicious of persons trying to lure you away from your residence with claims you must pick up a prize or you just won an item. Additional attempts might be for you to retrieve an item you left in storage, or by presenting you with a hospital notice of an injured family member. Verify the call with a return call before responding.
- Do not participate in surveys or opinion polls.
- Do not reveal any personal information to anyone whom you do not know or who does not have a right to the information.

HOME AND FAMILY GENERAL SECURITY AND SAFETY TIPS

The home should be our safe haven. There are a number of steps that can be taken to ensure home safety. In order to prevent or minimize the chance of a home invasion, remember the "three D's": deter, detect, and delay.

The following practices are recommended:

- Deterrence is critical since it might prevent criminals from targeting you in the first place. Nothing deters criminals more than lights and noise.
- An important first step is improving exterior residence lighting. Energy-saving spotlights utilizing motion detectors should be place strategically around the perimeter of the home. The spotlights should be directed to illuminate the dark corners and to expose areas where persons might conceal themselves. Shrubs and vegetation that would allow

for concealment should be trimmed down. Garage overhead and personnel doors should be equipped with deadbolt locks and peepholes.

- Security systems supplement the idea of deterrence. Systems will detect unwanted visitors while you are home or away. The system should include sensors on windows and doors used for entry. Large glassed areas like sliding doors should also have glass-break detectors. There should also be at least one motion detector strategically placed in an area that an intruder would have to pass while moving around the house. A siren should be located on the interior and exterior. In addition to the noise alerting occupants that someone has entered the home, a siren sounding in the neighborhood will also attract attention and assistance. The siren may cause the criminals to vacate the area quickly. Unless you live in a rural or isolated area, it may not be necessary to have the system monitored by a security company. However, many systems now allow for Internet/remote monitoring and alarm "call up."

- Should someone enter the home uninvited, you need to have a "safe room" or area your family can respond to once the alarm sounds. This area should be constructed to delay intruders until law enforcement or other assistance arrives. A room, usually the master bedroom, can easily provide this protection. The doors entering the bedroom should be solid wood construction with high-security deadbolt locks with a minimum 1½-inch throw. The door frame should be of solid, reinforced construction to further delay kick or blunt object attacks. The deadbolt locks should be operable from the inside of the bedroom only. Adding a slide bolt on the door interior top and bottom further reinforces the door.

- Inside the safe room you should have a cellular telephone, fire extinguisher, flashlights, and a list of emergency phone numbers. The cellular telephone is critical since the telephone lines to the home will probably have been cut in this type of situation. (One option is to have telephone lines buried or protected with conduit to lessen the chances of phone lines being cut. Alarm systems should also be equipped with cellular phone backups or phone line interruption devices that alert the alarm company to telephone lines being severed.) Preprogramming emergency numbers into the cellular phone is a good idea since dialing using a phone list is often difficult in emergency situations under duress.

- The entire family should have a plan for when disaster occurs. Most central home alarm systems have different alarm sounds for intrusion, fire, or medical emergencies. With a home invasion all members should know to immediately respond to the safe room when the alarm sounds. Alarm systems can be programmed to include a duress code that allows an additional "secret" number that can be entered if attempts are made to force the home occupants to enter the disarm code under threat of harm. The additional number would allow for the alarm to be disarmed and additionally indicate to the alarm monitoring company that there is a problem that requires immediate dispatching of law enforcement to the home and the possibility of the duress situation described. Additionally, alarm systems can be equipped with remote duress alarm indicators that resemble wireless garage door openers, small devices that can fit into a pocket and will remotely sound a duress indication (lights, siren, and notification—silent or otherwise) to the monitoring service. In the case of a fire you should have a plan indicating how and where to exit the home, and a collection point located safely outside of the home.
- Fire and smoke detection equipment should be part of the alarm system, along with safety equipment detecting noxious fumes and gas leaks. Systems may also include detection for flooding or water, such as in basements, near furnaces and hot water heaters.
- Precautions should be taken in case of medical emergencies. If possible, have members of your family attend first aid and CPR classes. A list of telephone numbers for doctors, hospitals, and ambulance services should be located near the telephones, and programmed into cellular and all telephones. If family members are taking medications or have allergies, keep a listing or notice of these nearby.

FAMILY MEMBER SAFETY AWARENESS

The following are general security precautions that should be discussed with all family members:

- Do not open the outside door to anyone until you know who is there and what he or she wants. Use the peephole in the door to see who is there. It is recommended that you have an intercom system incorporated into your front doorbell.
- If you do not recognize the person at the door, do not let him or her in.
- Do not give out information over the telephone concerning who is and who is not at home, where they are, or when they will be back.
- Do not answer questions asked by anyone saying he or she is conducting a survey, even if you are offered a free gift.
- Only give your home telephone number to those who have a legitimate need for it.

PRECAUTIONS FOR CHILDREN

It is important to teach children how to protect themselves when away from home and while alone in the home. Statistically, the risks of a stranger deliberately harming children are low. It remains a good idea to communicate security awareness to them without frightening them. Suggestions include:

- Children should be instructed not to talk to strangers, or accept their gifts or rides.
- A parent should accompany small children to school or the bus stop.
- Advise children of the actions to take should they be approached by a stranger.
- Instruct school administrators not to disseminate personal information to anyone.
- Determine your child's school absence notification policy. Parents should be notified within 2 hours of the start of

class if their child is not present and the school has not been notified of the absence.

- Request that school administrators not release the child from school without your written consent. The child should be met at the principal's office, not outside the building.
- Children should be encouraged to advise you of any stranger's attempts to talk to them.
- Teach your children what to do should they get lost, such as finding a policeman, shop owner, another person with young children, fire stations, etc.
- Advise them never to give out information to persons on the phone.

DOMESTIC HELP

You should always thoroughly prescreen any domestic help that you are considering hiring, especially those who will be assisting with the care of children. Once hired, establish family rules that you expect them to follow. Some prescreening suggestions are:

- Conduct criminal checks with local, state, and federal authorities.
- Conduct credit checks with the consent of the prospective employees.
- Verify prior employment and interview references.
- Verify education if the domestic help is being hired to work with children.
- Instruct all domestics with your rules regarding admission of strangers to the home.
- Remind the domestic help to remain security-conscious at all times and report anything suspicious.
- Brief domestic help on your procedures regarding the admission of repairmen, visitors, and answering the phone.
- Emergency phone numbers must be available to your domestic help.
- Do not discuss sensitive information in the presence of domestic help.

REDFLAGS AND CONCERNS FOR PROTECTING PROPRIETARY INFORMATION

- Inadvertent disclosure by the owner or by a person in authorized possession
- Marketing personnel, trade association meetings, supplier discussions, off-premises discussions by employees, public relations, government agencies (FOIA)
- Deliberate theft by an outsider—industrial espionage agent in the classic sense
- Competitive intelligence collectors/newspapers, document with locals, technical journals, articles, presentations, casual conversations
- Techniques of industrial espionage: romantic partners, recruitment ploys, unauthorized access to premises, examining trash "dumpster diving"
- Deliberate theft by an insider entrusted with access

ASSESSING YOUR VULNERABILITIES

- Where and when does the company's critical information exist?
- How is the information vulnerable to exploitation?
- When must the competition have the information in order to effectively respond to the company's initiatives?
- Who are our indirect employees or associates (vendors, suppliers, customers, distributors, consultants, and others)?
- What do they know about the company operations, plans, strategies, capabilities, and weaknesses?
- How do they treat information that is important to the company?

Key information convergence points identified:

- Security efforts are limiting access to these key points.
- Relax controls as goals or production efficiencies are achieved.

TIPS ON PROTECTING YOUR PROPRIETARY INFORMATION

- Effective access control system (if 100+ employees, positive systems of nonemployee identification, including photo ID badges).

- All visitors must sign in, wear badges indicating they are "visitors," and be escorted.
- All YOUR COMPANY employees must politely challenge persons whom they do not recognize as to their reason for being in the office space, lobby, etc.
- All employees must report suspicious activity immediately to their supervisors or to appropriate authorities.
- Key control: stamped keys ("Do Not Duplicate"), numbered by recipient, with biannual audit.
- Signed secrecy agreements. Place all visitors, vendors, suppliers, and contractors on notice ("Conditions of Entry" agreement form).
- Debriefing and execution of nondisclosure agreements upon termination.
- Preemployment screening (reference checks, previous employers, criminal background checks).
- Policy and procedural statements covering the recognition, classification, and handling of sensitive information.
- Preemployment screening techniques and incumbent employee review procedures to ensure that persons entrusted with sensitive data do not have any ascertainable motive or reason to exploit such data and are basically stable.
- Awareness program in which all employees are made aware of the existence of sensitive data in the company, their responsibilities in protecting it, and the required procedures.
- Nondisclosure agreements from employees, in which they acknowledge their fiduciary responsibility.
- Documented records of exposure for those employees to whom significant kinds and amounts of sensitive data are released. These records may also include periodic reaffirmations of nondisclosure responsibility.
- Noncompetitive agreements from specified classes of personnel to prevent them from taking employment with defined competitors within a stated future period.
- Physical measures, such as area and access controls, admittance controls, identification devices and routines, secure storage containers, regulated reproduction facilities, shredders, controlled trash disposal, and restrictions on use of communications

media to minimize the ability of unauthorized personnel to gain access to sensitive data on or off the premises.

- Follow-up efforts with new employees or former employees who were exposed to sensitive data but who were not required to execute noncompetitive agreements. Such programs include notices to the new employer of the former employee's exposure and responsibility to protect.
- Continuous and informed monitoring of routine activities in the field to detect appearances of one's sensitive data.

SOME TIPS ON RECOGNIZING SOCIAL ENGINEERING

Social engineering is the process of deceiving people into releasing or delivering private, confidential, or privileged information. The desired product can be computer logon passwords or contract bid information. People attempting to obtain information often use some of the following methods:

- Developing trust—apparently innocent actions, relationships, etc., are designed to gain access.
- Reverse social engineering—this can result from someone causing a problem, such as on a computer network, then repairing the "problem" and gaining trust and appearing to be the hero.
- Avenues and media—often attempts come over the telephone to obtain passwords, information on projects/status, and other useful tidbits. Often offices are visited, with an individual posing as a repairman, IT support person, contractor, or cleaning person. Information can be gathered from desktops, trash cans, phone directories, and organization or name charts.
- Persons seeking information often rely on the psychological effects one experiences, such as being startled if you noticed a strange person in your work area—and the person you notice is dressed in a suit or fits in with business casual. They might act as if they are lost, or looking for the business next door (they will have the company name and names of people who work there also). Often the approach is to cause employees to believe that their job depends on their actions (if you don't turn over PC controls, passwords, etc., the system might

crash), or the ever-present "Give us your personal information" (social security number, credit card, etc.), "You have won fabulous prizes," etc. Often, recruiting efforts come in as cold calls, with persons seeking competitive intelligence by posing as a headhunter who wants to know what types of projects you have worked on, etc.

- Additional methods of obtaining information include sensory overloading of the victim—too many facts or questions are posed to the victim, not allowing time to logically react.
- Reciprocation consists of a problem being solved, or a favor being done by someone seeking information—and the "favor" is called in later or immediately with a request of the victim.
- Deceptive relationships are engaged with the purpose of fooling the victim into revealing valuable information at some point in time.
- Persons may be looking over your shoulder while you are working on your laptop on an airplane, or may be attending a conference to steal laptops from it. Hostile foreign intelligence services may monitor electronic or other conversations, emails, and faxes, or may target hotel rooms for break-ins.

SOME TIPS FOR MITIGATING SOCIAL ENGINEERING EFFORTS

- Identify the product, information you have which is of value.
- The person on the phone may not be your friend. A new relationship may be an effort to gain access to information.
- Password protection is critical.
- Anyone can buy/steal/manufacture a UPS, Fed Ex, or Xerox uniform or ID.
- Conduct a reality check: Is the information that you are working on worth something to competitors, criminal enterprises, or terrorist organizations—domestic or foreign?

Don't be afraid to say no. Ask for a call-back number; offer to pass their request, information, etc., on to someone else (another means of verification and clearing the request).

A true hostile area security plan is a complex endeavor. See Appendix A for an example of a hostile area security and crisis management plan and for more useful security techniques, procedures, and recommendations.

ARMED ROBBERY PREVENTION AND PROCEDURES

Armed robbery is one of the most serious and potentially danger-ous crimes committed in the United States today. A robber commits a holdup because he or she believes that the profit will be worth the risk. By decreasing the possible profit and increasing the risk of apprehension, potential victims can reduce their chance of becoming a target. Personal safety is always the most important consideration when planning how to react to an armed robbery. This document provides basic information that can and will diminish the chance of becoming a victim.

ROBBERY PREVENTION AND MITIGATION

Businesses must face the possibility of robbery on their premises realistically, and they should give security training a high priority. Employees should be trained in the latest methods of robbery pre-vention, which will improve their chances for safety and their abil-ity to provide information that could help in the apprehension of the criminal. In addition, this preparation can lessen the emotional aftereffects of being involved in an armed robbery. Opening and closing procedures should be established. These could include:

- Have several employees present when opening and closing the business.
  - Inspect the business for forcible entry before entering the business.
  - One employee searches the premises before admitting others. If all is clear, the employee entering the store first can signal the companion with some prearranged sign.
  - At closing make sure no one is hiding in the business.
  - At closing one employee can enter the parking lot first and can signal the companion with some prearranged sign if it is safe.
- Keep a minimum of easily accessible cash on hand, both in cash drawers and in the safe. During evening and late-night

hours of operation, cash levels should be kept to a minimal amount per cash register ($50 or less) to conduct business. Transactions with large bills (over $20) should be prohibited. Use special quick-deposit drop safes in which money can be easily deposited when there is an accumulation of funds. Keep reserve funds locked in a money safe and deliver new funds only when required.

- Use a money safe that requires more than one employee to open and remove daily receipts. Always lock money safes after the day's operating funds are obtained. Every business should operate with a cash protection system. Each employee handling cash should be trained in the various possible types of attack, and the employee should follow good cash handling practices. The cash system should work two ways by protecting both lives and money. Periodic checks should be made to be sure all cash protection rules are being followed. By following these cash handling procedures, the business will make itself a less attractive mark and limit the robber's profit while reducing the business's potential losses. Loss can be reduced by having special, separately locked inner compartments or lockers where the change funds are maintained. Dual control of safes and two-key inner compartment money safes require at least two people to open the door, thus helping to prevent robberies.
    - Try not to open the cash safe too often. Do not maintain more surplus cash in the store than is absolutely necessary.
    - Always keep money out of reach of customers.
    - Make sure employees do not display large amounts of money. Cashiers should not balance their cash in the checkout area before closing. This procedure should be accomplished in an office or other secure area less visible and vulnerable than the checkout area. Bank teller station counters should be designed to keep cash out of sight.
    - Do not allow employees to count large amounts of cash in areas visible either to the public or to other employees. Large amounts of money exposed to view

represent a temptation not only to robbers but also to employees and customers alike.

- Exercise plenty of precautions when making bank deposits. These precautions include:
  - Try to make bank deposits during daylight hours with more than one person.
  - Vary the route to the bank.
  - Do not make any stops along the way.
  - Vary the time of day the deposit is made.
  - Disguise the currency bags in plain wrappings or in another container (i.e., brief case, etc.).
  - Vary the personnel doing the deposit, if possible.
  - Vary the vehicle used.
- Request police or armed guard protection when handling or transporting large amounts of money.

Physical security measures include:

- Maintaining a well-lit interior visible from the street. Make sure signs, displays, plants, etc., do not obstruct the view from the street of the customer service area. Maintaining visibility into the business establishment at all times is important.
- Physical barriers such as bullet-resistant enclosures between customers and employees provide the greatest protection for workers. Installing pass-through windows for customer transactions and limiting entry to authorized persons during certain hours of operation also limit risk.
- Storage rooms that have a lock that can be opened from the inside. Robbers sometimes lock employees in storage rooms. Hide a key in the room if the lock cannot be opened from the inside.
  - Marking the edge of the doorway at varying heights to identify the height of a robber.
  - Mechanisms that permit employees to have a complete view of their surroundings, such as convex mirrors, an elevated vantage point, and placement of the employee/customer service and cash register area so that it is clearly visible outside the retail establishment, serve as deterrents.

- Securing the teller and cashier operations. Install barriers to keep unauthorized persons out of these areas.
- For secure areas, use doors and gates with latches that automatically lock on closing.
- Install a timed delay switch to turn off exterior lights after the employees have gone for the night.
- Prominently displayed surveillance camera equipment. Be sure to have the equipment serviced regularly and to only use videotapes the amount of times recommended by the manufacturer.
- Use a dual-key, drop, or delay-action time-lock safe.
- A silent alarm system. This alarm system:
  - Could incorporate a daytime holdup feature that reports to a remote supervised area. Make sure employees know how and when, and *when not*, to activate the alarm.
  - Could be unobtrusively activated by an employee who is forced to open the safe or vault.
  - Should include standby power. Transmission method should be tested periodically. When accidentally set off or when it malfunctions, it should be reported immediately to the police to ensure an adequate response.
  - Should be taught to new employees and periodically reviewed with those employees who need to know.
- Seldom used rear and side doors, windows, and other accessible openings should always be kept locked. Doors should have viewers. Doors used for deliveries should be locked when not in use.
- Maintain good exterior lighting. Adequate outside lighting of the parking area and approach to the business during nighttime hours of operation enhances employee protection. Surveillance lighting to detect and observe pedestrian and vehicular entrances of the business can also help. Adequate lighting within and outside the establishment makes the store less appealing to a potential robber by making detection more likely.
- All shrubbery and trees, which a criminal could use to hide behind, should be cut back and maintained.

In certain high-risk areas or businesses, consideration should be given to the use of additional deterrents. These may include:

- The presence of off-duty police or uniformed guard
- The use of an armored car service for delivery and pick-up of cash
- Maintain a list of emergency contact telephone numbers near the telephone. Have witness description forms available for employees and witnesses to complete after a robbery has occurred.
- Vary lunch hours and coffee breaks so several employees are always on duty.
- Employees should be trained to watch for and report suspicious actions of people inside and immediately outside the premises. Don't hesitate to call the police when worried about a potential risk. Should the person leave before the officer's arrival, write down the description of the suspect and his or her vehicle for possible police use. A suspicious person that is seen today may turn out to be the robber who returns tomorrow. Examples of suspicious activity could include:
  - Persons monitoring business operations
  - Persons asking about closing times, volume of business, the amount of money on hand, etc.
  - Persons who appear to just loiter in the area checking the business layout and operations
  - Persons who may be waiting for a lull in activity and fewer customers
- Give every customer entering the business a friendly greeting. Look each customer directly in the eyes. A robber does not want to be identified, and such human contact may spoil it for some would-be robbers.
- Require that employees ask for the identification of workers, repair people, guards, police officers, etc., before permitting entry into secured areas.
- The counter or work area should be cleaned regularly to remove old fingerprints. This increases the possibilities that a robber may leave a readable print behind. Oil or wax-based cleaners should not be used.

- Try to have at least two employees on duty always. Employing two clerks is a form of "target hardening" because it may make a robbery more difficult to complete and, therefore, more unsuitable to a potential robber.
- Don't be tempted to use phony signs or equipment. The use of phony surveillance cameras, for example, can destroy the credibility of all other security precautions. Robbers soon learn to ignore them.
- Publicize the fact that the business uses good cash protection techniques and good protection equipment. Let potential robbers know their profits will be small and their risks high by using signs to convey this message. These visual deterrents (decals, placards, signs, etc.) should explain what safe method is used (dual-key, drop, or time-delay safe) in hopes of deterring a potential robber or explaining the method should a robbery occur.
- Many police departments have procedures for alarm verification and robbery response. Finding out what they are is advisable so that the employees will know what to expect in case of an armed robbery.

PROCEDURES DURING A ROBBERY

Proper employee training of the procedures to follow during a robbery is vital to surviving the confrontation. Conduct documented training and discussion periods so that every employee knows his or her part and has an opportunity to ask questions. A few minutes of brief review on a regular basis will help to ensure the proper reaction in case of a robbery. The overriding consideration in dealing with a robbery is to reduce the possibility of injury.

- Do not resist the robber. The money is not worth risking a life. Take no action that would jeopardize the safety of personnel or customers. Cooperate with the robber and do not try to become a hero. In most situations, robbers almost never hurt anyone who cooperates.
- Do not use or encourage the use of weapons against the robber. Introducing another weapon into the situation increases the chances of someone becoming injured during the

robbery. No amount of money is worth the risk of endangering a person's life.

- Try to inform the robber of any surprises. If someone is expected back soon or if you must reach or move in any way, tell the robber what to expect so he or she will not be startled. A suspicious move by an employee may trigger a violent reaction endangering the lives of many people.
- Follow the robber's commands, but do not volunteer to help. The longer the robbery takes, the more nervous the robber may become and more apt to become violent.
- If the robber demands a specific amount of money, only give them the amount they demand.
- Try to include "bait money" along with other cash. This bait money could be a bundle of currency with recorded serial numbers (record the denomination, serial number, and year of several tens and twenties on a piece of paper kept separate from the register) or concealed dye packs. The silent alarm may be designed to activate by the removal of the bait money.
- Try to keep customers and employees calm during the robbery.
- If the robber displays a firearm or claims to have one, consider it loaded and that the robber would use it.
- Activate the holdup alarm, if possible, only if it can be safely done without being obvious to the robber.
- Try to alert other employees of the situation by using prearranged signals.
- Be observant. Plan to be a good witness. Try to notice as much as possible about the robber.

Be sure to make mental notes of:

- The number of robbers.
- The robber's physical characteristics, including race, sex, age, height, weight, facial characteristics (head shape, color of hair, color of eyes, shape of eyes, nose, and mouth, etc.), speech patterns (i.e., accents), scars, marks or deformities, right- or left-handed.
- The robber's clothing description.
- Any names used by the robbers.

- Any peculiarities exhibited by the robber (i.e., smelled of alcohol, appeared to be high on drugs, etc.).
- Description of any weapons used—barrel length, barrel color, color of grips, whether a pistol is automatic or a revolver.
- If the robber uses a written note, try to place it out of sight to retain it as evidence.
- After the robber has the money, offer to have employees and customers lie down instead of waiting for the robber to decide what to do, such as knocking you down or tying you up.

PROCEDURES AFTER THE ROBBERY

If these steps are followed after a robbery, the business employee will be in a better position to provide information to assist law enforcement officers in arresting the perpetrator and, more importantly, in protecting the employee and innocent customers from harm.

- Establish which personnel will take certain actions if a robbery occurs. Decide now which employee will lock the doors, who will call the police, who will care for the injured, who will look for the getaway car, who will protect the evidence, etc. Don't assume these jobs will be done automatically.
- Do not chase or follow the robber. The robber may shoot at any pursuers or the police may shoot at you, too, thinking you are a robber.
- Secure the doors so the robbers cannot reenter the store. Stop business operations and place a sign on the door advising customers that the business is "temporarily closed due to an emergency." Do not let anyone in, except emergency personnel.
- Call the police immediately. Be sure to tell them if anyone is injured so they may dispatch medical personnel if necessary. Give the police the time of the robber's departure, his or her description, and direction and method of travel. Stay on the telephone until they tell you it's okay to hang up. The speed of reporting is critical to the apprehension of the offender.
- Care for any injured people.
- If it can be safely accomplished as the robbers leave, try to note their method of escape along with the direction of

travel. If a vehicle is used, try to find out the make, color, type, license number, and state of registration.

- Try to preserve any potential evidence. Protect the scene of the crime and do not touch anything the robber may have touched. Keep people out of the area.
- Write down the description of the robber. Witness description forms can be available to fill out descriptive data and other remarks, or if not available, use any available paper. Do not "compare notes" with others until a police officer arrives and conducts the necessary interviews.
- Ask witnesses to remain until the police arrive. If they insist on leaving, try to obtain their names and addresses.
- Contact any other individuals who may need to be contacted (i.e., store owner, bank security, etc.). Emergency telephone numbers should be accessible and the notification policy clearly established.
- Do not discuss the crime with outsiders until police give permission to do so. Refer all questions to the police.
- Do not tell or estimate how much money was lost to the robber unless absolutely necessary. The police can list the amount taken as an "undetermined amount of cash" until the exact amount is determined in an audit. Find out and record anything else that may have been stolen. If an exact amount of cash taken during the robbery should be released to the media and they report a large loss, other robbers could be attracted to the business or others in the chain.
- Assist the investigating officers in every way possible. Cooperate with the police by being available for interviews, not being reluctant to identify suspects, and giving evidence in court when notified to do so.

SOME SECURITY TIPS FOR OFFICE BUILDINGS AND RECEPTIONIST STATIONS

First and foremost, keep an eye on what is happening in the front-desk area. Avoid sitting with your head down, reading a book. Don't get involved in lengthy conversations with colleagues or lengthy personal phone conversations. Be aware of who and what is coming through the door. If someone sitting in the waiting area moves, be aware of where they are going.

If employee badges are required at your location, do everything you can to maintain 100% compliance. If a colleague, even one you know well, is not wearing his or her badge or if the badge is not visible, remind him or her of the requirements. If there is a metal detector, have everyone go through it. No by-passers allowed!

While it might be easier to just ignore some of these standard procedures—after all, it's your coffee buddy Sue or Joe, or maybe a company executive—there are policies and requirements, and it is your job to enforce them. No exceptions. Follow all security guidelines to the letter at all times.

If you have keys or an access card to the building or interior doors, keep them safe. Don't lend your keys to anyone or let anyone use a key or access card with which you have been entrusted. Don't leave your keys, access card, or ID card on a desk or countertop in your work area. It's best to always keep keys on your person or in a locked cabinet or drawer. Hiding places that you consider secret often don't remain secret for long. If your key, access card, or ID card is lost or stolen, report it to security, or others as designated, immediately. Don't label keys with a room number. If petty cash is kept at the front desk, always keep it out of sight and locked away.

If you must leave your work area for any reason, even for just a minute or two, lock everything. Don't leave a purse, briefcase, or bag at an unattended front desk.

If you're working on a computer, clear the screen and log off before walking away. Always follow all Internet/intranet security guidelines; even one exception can create a breach in computer security that may be widespread and costly. Do not leave your computer password where someone might see it or easily find it. Again, there are no perfect hiding places.

If you have work papers on the desktop, put them in a drawer. Avoid leaving documents in shared printers or facsimile machines in public areas. If you work with printed material that is in any way confidential or proprietary, do not simply throw it in a wastebasket in the front-desk area. If there is not one in place now, request a shredder for the front-desk area. If that is not possible, dispose of discarded papers in an area of the building not accessible to outsiders.

Avoid discussing confidential information or organization business in front of visitors, and remind your fellow employees to follow suit. Remember that even a seemingly insignificant conversation may include content that should not be heard outside the organization. Information that seems inconsequential to you may be of great interest to competitors or other outsiders, or even to employees who may use it to the detriment of the organization or employees. Your organization's business plans, customer information, and other sensitive data are an asset to be protected.

If possible, stagger the times you take breaks and leave the area to go to lunch. Don't be too predictable. Make it a point to brief the person relieving you. Who is in the waiting area and who they are waiting to see? Are any deliveries or service persons expected? Has anything happened that is out of the ordinary? Let your relief know what is happening and get answers to these same questions when you return.

Always be aware of your surroundings. Report any suspicious activity, such as an unfamiliar person remaining in the front-desk area for no apparent reason or someone who returns to the building multiple times in a short amount of time for no reason. Immediately report the presence of unauthorized building occupants, such as terminated employees, or outsiders who have been identified as being safety or security risks. If you have a no-solicitors policy, make sure it is enforced.

Always follow all access controls to the letter—no exceptions. Screen all visitors to verify that they have a legitimate need to be in the building and that they are expected. Have everyone sign in and issue them a temporary identification badge. Never assume that someone has a right to be in the building. Check the identity of unknown persons.

All visitors should be escorted while in the private areas of the building. Each visitor should be announced to the person he or she wishes to see by phone or intercom, and then be asked to wait in the front-desk area for the employee who will escort them. Following his or her visit, the person should be escorted back to the front desk to sign out. An enforced policy that requires all visitors to be escorted while in the building is both good security practice and old-fashioned good manners.

Some organizations are adding a requirement to check visitors' identification when they enter the building; in a more limited number of locations, two pieces of identification are requested. Other, more stringent requirements may include searching packages, purses, and briefcases taken into the building. Whether to add these additional check-in procedures is a decision that must be made by management based on experience and the level of security needed.

If you see someone begin to leave the front-desk area and head for other parts of the building without checking in, ask, "Can I help you?" or "Can I let someone know you are here?" Do not give them access and do not leave them unescorted. If the person is someone who should not be there, he or she may likely ignore you or may give you a curt answer and head for an exit, stairway, or elevator. Do not try to stop them. Call security or 911 immediately and provide a description of the person.

For example, imagine that near the end of the business day you see a man unknown to you enter the lobby and sit down in the waiting area. Upon asking how you can be of help, the barely audible response is that he is checking his appointment book for the name of the person he is to see. A few minutes later, as you are answering a phone call, you look up to see the man heading toward the door to the main part of the building. Without acknowledging your request that he check in at the desk, the man picks up his pace and, with an angry look on his face, continues into the building.

Without hesitation, call security or 911. There is an unknown person in the building. You do not know who he is there to see, exactly where in the building he is headed, or his purpose for being there. Stay at the front desk to be available to give a description of the person.

If someone is loitering or acting suspiciously in or near the front-desk area and you have any hesitancy about approaching them, call security or another preidentified source of assistance. Report the person's location and description. If possible to do so discreetly, keep an eye on the person until help arrives.

Any time you see a person committing an illegal act or criminal offense, don't hesitate. Call 911 immediately and inform security and others as identified in your organization's security procedures. While the details of the incident are still fresh in your mind, write down a description of those involved, exactly what happened, and the time and location of the offense. If the persons have left the area, report where they were last seen and their exit route. If your organization does not have an incident report form, you may want to create one to provide an outline of information to be noted.

Some front desks are also a central receiving point for packages. Even in organizations where most deliveries go through a central receiving area or a mail center, it is not uncommon for an occasional package or envelope to make its way to the front desk.

If deliveries are regularly received by the front desk, validate vendor lists of all routine deliveries and repair services. Take notice and report any suspicious packages. Even a briefcase that has been left unattended and for which you cannot readily identify an owner should be considered suspect. Do not handle or attempt to move any questionable item. It's important to keep track of what comes in the building—and what goes out.

Do not allow anyone—employee or visitor—to remove computers, peripherals, or other equipment from the building unless you know who they are and that they have permission to do so. In today's highly computerized world, while the equipment leaving the building does have financial value, it may also contain confidential or proprietary information that the organization can ill afford to let walk out the door. Some organizations have established a policy and system for tracking equipment taken home by employees. A form is signed by a manager giving permission for the item(s) to be taken from the building. These forms are tracked by the front desk, and items not checked back in within the specified time are reported to the manager who signed the permission form for follow-up.

Another security procedure being used by more organizations today than ever before, particularly where data security is highly critical, is to have all visitors check in their laptop computers at the front desk. The computer's serial number is recorded and then cross-checked when the visitor leaves the building with the computer.

This ensures that the same computers that enter the building leave the building and that no exchanges are made.

There may be a question about the necessity of these systems, seen as extreme by some. Based on the needed level of security, each organization must make a determination as to whether to adopt a policy requiring more stringent procedures to track articles passing the front desk. An incident that occurred at a large corporation a few years ago may present a good case for establishing these or similar policies and procedures at your location.

An employee discovered that an external computer hard drive was missing. While not being able to account for any equipment is always a nuisance, this missing hard drive caused great alarm and extreme concern as it contained the names, addresses, and bank account numbers of retired employees. The company took immediate steps first to rectify the situation by contacting all those whose information was contained on the hard drive, and then to institute strict procedures for employees and others leaving the building with any property belonging to the company. And for those wondering, the mystery was never solved, and the hard drive is still missing. We will never know if the hard drive was discarded by mistake, if it was taken by someone who intended to use the information on the drive for illegal purposes, or if it was just a case of someone wanting a hard drive for their home computer system.

Some safety and security procedures require you to say no or involve you in making certain that a person who would rather not do so follow established guidelines. When that happens, a few simple steps can make it easier for you.

IT'S OKAY TO SAY "NO"

Good front-desk professionals are polite, gracious, and often go the extra mile to accommodate everyone with whom they come in contact. While your comfort level in doing so is likely not always great, there are times when saying no is absolutely necessary for the safety and security of the organization and its employees.

You can't accept a package without the authorization of the person to whom it is addressed. You can't allow an unknown outsider to take pictures of the lobby. You can't permit a friendly, seemingly

nonthreatening person to go into the building without proper identification. You can't let a fellow employee bring friends or family
members into the building without appropriate clearance. These are
situations when saying no may be quite uncomfortable but is the
necessary and right thing to do. Here are some tips that may make
not saying yes a little easier:

First, remember, and mentally tell yourself, that saying no is the
appropriate response. If the organization's policies and procedures
are that the answer you are to give is no, then it is appropriate and
right for you to do so.

Consider this example: A woman with a notepad and pen in
hand approaches you and asks you about a recent downsizing at
your organization. She wants your opinion about how the layoffs
were handled, whether you thought they were necessary, and the
names of a few of the people who lost their jobs. It quickly becomes
apparent to you that the woman is a reporter. In a comeback to your
initial response that the organization's policy is that employees not
give media interviews, she aggressively reels off a list of reasons
why you should give her the information. I only need you to give
me a short statement. Don't you want to get the employee's side of
this story out there? The organization doesn't have anything to hide,
does it? Just give me a little insight on what's going on. You can trust
me; I won't repeat anything you tell me.

Remember that you don't have to respond immediately; take a
few seconds to organize your thoughts. You know what the policy is
and you are in charge.

Always maintain a professional image and avoid being argumentative or confrontational. Check to make sure you are not conveying a
nonassertive image by keeping your eyes downcast and avoiding eye
contact, having poor posture, fidgeting, or shifting your body. You
also don't want to exhibit an aggressive attitude or stance.

It is often easier to be assertive by starting your response with
the word no. "No, I cannot allow you to go immediately to Mr.
Smith's office. No unescorted guests are permitted beyond the main
lobby." This makes your response clear to the visitor and helps you
remain committed to your response.

Don't qualify or hedge your statements. "I think that you aren't
supposed to take that laptop home without your manager's approval"

makes it seem that you are not quite sure about what you are to do or that there's room for negotiation. A simple "The requirement is that all employees have written permission to take equipment from the property" leaves no doubt.

Sound confident and secure in your statements. Ending a statement by tagging on a question, either by asking an actual question or by an upward voice inflection, indicates insecurity and a lack of confidence. Avoid "Take a seat in the waiting area while I check to see if you are expected, okay?" Erase the "okay" that changes your assertive statement to a question and opens the door for discussion.

Using certain phrases destroys the authority of what you are saying. "You're not going to like having to take the extra time, but we require all parcels to be delivered to the loading dock." Don't preface your statements with comments that diminish their impact or importance. "We require that all parcels be delivered to the loading dock" is the message and all you need to say.

When saying "no," use assertive nonverbal skills. Keep your voice firm, clear, and direct. Avoid speaking too quickly. Pay attention to what the other person is saying. Letting them know you are listening to them does not indicate that you agree or that you will give in to their request.

Here's an example: A customer is at the front desk, demanding to see the manager of customer service immediately about a billing adjustment. You know that policy requires that all requests for adjustments must be made in writing. First, remain calm and diffuse the situation by saying, "Tell me about what has happened, and then I'll see how we can help you." While she tells you about her situation, occasionally nod or say "Go on" or "I see" to let her know you are listening. While it will still be necessary to deny the woman's request to see the customer service manager, just having someone listen will give her a chance to calm down. You can then say no to her original demand and provide an alternative way for solving her problem.

If it helps you to take a more assertive approach, stand up. Whether sitting or standing, square up your shoulders and look the person in the eye. Simultaneously shake your head and say no. When standing, keep your arms relaxed at your sides, your feet slightly apart, and your knees slightly flexed. You'll look as though you're ready to move and take action. When sitting, keep your head up and keep your hands above the counter or desk.

If there are times when you're not sure that no is the best response or if you are being repeatedly cajoled or coaxed to change your response, take a breath and take the time to think it over. Remind yourself that the decision is entirely up to you. You are in charge of the front desk. You know what you need to do; don't be forced into a decision you will later regret.

Remember that if you do say yes when you need to say no, you may endanger the safety and security of your organization and fellow employees.

DEALING WITH ANGRY PEOPLE

There may be times when a visitor to your building will become angry when hearing no, or when an angry or hostile customer or client confronts you about a problem. Dealing appropriately with these individuals may head off a potential emergency or disaster.

Dealing with unhappy, sarcastic, angry, or abusive people at the front desk is stressful and can take a great deal of your time. While we need to accept that people will get angry at times, such people are a challenge to deal with at best. In more extreme cases they may even swear at you, attempt to intimidate you, or make threats. Most of these situations are easily handled, and while every hostile situation is different and must be dealt with on a case-by-case basis, there are some suggestions that will help keep a bad situation from escalating into disastrous one.

For example, you see a man walk through the door and stride quickly toward the front desk. He is tight-lipped, red-faced, and has a tense body posture. Glaring at you, in a very agitated tone, his first words are, "I have left several phone messages for John Gray over the past 2 weeks, and he has not returned my phone calls. I have to see him, and if he doesn't see me now, there's going to be real trouble." He slams his fist down on the desk. What do you do?

- First, be aware of the signs that indicate that a person approaching the front desk may be irritated or upset. Even before they speak, angry and hostile people often telegraph their mood with nonverbal messages. Watch for hunched shoulders, clenched fists, an angry expression, or perhaps a red face, or heavy, stomping footsteps. Restlessness and either staring you down or avoiding eye contact are other indications that the person approaching will require some special attention.

- If you believe an approaching person may be angry, prepare yourself. Take a deep breath and remind yourself that you are absolutely capable of handling the situation.

- Let the approaching person see a calm, friendly, yet businesslike person. Don't react too quickly; take things slowly. Avoid becoming angry yourself. Responding in kind to shouting or trading insults will only exacerbate a bad situation and might result in negative consequences for you. Remember that the person is not angry with you personally. While you are the first person with whom he or she has contact, his or her issue is likely with the organization in general, a situation, a product or service, or perhaps another individual in the organization.

- Speak in a friendly manner and greet the person cordially, by name if possible. Show your interest and concern. Listen carefully to what the person is saying before beginning your response. In the majority of cases, while he or she does want the problem fixed or the situation changed, an angry person does not necessarily expect you personally to do so. He or she wants to be heard. Empathize, perhaps with a phrase like, "Most people would be angry if their bill was incorrect 3 months in a row." Remember that an angry person doesn't really hear anything that you say and is not ready to solve the problem. Keep listening; focus on acknowledging the person's feelings. Only after he or she starts to calm down after having vented his or her anger and having made clear to you how upset he or she is, is it possible to move toward finding a solution to the problem.

- Monitor the situation and the person's actions. If your attempts to calm the individual are unsuccessful, and if you have any reason to believe that the situation is worsening or that your own safety and that of others in the area is in any way in jeopardy, do not deal with an escalated situation. Remember that you are not obligated to tolerate foul language or abusive behavior. If your threshold of tolerance for abusive behavior is crossed or if threats are made, take the steps necessary to deal with the situation. Contact security. Use the panic button. Signal someone to call 911. Do whatever the specific situation requires to ensure everyone's safety.

- When the angry person is on the phone rather than standing in front of you, follow the same general guidelines. As with an angry person standing at the front desk, take any threats the caller makes seriously and take the appropriate actions immediately.

FRONT DESK MITIGATION

Mitigation in the front-desk area may require that you be proactive and take the lead. For the safety of visitors and employees, check to be certain your front-desk area does not present any safety risks. Work with facilities or engineering to check for and correct any such risks. For example, are rugs and floor mats in good condition? Is there a possibility that frayed rugs or mats or a slippery floor could cause falls?

Coordinate with facilities and security to make the front-desk area as easy to monitor as possible. If feasible, in a front-desk area that has more than one entrance, designate only one door to be used by everyone for entrance and exit. This makes it easier to observe who is coming into and leaving the building. Doors not intended for ingress and egress should not be propped open to allow people to enter unseen. Are entrances kept clear of obstructions at all times?

Position the front desk to make it as easy as possible to see all those coming and going and to provide the best possible view of doorways and of persons who have not yet signed in. This may include moving large plants and rearranging furniture in the guest waiting area. A flat surface at a suitable height for visitor sign-in is a plus. If you do data entry at the front desk, position the computer monitor to allow you to simultaneously use the computer and keep an eye on the front- desk area.

Consider adding entry or lobby signage that directs all visitors to sign in at the front desk or, if it is part of your security procedures, an advisory that all packages, handbags, and briefcases carried in by visitors are subject to being searched.

Silent duress alarm switches, often referred to as panic buttons, are an invaluable security tool at reception points. A simple touch triggers these hidden buttons, summoning assistance without overt actions. Increasingly common tools at front desks, panic buttons are also used in the offices of executives and their assistants and other high-security areas. If a panic alarm is not in place, check the feasibility of having one installed. Work with security experts to choose a location for the alarm; it needs to be easy to activate without drawing attention.

The ability to lock the main entrance door remotely from the front desk is another step that may be considered. This is particularly advisable in areas where public demonstrations are a frequent occurrence or in generally unsafe locations.

Working with security, facilities, and as appropriate, others in your organization, establish code words that can be used to quickly request assistance. Delivered by phone or in person, these code words summon immediate help without letting others know that the request is being made.

In some organizations the front-desk area is removed from the rest of the building or in a somewhat remote area. If that is true for your work area, a good security procedure is to establish set times during the day when you will check in with a specific person, perhaps in security or facilities. If the designated person doesn't hear from you, for example, when you first arrive at work, at 9:10, 11:15, 1:20, 3:25, and again just before you leave the building, he or she will phone you or come to the front desk to make sure there are no problems.

PREPAREDNESS RESPONSIBILITIES

As with most things in life, when you must take action to respond to a safety or security threat, the better prepared you are, the more effective the outcome will be.

Depending on the size of the organization, you may be asked to be a member of the emergency response team for your area of the building, or your role may be to manage the emergency response in the area of the front desk. In either case, it is important that you know what actions you are expected to take, that you be familiar with the role and responsibilities of the emergency response team, and that you understand how you are to collaborate and coordinate with the emergency response team organization.

Know which employees have been trained and certified in CPR and first aid, their work locations, and their extension numbers. Update this list no less often than twice annually to add newly trained employees, delete those whose certifications may have expired, and correct for changes in work locations or extension numbers.

While the first telephone number to call for any type of emergency or disaster is 911, to contact the fire department, local police or law enforcement office, and paramedics, there are other numbers that you should have at your fingertips. Include the internal numbers for security, the emergency response team coordinator, and facilities. An ambulance service, the nearest hospital or urgent care facility, your alarm company, the local postal inspector, and local FBI officials are some of the other numbers you may want to add to your list.

While it's a good practice to have these numbers programmed in your automatic dialer, in some major emergencies and disasters, the phone system may not work. Automatic dialers not equipped with battery backup will not function when the emergency results in a power outage. Having a printed list available is essential. Print the emergency contact list using a large, readable font. Consider using colored paper, yellow, orange, or lime green, and laminating the list. Keep it where it is always visible, and be certain everyone who staffs the front desk knows exactly where it is located. Check all numbers for accuracy at least quarterly and make any necessary changes or corrections.

Keep a flashlight and two sets of extra batteries at your work area. In the event of a power outage, it will help you carry out your emergency responsibilities and can also be used to help reassure and guide visitors.

A small portable radio often comes in handy to monitor weather conditions in natural disasters or to listen to news reports for updates on other disasters. If you are in an area that frequently experiences severe weather, e.g., hurricanes, tornadoes, or severe winter storms, a National Oceanic and Atmospheric Administration (NOAA) weather radio with a tone alert feature that signals when severe weather is approaching and provides information about what to do is particularly helpful. Again, keep two extra sets of replacement batteries. Replace both the flashlight and radio batteries every 6 months or when their expiration date nears to ensure that they will work when needed.

Review all emergency plans at least once a quarter. If you note areas needing updating or a need for additional procedures, talk with the person in the organization who is responsible for maintaining the plan.

Be familiar with the layout of the front-desk area and the surrounding areas. Know the location of the nearest fire alarms, fire extinguishers, first aid supplies, and emergency equipment. Know the location of the emergency exits, evacuation routes, and designated outdoor assembly areas. Walk through the evacuation route for your area once a month. Check monthly to see if there have been any changes in the emergency response team members on your floor or the first aid– and CPR-trained employees nearest the front desk. These individuals may change frequently as people are reassigned or leave the organization.

Attend any offered safety and security training. If you feel that you need additional training, check to see if it can be made available to you. Participate in all evacuation drills and emergency exercises.

As an additional preparedness measure, some organizations provide visitors with a one-page list of basic emergency instructions that includes an evacuation map for the floor they will be visiting. Discuss with those in charge of your emergency management program whether this may be a good option.

Making the necessary preparations now will enable you to act quickly and efficiently when an emergency or disaster happens.

EMERGENCY RESPONSIBILITIES

Your responsibilities in an emergency response will depend on your organization's emergency management program and related safety and security plans and procedures.

Whatever your role, here are some basic guidelines.

- One rule to remember above all others: Protect life, including your own. Never put your own well-being in jeopardy.

If you are injured, you will not only need assistance, but will be unable to help others.

- Stay calm. Breathe deeply and slowly to help control your stress. Remember, visitors and fellow employees will look to you for reassurance. Stay focused on what needs to be done now. Be decisive. Take control of the front-desk area and provide clear, concise instructions in accordance with established procedures. Remember that visitors are not familiar with your building or procedures; they will rely on you. Make sure they understand what they are to do and how they are to exit the building. If necessary, personally guide them out of the building and to the assembly area.

- A long-standing principle in first aid is to do no harm. Never attempt to provide assistance that is beyond your capabilities or for which you are untrained. Remember that you can't be all things to all people. Each person has ultimate responsibility for his or her own safety.

- When you are in doubt, always err on the side of caution. If you are not certain whether you need to call 911 or security, don't hesitate. Make the call. Wait for emergency personnel to arrive. If the professionals require your help, they will let you know what is needed.

- Follow established plans and procedures to the extent possible. In cases when, because of unusual or unforeseen circumstances, doing so will not be safe, or in situations when established procedures, for whatever reason, will just not work, be flexible and creative. First, assess the situation, and then act to best address it.

Based on factors including the location of the front-desk area, building configuration, and staffing, you may be assigned to an emergency response team (ERT). Whether or not you are a member of the emergency response team organization, it is important to understand how the teams are organized and the roles of the team members.

As required by the specific emergency situation, the ERT members direct and coordinate response by individual employees, conduct basic search and rescue, and assist in accounting for building occupants following an evacuation. They provide first aid or make the notifications necessary to get medical help for ill or injured persons. They calm and reassure people to help prevent panic. Often just knowing that there are trained teams responding to the situation allays fears and provides reassurance.

One of the benefits of ERT members wearing identifying vests and perhaps hard hats is that it lets people see that there is an organized and trained team taking charge of the emergency situation. Some organizations take the additional step of identifying ERT members and their normal work locations with special signage to provide another way to reassure employees and visitors that there are people who will assist them when an emergency occurs.

The emergency management director has responsibility for managing and coordinating the organization's entire emergency management program. Specific duties typically include organizing ERTs, procuring supplies and equipment, arranging for appropriate training for ERT members and the general employee population, and coordinating with security and other departments as necessary.

The building ERT coordinator directs the ERT members and reports to the emergency management director. The building ERT coordinator has full life-safety-related decision-making authority for the facility during emergencies. The building ERT coordinator may also have responsibility for coordinating with security, facilities, and any outside agencies involved in responding to the emergency. In organizations with multiple buildings, a building ERT coordinator is appointed for each building.

The floor warden oversees the emergency preparedness and response program on the assigned floor. When an emergency occurs, the floor warden is typically responsible for directing the other ERT members on the assigned floor, employee and visitor response, compiling status information from other team members on the assigned floor, and reporting to the building ERT coordinator. Additional floor warden responsibilities may include conducting preliminary damage surveys and providing status reports to the building ERT coordinator once the initial response is concluded.

Coordinating with the floor warden, monitors direct employees and guests toward the emergency exit while helping to keep everyone calm and providing assistance as needed.

On upper floors, elevator monitors direct everyone away from the elevators and toward the emergency exits, again keeping people calm and aiding anyone needing assistance. Both exit monitors and elevator monitors remind employees to report to their assigned assembly area after exiting the building.

Searchers, always working in pairs, ensure that the assigned area has been vacated in the event of evacuation. They conduct a systematic search of the assigned area, including rest rooms, file rooms, lunch and coffee rooms, conference rooms, and storage areas to ensure that everyone in their assigned area heard the alarm and completely vacated once the evacuation was ordered. Searchers close all doors as each room and area is checked.

The assembly area coordinator is typically responsible for reporting to the designated outdoor assembly area following a building evacuation and directing all employees to congregate by department, work group, or building area as predesignated. Once employees have gathered, the assembly area coordinator collects reports from all floor wardens and confers with work supervisors and coworkers to see whether everyone has made it to the assembly area; he or she then provides a complete status report to the building coordinator that includes a list of those unaccounted for and their last known location.

A discussion of ERTs always reminds me again of the importance of tailoring every aspect of an emergency management program, not only to meet the organization's requirements and capabilities, but also to fit with the organization's culture.

As a case in point, at one company it was even necessary to change an ERT position title to mesh better with the company's culture. In introducing the ERT organization structure to the employees of the company, where the average employee age at the time was approximately twenty-six, there was immediate and extreme dissatisfaction with the term *floor warden*. Many employees viewed the title *warden* as one that belonged in a penal institution, not in their company. To maintain a satisfactory comfort level for everyone, the *floor warden* became the *floor coordinator*.

Was this an insignificant, unnecessary change? While the initial response may be a resounding "absolutely," the importance of integrating emergency management into the organization's culture cannot be overstated. It is the organization's culture that dictates employee behavior and ultimately has much to do with the extent to which all employees support (or fail to support) the emergency management program and ERT members. Something as small as changing a position title may have great long-range value to the success of the emergency management program.

All employees need to fully understand that during an emergency, the ERT has full authority over the response by occupants on the assigned floor or area regardless of team members' day-to-day positions or responsibilities. Everyone is to follow all directions given by ERT members, building safety and security staff, or public safety officials.

Another possible scenario for you is that that the duties of some of the ERT members will be collapsed and the person staffing the front desk will fulfill multiple ERT duties for that area, typically those of the exit monitor, elevator monitor, and searcher. If that is the case, you will be responsible for directing employees and visitors in the front-desk area along the designated evacuation route to the emergency exit, and away from any elevators in the front-desk area, as well as advising everyone of where they are to assemble once they are outside the building. Before you leave, conduct a sweep of the front-desk area, and after ensuring that all employees and visitors have vacated the area, close, but do not lock, all doors.

Once outside the building, report to your designated assembly area and, to the extent possible, account for everyone who was in the front-desk area at the time the evacuation was ordered. Follow all established reporting channels. If you are not able to account for everyone who was in the front-desk area, immediately tell the assembly area coordinator or other appropriate person(s) who is missing and where you last saw him or her. Request first aid or medical attention for anyone who may have been injured during the evacuation, and continue to calm and reassure people who may be upset.

If there are reporters on the scene, do not make comments or give interviews, and discourage others from doing so.

Once the danger has passed, there is still work to be done. Comprehensive emergency plans include actions to be taken after the emergency or disaster has ended.

POST-EMERGENCY RESPONSIBILITIES

Check to see what is expected of you post-emergency, once people are safe or have received medical attention, and public safety officials who may have responded have left.

If a formal debrief is conducted, attend and give your assessment of how well the response was handled. In place of, or in addition to, the debrief, you may be asked to provide a written report either by completing a standard report form or by writing a narrative of your perspective of what occurred. Even if you are not asked to do so, write a report and send it to those in the organization who oversee emergency programs. Include in your report both what worked well during the response and what needs to be improved. Based on your evaluation, include a list of additional equipment that is needed, any procedures that are missing or that do not provide sufficient details, or the need for better training for designated response team members or all employees.

To the extent possible, move forward with making the corrective actions that you have identified as being necessary. If you can't personally make the changes, follow up with those who can to avoid having the same items become problems again when the next emergency or disaster occurs.

Good emergency management requires a team effort. You can't do it alone.

YOUR SUPPORT SYSTEM

You have many allies, both in your organization and in the community, to assist you in preparing for and carrying out your safety and security responsibilities.

Establish and maintain open lines of communication with others in your organization who play a role in protecting the safety and security of employees and visitors. These channels of communication are of significant help not just when an emergency happens, but in the mitigation and preparedness processes as well.

If your organization has a safety coordinator or an emergency management coordinator, meet with them to learn exactly what programs are in place, what your role and responsibilities are, and what support is available to you.

The security director and the on-site security staff have likely identified the risks that are the greatest threat to the organization in general, as well as those that are specific to the front desk. They will provide you with guidance on what to do in the event of a security threat or breach. Coordinate with them when emergencies occur. Call them if extra help is needed, or if you are just not comfortable handling a situation on your own.

The human resources (HR) management department or personnel department is your best source of detailed information about your organization's policies on violence in the workplace. They can also help you obtain needed safety and security training. If HR has oversight of Occupational Safety and Health Administration (OSHA) compliance, they may take ownership of conducting a facility risk survey, occupational health and safety issues, and placement of needed safety equipment. HR can take the lead in developing a communications plan to disseminate correct, rumor-free information to employees to prevent panic immediately after an emergency, and to provide appropriate updates in the days or weeks following a disaster. If your organization has an employee assistance program managed by HR, that program is the natural link to an excellent source of posttrauma stress counseling following an emergency.

The facilities or engineering department can help facilitate mitigation measures such as repairing nonfunctioning exit signs or rearranging the front-desk area.

Check around. These are just some of the internal resources you have to assist you. There are likely others. Outside the organization there are also many sources of valuable information and assistance that are prepared to help you and your organization.

Public safety officials are the professionals who will respond and take charge when an emergency occurs. The two primary local agencies providing assistance are fire and law enforcement. In addition to responding to emergencies, these agencies are experts and are a great source of information and guidance in emergency preparedness planning. Available services vary from one jurisdiction to another, and there is seldom a charge for any assistance provided. In some instances fire authorities will initiate contact with your organization as part of their code enforcement and fire prevention program.

Both the fire department and law enforcement agency will review your safety and security procedures and emergency response plans and provide feedback for improvements. They may also review the related employee training curriculum.

The local fire authority can provide information on the possible threats and hazards in your area. They will check to ensure that your life safety systems and emergency procedures meet local codes and ordinances, and make suggestions to bring your organization into compliance. They will review your evacuation plan and offer guidance on mapping the best exit routes from your building. Representatives from the fire department can help you plan an evacuation drill, observe the drill, and provide valuable feedback that will help your employees get out of the building more quickly and safely. Some fire departments will present on-site employee training in the use of fire extinguishers, often giving everyone a chance to participate in some hands-on practice.

A tour of your building and grounds by fire officials provides an opportunity for them to meet with your emergency response personnel and become more familiar with your facilities. They may also request a drawing of your building indicating all entrances and exits, the location of gas and electric shutoffs, elevators, stairwells, and fire alarm panels. These steps help firefighters preplan responses to emergencies that occur at your organization.

Many local police agencies offer a security inspection service. They will work with you and your security staff to review building security measures and alarm reliability and effectiveness and make suggestions for improvements. A building exterior inspection that includes checking for possible entry points will be conducted. The inspection may also include identifying places outside the building where vision is obstructed by trees or bushes, and areas that need improved lighting. The police department will offer advice to help reduce employee theft and make presentations to staff on security and safety. Officers will also offer suggestions for arranging your front-desk area for better security and help in determining the best location for a panic button or silent alarm.

There is also help at the federal government level. Check the Federal Emergency Management Agency's (FEMA) website for information and downloadable forms and publications, and be sure to request a catalog of free printed material related to preparing for and responding to disasters.

Work with representatives of facilities, security, engineering, and other appropriate departments to identify areas where emergency professionals can be of help to you. Then give your local agencies a call to learn exactly what services they provide and how they can work with your organization to help prevent emergencies and improve response when emergencies happen.

Some additional suggestions for an overseas security, safety, and evacuation plan are included in Appendix D. A brief "Workplace Violence Procedures" worksheet is included in Appendix E.

KEY POINTS

Protection of people and assets includes property protection, protecting your employees, and protecting information. The standards of security historically include the three Ds of deter, detect, and delay. I like to speak about response as part of the security three D trilogy. As with security management, crisis management, or response, must be part of your agenda. I suggest you consider awareness as a critical factor in your protection programs. Awareness consists of creating the environment among employees that your goal is to protect them and the company's assets. You will also be able to enlist their assistance while imparting to them ownership and control over much of this program.

CASE STUDY

Some employees were based in the southern part of a country that was occupied by occupation forces, and insurgents were battling for control of regions that were not yet stabilized. The employees were U.S. expats, who relied not only on the protection of company-hired heavily armed security professionals, but also on the capabilities of an armed forces unit stationed nearby. One hot Friday evening, the job site began to hear car bombs, followed by mortar fire, small arms fire, and any number of frightening sounds. The facility itself came under direct attack by rocket and mortar fire. Damage was minimal, but nerves were frayed rather quickly. As per the crisis management plan in place for the project, calls were immediately made to the security management in the United States, and to contacts within the armed forces stationed in the nearby city center. The security manager began by asking if the local emergency management plan had been initiated, which it had. Employees were in bomb shelters and bunkers, and all preparation had been made in the event that the location would need to be evacuated. Per the crisis management plan, the project employees were in contact with the nearby foreign military force, which was in charge of the area and city where the project was located. The military advised they were under attack, pinned down, and could not get to the employees. Thus ensued a frantic weekend of phone calls, with the employees contacting the security manager in the United States with updates, and phone calls to mobile phones at the project site to determine the status. Private evacuation resources were out of the question. If the military could not travel, no one would be in the air or on the road. The project site security and crisis management plan binder got a major workout. It was 2 weeks before the roadways were clear enough to send a response force to the project site. When the U.S. military arrived, they asked employees if they wished to remain on the project or be evacuated. All chose to remain. Without a well-written and crafted plan, panic might have ensued and loss of lives might have occurred.

8

Predeployment and Security Awareness Training
"Tell Me Everything I Need to Know about This Country in about 15 Minutes"

Those with the greatest awareness have the greatest nightmares.

—Mahatma Gandhi

Preparing people for deploying across the world can be both challenging and rewarding. Challenging in that if you think it is going to be easy to convince a busy junior executive, lawyer, engineer, IT specialist, or any other professional that they should sit through a predeployment course on their country of destination, then I have some condos on the lunar surface I can let you have for a song. Nevertheless, predeployment training is critical to the success of your security and crisis management operations since these employees are going to be in the front line of your operations. The success or failure of your planning for their protection will rely on how well you construct your plans, train these individuals, and they and you execute the plans in an actual emergency.

Predeployment training can be as basic as the travel tracking email pushes received from web-based monitoring services such as iJet. These provide travelers with notices and pertinent timely information relating to health, safety, and security concerns. Predeployment training can be as detailed as bringing in country security and safety experts for lectures and seminars for your travelers, such as the previously mentioned occurrence of the retired CIA case officer instructing a group of pharmaceutical research scientists on the do's and don'ts of getting around in what was the then Soviet Union.

You will obviously need to tailor your information to your audience, but also their protection needs. Make sure you are giving your employees the best, most current and useful information possible. I was not an expert on the Soviet Union, by any means, so why not bring in someone who was? If your employees are going to be exposed to risk in the form of natural disasters, landslides, severe storms, or health risks such as malaria, it is important to get the correct information to them with the proper instructions.

I want to point out what I feel is one of the most important tools in detection when working in volatile regions. Investigations have verified that in most terrorist attacks, surveilling the target has been utilized. The surveillance can be directed toward individuals, vehicles, residences, office buildings, job sites, and other locations, such as restaurants and clubs. It seems almost cliché, and once you bring this up to employees and project personnel, you might be rewarded with the rolled eyes or sideways glances. This seems a little too James Bond, a bit much of Le Carré. They will check to see if you have a Robert Ludlum novel tucked under your arm. Trust me on this one: it can and does occur, but it looks about as much like what you see in the theater or on TV as my signature looks like a painting by Cézanne. I know of several instances where employees operating on projects I was associated with were surveilled.

I would suggest developing your ideas on identifying and dealing with foreign surveillance into a training module or program. You could do a "stand up" in the classroom or online training sessions. I have even discussed these ideas on conference calls with multiple attendees in different countries. Obviously, you are counseling everyone to be alert. Not always an easy call when you have employees heading to meetings, working 16- or 18-hour days, and given the hustle and bustle of many foreign cities. The bad guys have the advantage; they conduct this activity for real and every day. They know the terrain and areas. You are the one who is going to stand out by your mere presence; you will make an ideal target.

As mentioned, the criminals (yes they do this too) and terrorists, would-be attackers, are looking to find out who or what (office, residence, job site) would make for the most ideal target. Perhaps there are more employees present at one entrance (such as a vehicle entry point) that creates a choke point and a larger potential target for a vehicle-borne improvised explosive device (VBIED) or package bomb, attack with automatic weapons, or other means. They might determine that every Friday an employee walks to a local automatic teller machine, withdraws some cash, and then walks to a nearby mall to pick up items and kill some time. Driving to a job site each day at the same time, using the same route, and making the same stops along the way also set a routine out for those who might be surveilling you. The surveillance might go on for some time until such routines and weaknesses are determined.

Those who are conducting the surveillance must take care not to stand out themselves or risk being observed by police or military, nearby shop owners, or others. They may go as far as to check out what types of activities would not draw attention, such as being in a business suit when the locale is a fishing village. This will be easy for the surveillors to overcome. In addition, they may have assistance from members of the community, shop owners, even police or military who are supportive.

There is moving and stationary surveillance. If you are out walking, you could be followed on foot. Those who are watching you may use one person only, which could alert you if you start to see the same person behind or around you wherever you go. If they use more than one person, then it will be harder to detect since they can trade off positions and people. If three or more persons are added, it will be increasingly difficult to spot what is going on. The experts in countersurveillance would tell you to look for footwear, the types of clothing worn on the lower body, such as pants for men, skirts for women, which if someone is trying to appear differently clothed, will be harder to cover up or change out of.

The experts will also advise that you might suddenly stop and turn around while walking, change your direction suddenly, change your walking speeds, enter shops or stores to see who lingers, or use windows, mirrors, or reflective services to observe who might be watching or following. Vehicle surveillance can be both easier or more difficult to detect, given the means with which this type of surveillance is conducted. As with foot patrol, one vehicle will be easier to spot than two or three. If your employees use the same routes and times in order to travel to and from work, the chances of you being successfully surveilled increase. Vehicle surveillance can be conducted, if you are using the same routes each day, in a manner that is extremely difficult to detect. A vehicle might follow you to a particular point or intersection one day, then turn off and break off contact. The next day, the surveilling vehicle might pick you up at this same intersection and continue on, turning off at some farther point. Each day the surveilling vehicle might get closer and closer to your end location until it succeeds.

Some of the same methods for detecting foot surveillance apply to the detection of being followed by a vehicle. If you can do so safely, you might make a U-turn to see who is following from behind. Changing direction will shake things up. Turn off the street to observe who follows your movement, possibly continuing on to circle a block. You can pull off the street and park, or delay and hesitate over the top of a hill or around a corner. I have recommended and had success with attempting to time a traffic light so that you can pass through but a vehicle that might be following is caught on red at the other side of the intersection.

Be careful in these situations. Keep in mind that an expatriate driving in foreign countries is a risk in and of itself. Walking around on many foreign city streets in some areas is not recommended. You can instruct drivers you might be utilizing in these methods, or you can ensure that employees can pass along instructions to drivers while they are able to take note of observed information.

It has been noted by security services that terrorists often employ surveillance of fixed targets by methods such as parking a vehicle in a location, with surveillors remaining in or nearby these vehicles. If vans are used by surveillance teams, a driver might park a vehicle and leave a team within a van. Teams might appear to be conducting vehicle repairs, chatting with persons who might be on a park bench or on a bicycle or motorbike. There may be children or couples present. Vehicles that are frequently seen in the same places around the same times should be noted. Ask yourself, "Wasn't that van here this morning, and weren't the same people inside the van?"

Reporting suspicious persons and vehicles to law enforcement or security personnel can keep one safe.

As I mentioned, I have also provided a guide to foreign national employees who are visiting the United States for the first time. The information is intended to provide these employees with some practical information regarding travel and general security within the United States. I think it can provide informational prompts for those non-U.S. citizens and others not familiar with the United States customs, laws, and how to remain safe while in-country.

Terrorism is a threat throughout the world. The U.S. Homeland Security Advisory System Threat Level provides the current threat-level status and explanation of each level. The link to the Department of Homeland Security is listed at http://www.dhs.gov/dhspublic/. Should terrorist acts take place within the United States, local, state, and federal law enforcement and government agencies will advise citizens how to respond. For more information on the types of emergency medical or other supplies to keep on hand, visit the American Red Cross website at http://www.redcross.org/services/disaster/0,1082,0_601_,00.html.

Crime takes place in the United States, as it does in other countries around the world. Crime rates in the United States tend to be higher in larger cities, but also in some smaller urban areas. It is best to be wary of venturing into areas either on foot or by automobile if you have not at least asked advice of colleagues, hotel concierge, or law enforcement agencies. Visitors and tourists can be targeted for pickpocketing or petty crimes. Crime statistics in the United States are a matter of public record, and often may be retrieved utilizing police department or sheriff's office websites. In addition, many newspapers carry crime statistics, supplying postal zip code and blocks where the incident took place, as well as the time and type of incident. The U.S. Department of Justice compiles crime statistics by state and city. Visit their website at http://www.ojp.usdoj.gov/bjs/.

The United States experiences various natural hazards, including hurricanes, volcanoes, and earthquake activity around the Pacific Basin, including Hawaii; tornadoes are more prominent in the Midwest, but may occasionally occur in other locations; mud slides and earthquakes may take place in California; forest fires in the West; and severe snow and ice storms, and flooding in various locations. Local media will keep persons advised of weather and other conditions, and of any evacuation notices. Some useful links include:

Federal Emergency Management Agency: http://www.fema.gov/
National Weather Service: http://www.nws.noaa.gov/

Concerning handling money and valuables, a good way to handle payments while traveling is to utilize travelers checks. If using credit cards, do not carry more than you require. If using an automatic teller machine (ATM) card, ensure it will operate in the United States, and then utilize only ATMs located in safe areas, such as hotel or bank lobbies. A common means of robbery in the United States is to accost persons using outdoor ATMs. Make two photocopies of valuables, such as your passport, tickets, visas, and traveler's checks. Keep one copy with you in a separate place from the original, and leave another copy with someone at home.

It's a good idea to keep the cash you carry to a minimum and consider utilizing a concealed money belt, or carry billfolds in front pockets to deter pickpocketing. Avoid flashing large amounts of cash or expensive jewelry or watches.

Travelers should keep passports in a safe place (such as a hotel safe) when not traveling. Keep at least two photocopies of your passport, one secured in a safe place or with a relative/friend.

If you are traveling with children, explain safety and security precautions to them. Children should be especially cautious around any strangers, and should be supervised whenever possible.

Immediately report any suspicious or unusual activity to law enforcement, management, or security officers. Dial 911 from landline or cellular phones. Know the phone numbers for local law enforcement in your area and the location of police and fire stations.

Identity theft is a growing issue around the world, and the United States sees its share of such victimization. Despite your best efforts to manage the flow of your personal information or to keep it to yourself, skilled identity thieves may use a variety of methods to gain access to your data.

The following is a list of how information is obtained from businesses or other institutions:

- Theft of records or information while the thieves are on the job.
- The use of bribes to an employee who has access to these records.
- More technically competent thieves might hack your information.
- Employees can be tricked into unwillingly providing detailed information of use to thieves.

Thieves may obtain your mail, including bank and credit card statements, credit card offers, new checks, and tax information, while others might dumpster dive for your trash, the trash of businesses, or public trash dumps.

- For more information, see *How Not to Get Hooked by a 'Phishing' Scam*, a publication from the Federal Trade Commission (FTC).
- Treat your mail and trash carefully.
- For more information, visit http://www.ftc.gov/bcp/conline/pubs/credit/idtheft.htm.

Concerning keeping travel plans and itinerary information secure, employees should make travel reservations through corporate travel or your designated travel service. Employees should complete/ensure a traveler profile (including "tertiary" for lifeline contact) is current and correct. All travelers should follow country travel advisory and visa/customs rules. Employees should establish a check-in/checkpoint schedule (call in to your manager or coworker at designated times each day while traveling).

ROBBERY AND ASSAULT PREVENTION: AVOIDANCE/PRECAUTIONS

Below are a series of checklists and security rules to follow regarding personal security that you can pass along to your employees.

ON FOOT

- Be alert of your surroundings.
- Know where you are going. Utilize MapQuest, directions, GPS, road maps.
- Know the location of the nearest police department.
- Plan your route in advance.
- Avoid dark corners.
- Carry a flashlight if going to be walking after dark.
- Avoid parking too far away.
- If you sense you are being followed, change directions and continue to a public area, business, fire station, police station, fast food restaurant, etc., and ask for help.
- Maintain a safe distance from others.
- Alert others when fleeing from danger.

IN VEHICLES

- Park in well-lit areas.
- Have keys ready when approaching vehicles.
- Inspect vehicle before entering for signs of break-in, tampering, or persons inside the vehicle.
- Ensure the vehicle is routinely serviced and maintained.
- In high crime areas, do not carry credit cards and bring only the cash you will need.
- Make sure you have a cell phone and utilize 911 for emergency calling in case of trouble.
- Keep vehicle doors locked.
- Preplan your route of travel.
- Do not stop to assist stranded motorists, but call in safely from your cell phone.
- Drive to the nearest police or fire station if being followed, etc.

- If rear-ended by another vehicle, pull over in a public place to exchange information.
- If your vehicle breaks down, use your cell phone to call for assistance.
- Blow your horn if someone suspicious approaches your vehicle at a stop sign or traffic light.
- Do not pull over for flashing headlights. An emergency or police vehicle will be equipped with red and blue flashing lights.
- If you become lost, find a public place such as a gas station or other well-lit public area to ask for directions or call for assistance.
- Use automatic teller machines only in bank or hotel lobbies, or drive-up units, and only during business hours in safe sections of town.
- Use steering wheel locking devices (such as those called "the Club").

INSIDE BUILDINGS

- Be aware of persons who may be loitering near building entrances or doorways.
- Use the elevators (except in case of fire); avoid stairwells.
- Lock doors to any equipment rooms or spaces where you are working immediately upon entering if ingress is available from public space.
- Notify building security/maintenance/coworkers/managers if you are working after normal business hours.
- Leave yourself an "out"—a means of escape while you are working and if you are approached by suspicious persons.
- Move or drive away from individuals or groups who will not take no for an answer or make you feel uneasy. Go for help or ask someone nearby for help.

ASSAULTS AND DEALING WITH POSSIBLY MENTALLY DISABLED PERSONS

If you are confronted with persons who appear to be deranged, mentally challenged, unstable, aggressive panhandlers, or abusing substances, do not be aggressive in response. Make eye contact and use a calm, but firm voice to reply no to solicitations for money or other such requests. Make no sudden movements or hand gestures. Use open hands, palm up and arms spread shoulder width apart (this action denotes "no harm").

IN THE EVENT OF A ROBBERY

- Remain calm.
- Keep it short and smooth—handle the robbery as if it were a normal transaction.
- If you must reach for something, tell the robber first.
- Let the robber know you intend to obey.
- Follow the orders of the robber immediately and exactly as instructed.
- If you are not sure what the robber is telling you, ask.
- If someone else is working with you or there is a possibility they will enter the area, let the robber know to avoid surprises.
- If any shots are fired, immediately fall to the ground or take cover.
- Calmly observe what the robber(s) looks like and what clothes are worn. Memorize peculiarities such as tattoos, scars, and prominent physical features.
- Obtain the direction the robber(s) fled on foot or vehicle description and license number.
- Immediately upon the exit of the robber(s) dial 911.
- Preserve the area where the robber(s) may have touched.
- Contact your manager.
- If there are witnesses, ask them to remain there until the police arrive.
- Begin to assess what has been taken or lost.
- Do not argue with the robber(s).
- Do not resist, arm yourself, or in any way fight with the robber(s).
- Do not chase or follow the robber(s).
- Do not activate any silent panic/holdup alarm unless you may do so without the knowledge or observations of the robber(s).

PARKING LOT SECURITY TIPS

- Park in well-lit areas or areas visible to the workplace/lodging, etc.
- If you can't see more than 100 feet at night, park elsewhere.
- Park in areas of the lot that have higher traffic.
- If you are going to work after dark, move your car at some time during the day to a better, closer location.
- Keep all valuables in the interior from being seen from the vehicle exterior, or secure in trunk.
- Lock vehicle doors and keep windows rolled up—"venting" for heat provides easy access for thieves.
- Use a steering wheel/column lock, such as "the Club."
- Car alarms and decals/stickers are effective deterrents.
- Make use of restaurant or hotel valet parking.

REMINDERS FOR PARKING LOT

- Lock car doors.
- Roll up windows.
- Remove keys from ignition when exiting vehicle.
- Park in well-lit or easily viewed areas.
- Be aware of your surroundings.
- Be cautious of and alert to male predators in parking lots.
- Plan where you are going to park.
- If you see suspicious persons in the area, do not exit your vehicle.
- As you exit buildings and head to your vehicle, scan the area.
- Advise children and family members to enter vehicles quickly and lock doors once inside.
- If you believe someone is following you, yell at them to stop, but do not confront them.
- Quickly return to the business or office and ask for assistance if you observe or experience something suspicious.
- Have your keys ready when you exit.
- Keep your hands as free as possible.
- Keep a cell phone with you.
- Dial 911 in emergencies and know the number for police or sheriff's office dispatch in your location.

- When you are safe, call the police or notify security if you see anything suspicious.

LODGING SAFETY TIPS

- Do not use hotels or motels with outside or exterior entrances.
- Do not use lodging that issues actual keys for rooms.
- Avoid mentioning or having your room number mentioned by you or the front-desk clerk.
- Knock before entering your room for the first time.
- Don't answer the door without verifying who it is.
- Use your door peephole to view who is at the door.
- Keep your room key with you at all times and don't needlessly display it in public.
- Close the door securely whenever you are in the room and use all locking devices.
- Check to see that any sliding glass doors, windows, or connecting doors are locked.
- Do not invite strangers to your room.
- When away from your room, keep the TV or radio on so that persons who may be interested in breaking into and entering the room may think someone is present. Utilize the "Do Not Disturb" sign for the same effect.
- Do not draw attention to yourself by displaying large amounts of cash or expensive jewelry, laptops, or other items.
- Place all valuables in the hotel front desk or room safe/safety deposit box.
- When returning to or leaving your room late in the evening, be aware of your surroundings, stay in well-lit areas, and use the main entrance.
- Take a few moments and locate the nearest exit that may be used in the event of an emergency.
- If you see any suspicious activity, notify the hotel operator or staff member.
- Attacks may take place in hotel or motel parking lots. Practice safety and security consciousness while parking or walking to your vehicle.
- Report anything suspicious and be safe!

AIRPORT CONCERNS AND PRECAUTIONS

When arriving at a foreign airport, pick up your ticket and quickly move from the public areas to the secure section located beyond the metal detectors and x-ray machines. Move away from areas where there are unattended packages or luggage. Be careful who you talk to and what information you give out, as well as who is listening to your conversations. Be more aware of what is going on around you and who may be paying attention to you. Staying alert and being aware of your surroundings will decrease your chances of being in the wrong place at the wrong time.

Be aware of the various airport scams, some of which occur at the entrance to the secure area. In one common scenario, your attention is distracted when you place belongings on the conveyor of the x-ray machine, and an accomplice takes them. Targets include laptop computers, purses, and expensive briefcases.

Baggage claim is an area where criminals can target their victims. They are looking for people who appear to be wealthy, such as those wearing expensive jewelry or clothes, or those who have expensive luggage. Those wearing logos designating major corporations or American universities may also be targets. Be aware of anybody that may be watching you, and note if they happen to appear at your hotel later. If you are in a reputable hotel, you may give the staff a description of the person who you believe is following you.

Prior to leaving for your trip, contact your local office, if you have one in your destination city, and determine which taxi companies are reputable or what other means of transportation is available. Many foreign airports have licensed taxicabs, as well as individual cabs that are not licensed or regulated. You should have some idea of the route from the airport to the hotel or office to which you are going. Make sure you negotiate the rate before you leave the airport; once you are in the cab, you are at their mercy. Having a limousine service pick you up is not a bad idea, but do not have them display a placard with your name. By using a limousine, you are effectively publicizing your wealth; displaying your name unnecessarily reveals your identity.

STREET SMARTS

The same commonsense procedures used in the United States are also effective in other countries. Being alert and aware of what is going on around you will keep you out of potentially dangerous situations. The problem with most travelers is that they are so preoccupied with sightseeing or business that they have to conduct that they do not pay attention to what is going on around them. If you do nothing more than give the impression that you are alert and aware, you will dissuade most criminals from making you their next victim. Why? Because there are too many easy targets out there who are not alert and aware. Do not ask strangers on the street for directions. Go into a place of business, such as a hotel or restaurant, and inquire of them.

Most criminals conduct surveillance prior to committing the criminal act. That surveillance may last seconds or days, depending on the sophistication of the criminal, but it will happen. In order for someone to watch you, they must be close enough that you can also see them. To detect surveillance, you must first identify anyone you have seen repeatedly at different locations. Also look for people standing around who begin to walk when you walk and stop in the same manner. Use store windows and car windows to observe people who may be following you. If you suspect that you are being followed, do not confront the individual(s). Go into a store or restaurant and call your company security personnel or local police.

When you are out walking, walk with confidence. Stop and look around occasionally, giving the impression that you are security-conscious. When you come out of a building, look around as you exit, again giving the impression that you are alert and aware. Remember, the bad guy does not want to get caught. Prison in foreign countries is feared. The criminal will look for an easier target, and those who appear to be security-conscious will not be very high on their list.

If you think you are being followed while in a car, make several stops and see if the other car stops. Do not be obvious in what you are doing. You can pull into a shopping mall, drive through the parking lot, and exit the mall without getting out of the car. Did the car following you take the same route? Another technique is to make a U-turn when it is safe to do so. If you determine that you are being followed, go to a police station or a well-populated, well-lit area to exit your vehicle. You may then contact law enforcement. If it is safe to do so, you may also use your cellular phone to contact law enforcement or your security personnel.

When driving a car in a foreign country, park in areas that are well lit and near public buildings if possible. Do not park in dark or remote areas. As you approach your car, glance underneath it, as well as in the back seat. A favorite trick of criminals is to hide under the car and, as you attempt to open the car door, pull your legs out from under you. If while walking to your car you feel you are being followed, do not go to the car, but instead go back to where you came from and get help. Use common sense. If a situation does not feel right, avoid it.

Do not use ATM machines if possible. If you do use them, do so during the day and try to find machines located inside of buildings, such as secure airport areas, banks, or hotels. So-called express kidnappings are very popular in South American countries. The criminal will target an individual because he or she has used a credit card at an ATM machine. The criminal will then wait for the opportunity to kidnap the individual, and drive him or her around in a car at gunpoint while visiting different ATMs until the victim's account is depleted.

Should a stranger approach you and attempt to engage in conversation, be polite but excuse yourself immediately. If you go out, try to have someone with you. There is truth to the adage of safety being in numbers.

If you are staying in one location for a period of time, vary the routes that you travel and the times of the day that you leave and return. Unpredictability is your ally. If your movements and locations cannot be predicted, the chances of you becoming a victim are diminished.

SOME ADDITIONAL RULES FOR TRAVELING SAFELY

Events such as the bombing of a U.S. embassy and increasing incidents of terrorism, kidnappings, and assaults demonstrate just how vulnerable business travelers are, especially when working overseas. While it is impossible to completely guarantee safety in every situation, there are many steps that an individual can take to decrease the likelihood of becoming a victim of random violence or terrorism. Staying alert and being aware of your surroundings are the first steps to reduce risk. Traveling or living in a foreign country can and should be a pleasant, enjoyable experience if you are prepared.

Four basis principles to remember are:

1. Be aware.
2. Be low-key.
3. Be unpredictable.
4. Maintain good communications.

Even before you leave for a foreign country, there are certain steps that you can take to minimize your chances of being victimized or inconvenienced:

- You should be informed about the country that you plan to visit; know the customs, holidays, politics, climate, and currency.
- Make sure your passport is valid for at least 6 months. You should make copies of your passport and keep them in separate pieces of luggage along with passport photos. If your passport is lost or stolen, it will be much easier to get the embassy to replace it if you have these duplicates. If visas are necessary, make sure you apply for them at least 2 weeks prior to departure.
- Know the entry requirements of the country you are visiting. In some countries, you cannot bring a laptop computer. In others, you can bring a laptop computer into the country, but you cannot take it back out. Prescription drugs are another major problem. If you are required to take prescription drugs, have a doctor write you a prescription to take with you as well as a letter describing your condition and need for the drugs. Over-the-counter drugs in some foreign countries exceed the dosages in the United States and are illegal. Do not attempt to bring over-the-counter drugs back into the United States. For more information, check the U.S. State Department website: http://travel.state.gov/travel_pubs.html.
- You should be aware of the medical facilities available to you in the destination country and their required means of payment. Most countries do not accept American medical insurance. Be aware of the medical problems in the country to be visited. Obtain all suggested vaccinations prior to leaving.
- Take an active part in making your flight arrangements. If possible, schedule only direct flights and stay away from high-risk airports. Should you have to schedule a layover, be aware of what time you arrive and the amount of time between flights. Many foreign airports have poor security during very early morning hours.
- Do not take or wear any clothing or other items with corporate logos or other insignias on them that identify you as an American. This includes baggage and luggage tags that can be exposed so that your name and your company name can be readily seen. Do not take or wear expensive jewelry. A good rule of thumb concerning jewelry is to leave behind anything that you would not want to lose.

KEY POINTS

In my opinion, you can't give employees enough or too much information to prepare them for deploying to hostile areas. You do, however, have to give them enough information to do their jobs, while not having to focus on security to the extent that it interferes with them doing the job. I developed a motto or mantra over the years, which goes something like this: If we (our company) can work in a war zone, we can work anywhere. And it's true. Think about your most difficult project locations, foreign or domestic. Now think about the issues you faced there and how these were resolved. Did your company pull up stakes and shut down the project? Or, did you have to scramble and fumble until you came up with a workable solution that resulted in a safe and secure work environment for everyone concerned? Maybe you did not foresee all the issues that might develop, but you adapted and achieved a level of success over these. I believe it is a company's responsibility and the employee's right to expect that you have thoroughly researched the risks they might face on foreign assignment, and that you have provided them with security awareness training, personal protective equipment, and any and all resources one might reasonably assume necessary for them to do the job safely.

CASE STUDY

I once was required to brief employees who were traveling from the United States to Iraq to work. Some of the employees had never been outside of the United States, let alone the Middle East, and surely not Iraq. I sat down with their project management, human resources, our legal and travel department, and corporate communications employees in advance, and we decided as a group which key areas would need to be covered, and by whom. There would be health concerns: which immunizations were required, for example. We decided to develop not only a predeployment training program but also a predeployment checklist, since so many areas had to be covered with employees prior to their departure. Our human resources employees decided, along with those responsible for health benefits, to provide a pretrip physical with stress test for all employees to be deployed. These employees were going to be traveling into a war zone, and an area that, with or without war, was inhospitable to human habitat due to temperature extremes, and my personal favorite, snakes, spiders, and scorpions. We would need to have detailed emergency contact lists for these employees. As I had rightly predicted, and given this was 2003, every bad report that reached the news would send a wave of concern through the friends and dependents of the employees, who would require immediate updates regarding the welfare of the employees. We realized early on that the news media, and others, would begin to obtain online information as to which companies had been awarded contracts and would contact these corporations for comment. I advised from the outset that we would never issue the number of employees we had in-country to anyone, and especially would not indicate where they were working. If employees within the company who did not have a need to know asked these same questions, they were not answered. We took into consideration operational security, and instructed the employees who were to be deployed to take this to heart, and asked their friends and dependents to act accordingly. Too many times, prying ears or someone trying to impress another could provide information that might actually place our employees at risk. When it came to personal protective equipment (PPE), our employees would be wearing the latest model ballistic helmets and vests. I brought these into the training room and demonstrated how they were worn, why, and at what times, and issued the sets to the employees. They were shocked at how heavy the vests were, up to 30 pounds. I instructed them to wear them at home, around the house, and even outside in the heat, to get an idea of just how uncomfortable, heavy, and hot these units were. Early on, we were issuing protective gas masks, and it is then, that while looking for training materials on these, that I stumbled upon civilian contractor training conducted by the military that would be available for our employees. I took three employees to this course and attended myself. When I returned, I was weighted down with all of the unclassified training materials I could carry in order to bolster our predeployment courses. My goal in briefing the employees who would be going to Iraq (and later Afghanistan) was to leave out the sugarcoating. I told them exactly how it was going to be, and pulled no punches. One employee asked me if I could guarantee their safety. I replied I could not. I did tell them that I think our company was doing many good things in order to protect them while in-country. I also advised the employees (and I hope your company official policy is similar, or words have been communicated by your senior management on down) that if you (the employee) are ever in a situation that you do not feel is safe, whether it be for a safety or security reason, you have the right and the obligation to say that you won't perform or continue the task. If, for example, an employee feels that their method of transportation has become unsafe, such as self-driving back and forth from lodging to the job site, and he feels he needs a driver, he needs to bring this up. If he feels his lodging security is inadequate—perhaps he feels a monitored alarm system is needed—he should report this. Your employees are going to know the security situation better than you, in some respects. They know what they do and don't feel comfortable with, and provided that what they feel comfortable with is a sound safety and security program, I am cool with that. I have had, on at least two occasions, employees who some time after the briefing (one employee while in transit and on the last airline stop before arriving at the final foreign location) decided not to accept the position or turned around and came home. I would much rather have it take place at that time then at some future time on the project.

HOSTILE COUNTRY X ASSIGNMENT CHECKLIST

Below is an example of overseas/hostile area assignment predeployment checklists.

Note: All correspondence relative to processing of personnel to and from Hostile Country X is to be coordinated through John Smith.

HIRING PROCESS

1. John Smith will contact Mabel Johnson to initiate the requisition and paperwork process. John is responsible to follow up with an official approved requisition and appropriate charge number.
2. All Hostile Country X assignment professionals will be hired into the Project Systems Division (Section 22A).
3. All offer letters shall follow the previously approved format with references to the work's temporary nature and that the offer is contingent upon the applicant passing the required preassignment physical.
4. Mabel Johnson will work with other parties to ensure the package sent to the candidate is complete and accurate. Contents include:
   - Hostile Country X Assignment Policy and tax information
   - Corporate card (T&E Card) application (email with return fax number)

- Offer/acceptance letter
- Medical questionnaire (email for completion prior to arrival)

5. Joyce will gather the following information and forward it to Mr. Security Manager so he may begin the process of obtaining "orders" and a "letter of invitation" and setting up to obtain an ID badge for each individual.
   - Full name (first, middle, last)
   - Social security number
   - Home address and phone number(s)
   - Passport number, expiration date, place of issue
   - Date and place of birth

6. Judy Craft will work with Travel to arrange to bring the candidates into Our Fair City for processing.

7. Mabel will notify the following people of the candidates, as well as schedule time for each person to brief/discuss his or her area of responsibility:
   - Sally Helpful will complete insurance coverage information. She will then forward quotes to John Smith for review and approval to bind coverage. Sally will also go over all benefits and make sure all forms are completed.
   - Mary Jane will schedule a physical, dental x-ray and checkup (as needed), inoculations, etc.
   - Becky Trueheart will discuss pay packages and policy.
   - Polly Thomas will:
     - Arrange for and manage the application process for Nearby Country Y visas for all personnel being assigned to work on any Mega Corporation project. If we begin processing visa prior to employee's arrival in Our Fair City, the passport should be sent to Becky via Fed Ex. Additionally, all approved visas should be delivered to employees via courier in Washington, DC, rather than being sent to their residence via Fed Ex.
     - Coordinate with Mega Corporation Travel/HR personnel regarding travel arrangements to Washington, DC, and on to Nearby Country Y City and Hostile

Country X Capital. This is only for personnel being assigned to work on any Mega Corporation project.

- Arrange for travel from Our Fair City to Nearby Country Z and on to Hostile Country X Capital for all personnel being assigned to work on any Mega/ Super Big joint venture project. This travel will be booked and paid directly by Super Big Corporation.
- Schedule a "new hire" orientation to complete all HR forms. Professionals will also be given a supply of hard-copy time sheets and EBER forms.
- Mr. Security Manager will:
  - Arrange to get "orders cut."
  - Arrange for getting the "letter of invitation"/"travel orders."
  - Perform a security briefing for each employee going to Hostile Country X Capital. All briefings shall be documented. The original documentation of the briefing, as well as a copy of the material, shall be issued to John Smith for placement in the project file.
- Ms. Safety Manager will perform a safety briefing for each employee going to Hostile Country X Capital. All briefings shall be documented. The original document of the briefing, as well as a copy of the material, shall be issued to John Smith for placement in the project file.
- John Smith will coordinate travel arrangements with Joe Schneider for all Mega Corporation assigned personnel and directly manage all Mega assigned personnel.

8. John will coordinate the issue of an EPCN to cover the uplift and work location change through Lara Simmons.
9. John Smith is responsible for managing the overall process.

TRANSFER PROCESS

1. John Smith will contact Janice Cameron or other division administrative managers to discuss staffing needs and potential internal candidates. *This shall be performed prior to looking to outside personnel.*

2. All Hostile Country X assignment professionals will be transferred into the Project Systems Division (Section 22A). Janice Cameron will coordinate with Lara Simmons.

3. John will communicate to all candidates that the position is contingent upon the applicant passing the required pre-assignment physical.

4. John Smith will gather the following information and forward it to Mr. Security Manager so he may begin the process of obtaining "orders" and a "letter of invitation" and setting up to obtain an ID badge for each individual.
   - Full name (first, middle, last)
   - Social security number
   - Home address and phone number(s)
   - Passport number/expiration date/place of issue
   - Date and place of birth

5. John Smith will work with Travel to arrange to bring the candidates into Our Fair City for processing.

6. John Smith will notify the following people of the candidates, as well as schedule time for each person to brief/discuss his or her area of responsibility:
   - Sally Helpful will complete insurance coverage information. She will then forward quotes to John Smith for review and approval to bind coverage.
   - Mary Jane will schedule a physical, dental x-ray and checkup (as needed), inoculations, etc.
   - Becky Trueheart will discuss pay packages and policy.
   - Polly Thomas will:
     – Arrange for and manage the application process for Nearby Country Y visas for all personnel being assigned to work on any Mega Corporation project.
     – Coordinate with Mega Corporation Travel/HR personnel regarding travel arrangements to Washington, DC, and on to Nearby Country Y City and Hostile Country X Capital. This is only for personnel being assigned to work on any Mega Corporation project.
     – Arrange for travel from Our Fair City to Nearby Country Z and on to Hostile Country X Capital for all personnel being assigned to work on any Mega/

Super Big joint venture project. This travel will be booked and paid directly by Super Big Corporation.

- Mr. Security Manager will:
  - Arrange to get "orders cut"
  - Arrange for getting the "letter of invitation"/"travel orders"
  - Perform a security briefing for each employee going to Hostile Country X Capital. All briefings shall be documented. The original documentation of the briefing, as well as a copy of the material, shall be issued to John Smith for placement in the project file.
- Ms. Safety Manager will perform a safety briefing for each employee going to Hostile Country X Capital. All briefings shall be documented. The original document of the briefing, as well as a copy of the material, shall be issued to John Smith for placement in the project file.

7. John will coordinate the issue of an EPCN through Lara Simmons.
8. John Smith is responsible for managing the overall process.

RETURN PROCESS

1. Return travel arrangements shall be coordinated as follows:
   - On all Mega Corporation projects, return travel shall be made from site and communicated to John Smith. John will then notify Lara Simmons and other parties as appropriate.
   - On all Mega/Super Big projects, John Smith will work with Polly Thomas to coordinate all travel needs. John will then notify Lara Simmons and other parties as appropriate.
2. Post physicals will be scheduled through Mary Jane for individuals whose assignment exceeds 6 months (per standard Super Big policy).
3. John Smith will coordinate with Lara Simmons to do an EPCN to return the professional to his former department and ending his allowance. For those professionals that do

not have a position in another department, John Smith will work with Lolita Clark to process an employee termination.

4. Project Systems Division will calculate R&R and provide time off or pay-out as appropriate.

5. Upon return, Project Systems Division will conduct a postassignment debriefing and lessons learned with the returning employee.

FOREIGN TRAVEL SAFETY TIPS

- Use traveler's checks and avoid carrying large amounts of cash. Visa, Thomas Cook, and American Express are the most widely accepted traveler's checks.
- Limit the number of credit cards brought on the trip.
- Do not carry cash and credit cards in the same place (i.e., same bag, pocket, etc.).
- Never exchange money on the black market.
- Always carry some smaller bills for tipping.
- Know the exchange rate of the country you are in.
- Prescription drugs should be checked for legality at your destination.
- Carry prescription drugs in their original container.
- Memorize your passport number.

AIRPORT AND AIRLINE SECURITY

- Do not put items on the x-ray conveyor until you are the next to walk through the metal detector.
- Utilize baggage locks (many locks are sold that allow TSA to unlock the bag if necessary).
- Never carry bags for strangers.
- Do not pack valuables in your luggage.
- Be alert whenever bumped or jostled. This is a common pickpocket tactic.
- Minimize your stay in the airport.

TAXI SECURITY TIPS

- Avoid using unofficial or unmarked taxis.
- Know the fare rate before getting into a taxi.
- Have change and small bills ready to avoid a payment dilemma.
- If possible, avoid putting luggage in the trunk.
- Avoid sharing a cab with other unknown passengers.

HOTEL SECURITY TIPS

- For safety reasons, avoid rooms on the first floor and above the eighth floor. Generally, the fourth and fifth floors are the safest.
- Knock before entering your room in order not to startle persons who may have not checked out of the room—or if an incorrect key/room has been issued. Quickly scan the room before entering.
- Immediately close and double-lock/chain your door once you are inside.
- Ensure that sliding glass doors, room-connecting doors, and windows are secured.
- When away from your room, leave the TV or radio on (another useful tactic is to keep the bathroom door closed but slightly ajar, and the bathroom light turned on).
- Utilize the "Do Not Disturb" sign for your room, and request service to be conducted while you are in the room.
- Never leave keys or personal belongings unattended at hotel facilities.
- Use the main hotel entrance, especially after dark.
- If an unexpected delivery comes to your room, do not open the door without checking with the hotel front desk first.
- Stay at reputable hotels since they tend to have better overall security.
- Once in your room, identify all the fire escape routes.
- Read fire safety instructions provided in your hotel room.
- Use the room or front desk hotel safe for valuables.
- Do not leave business or classified documents or laptop computers in your room. Recognize that in some countries business information along with emails, faxes, and telephone conversations may be compromised.

SECURITY AWARENESS FOR THE BUSINESS TRAVELER

Do's

- Do try to book a nonstop flight on a U.S. carrier to minimize your exposure during multiple takeoffs and landings.
- Do maintain control of your briefcase and carry-on luggage at all times.
- Do request a hotel room between the third and seventh floors, which is high enough to prevent break-ins but low enough to facilitate evacuation during a fire or other emergency.
- Do take steps to avoid having your communications overheard or intercepted. Avoid the use of cell phones as much as possible, and be sure that you do not discuss sensitive topics in crowded public areas.
- Do contact the local U.S. embassy if you feel that you are being followed or are under surveillance.

Do Not's

- Do not wear clothing with corporate logos or other insignia that identifies you as an American business traveler.
- Do not use laminated business cards as identification tags on your luggage.
- Do not publicize your travel plans.
- Do not pack sensitive or proprietary information in your checked luggage.
- Do not wear valuable jewelry while traveling. Avoid anything that draws attention to you and conveys affluence.
- Do not develop a routine for traveling between your hotel and places of business. Vary your routes and departure/arrival times as much as possible.
- Do not accept packages or letters from or deliver them for anyone unknown to you.
- Do not open your hotel room door to persons unknown until you have verified their identity with the hotel front desk.
- Do not travel in taxis that are unmarked or do not have an official license prominently displayed.

9

Establishing and Maintaining Contact and Coordination with Local, Regional, and International Authorities
"We Need a Favor, We Have People in Your Country That We Need Evacuated Now!"

We may have all come on different ships, but we're in the same boat now.

—Martin Luther King Jr.

In order to operate effectively in volatile regions around the world, I would very strongly recommend you establish effective liaisons with law enforcement, U.S. government agencies, and private sector personnel—even competitors. If operations are going to operate on a safe footing, and to be plugged into the critical information required for conducting business in a safe manner, these liaisons are critical. Whether it be something as simple as reporting a minor criminal act, vandalism, for example, to contacting someone when your people or assets have been victim to an extortion attempt or act of terrorism, having a relationship in advance with the correct officials can not only cut through red tape and save time, but it might also save lives.

When working in more dangerous regions and countries, U.S. government agencies should be made aware of:

- Nature/description of your project
- Number of expats working on the project
- Lodging/accommodations for expats
- Expat travel within the country and neighboring countries
- Other U.S. or foreign national business partners
- Other U.S. or foreign national contractors/subcontractors

I have invited U.S. State Department personnel to visit the job site or project on many occasions, and they have taken me up on this offer. I have appreciated their taking the time to travel to these locations. It makes an impression upon them to see Americans working on these projects, and I can guarantee you that U.S. expats will not be forgotten in extreme situations. But, this is not always necessary, and in some regions, such U.S. government personnel may decline to attend or visit, due to security concerns.

As far as contacting the law enforcement and government agencies of your host governments, I would recommend some caution (see the case studies at the conclusion of this chapter).

A word or two concerning the men and women of the U.S. Department of State: I have traveled the world a couple of times over, and wherever I go, whichever country I might be in, I make it a point to visit the U.S. embassies and consulates. I enjoy meeting and speaking with the regional security officers and their staffs, the U.S. Marine Corps on duty at these locations, consular officers, and many others. I do this to pay my respect to their efforts and commitment to keeping expatriates safe in foreign locations. The men and women who are employees of the State Department based here in the United States, particularly those who work with the Overseas Security Advisory Council (OSAC), I respect as extremely professional, dedicated, knowledgeable, and competent.

Having mentioned the work of the RSOs, I would be remiss to not mention the efforts of the U.S. embassy legal attaches, or LEGATs, as the Federal Bureau of Investigation refers to them. Not every embassy of our country has LEGATs, but the agents assigned to these duties can be of extreme benefit. LEGATs are assigned to the embassies due to the nature of U.S. business and our government's efforts in other countries. LEGATs do not have jurisdiction in these countries, of course, but they do have strong ties and work cooperatively with the law enforcement agencies of the host governments. LEGATs do investigate crimes against American citizens and companies internationally. LEGATs are involved in the search for missing Americans, kidnapped Americans, and many of the crimes perpetrated against Americans overseas. LEGATs are not going to be the in-country authority on terrorism concerns and how Western companies go about protecting their employees; that responsibility falls within the purview of the RSOs. However, whenever I visit RSOs on my trips, I make it a point to visit with the LEGATs. I view law enforcement liaison as a critical part of my domestic security programs, and through contacts with FBI agents in the United States, they can help facilitate meetings and consultations with LEGATs around the world.

RSOs are a busy bunch of people. Their duties include protecting the Americans and local nationals assigned to the embassy or consulate. They provide protection for visiting State Department and other U.S. government officials and employees. I personally don't know when they sleep, and I don't know if they have a minute of free time. But, by all means necessary, if you can arrange to sit down and meet with them, you will be doing yourself and your company or client a favor. But, do not expect the RSOs to be at your beck and call. They are very busy people. Their primary charge is to protect the U.S. embassy or consulate employees working in the country, and any visiting State Department personnel. Among the million other things they do, they would be glad to meet with you. I would suggest you try to arrange a telephone discussion long before you actually visit the country, and set up an in-person meeting well in advance of your arrival. Something may come up when you arrive and you might not be able to meet with them; this is just the nature of their jobs. Don't take it personally and go with the flow.

Another very worthwhile service RSOs and LEGATs may provide is one security managers seem to always be searching for internationally. These government employees can advise you which U.S. corporations are using contract security services in that country. They might even know which companies are doing the work for them. Of course, U.S. embassies and consulates often utilize local contract security services at their locations, and they might be able to provide you with contact information for these private companies. These are not recommendations, keep in mind, but merely contact information. It will be up to you to determine if the companies you discover are providing the types of security services you desire or find appropriate and whether these services are of a quality nature.

Questions you will want to ask the RSOs (or assistant regional security officers (ARSOs) should the RSOs be too busy to meet with you) include concerns about the types of security situations, dilemmas, and resources that might be present for U.S. or Western corporations working in the country or region. Are companies the targets of crimes such as extortion or kidnapping? Are employees of these companies victims of the same types of crime? Are there issues with random street crimes, and is violent crime being directed at these employees, visitors, tourists, or students? What has worked or seems to work in the way of mitigation? For example, have U.S. citizens begun to avoid going to certain areas of the city, such as markets? Is it sensible to avoid being nearby mosques on Fridays after prayers? Has driving into the countryside become too dangerous? Do Western companies mostly employ armed or unarmed security personnel to protect their employees? Are these companies utilizing armored or unarmored vehicles? By having these discussions with the RSOs, ARSOs, and LEGATs, one can begin to piece together not only the risks involved in working in these countries, but also the security plans and mitigation efforts for doing so safely.

RSOs can also provide you with the names of those in-country law enforcement officials from whom you might require ongoing assistance. For example, say you are working in a remote area of the country, far from the U.S. embassy, consulate, or any of the host government's civilian or military resources or facilities. The RSOs may provide you with names and contact information for police or military contacts who are based in or are responsible for the areas where you will be working. Should you have questions or need their assistance, these can be very valuable contacts.

RSOs provide much in the way of community outreach—the community being the Western companies that are operating in the country. Often, organizations such as OSAC initiate country councils, which are made up of the employees representing companies working in the country, who get together to share security concerns and information, discuss methods of dealing with security issues and problems, and can provide mutual assistance to each other for their common goals—a safe operating environment for employees and businesses. One of the first questions I ask of RSOs when I am looking into a country or region for the first time is: What other Western companies are operating there? But, more importantly, are there companies that do the same type of business that my company does—which might range from building widgets to chemical manufacturing to retail sales?

KEY POINTS

Successful liaison is critical to having an efficient security and safety management system in place for employees working overseas. The liaison begins with people such as State Department regional security officers (RSOs). Other U.S. government employees you will find it useful to meet with include Federal Bureau of Investigation legal attaches (LEGATs). Through these personnel, you may be able to determine availability of additional private and public sector assistance. You might become part of State Department OSAC country councils and receive extremely worthwhile safety and security information at these meetings; or you might obtain the contact information for local police or military officials who can provide resources you might otherwise be unaware of.

CASE STUDIES

One word of caution in dealing with law enforcement or military in foreign countries: they are not always what you have come to expect from dealing with those in many other countries. That is to say, don't be surprised if you become faced with a quid pro quo situation. Be careful to not get more than you bargained for, or to use another cliché, don't get boxed into a corner. Let me cite a few examples.

One situation involves a country where the security arrangements went something like this: The host government understood that terrorist acts had concerned many Western companies doing business in certain regions. Frequent calls for government assistance went unheeded, and Westerners had lost their lives in attacks. The government responded by requiring that all Western companies doing business in the country have the blessing, cooperation, and assistance of their military. What might sound like a monumental administrative nightmare became more efficient as the wheels of the bureaucracy began to turn. From the outset, when Western companies began to request visas and work permits for their employees coming into the country, the government had the ability to determine which company the Western citizen was working for, which cities they would be visiting, and which job site or facility. Next, the government initiated a program where these employees would be met at the airport by a military security detachment, and would be escorted to their destination by armed military personnel. Westerners were working, for the most part, in industrial parks that were guarded by a combination of private and military security personnel. Whenever companies had someone coming in for a site or facility visit or departing from the airport, they would contact a local military garrison and advise them of the time the flight was to arrive and the airline, and the convoy would set off to make the pickup or drop off. The system seemed to be working well, with no real glitches. Arriving or departing employees could expect to make their flights on time, or would not have to wait until their military escort arrived. One day, however, a military captain who was in charge of the local garrison and the escorts contacted the security manager. After some small talk, he got right to the point. The difficulties of his job protecting the project employees had led to problems at his home. His wife was mad at him for being gone all the time. What would really make her happy would be a pickup truck and a new refrigerator. After getting over his shock, the security manager replied that this was not something that was possible. The captain some months later requested a transfer out of the garrison and was never heard from again.

Another occasion arose with an individual who was a retired local national military officer placed in charge of security at a large public-private infrastructure project. The area was prone to protests by local residents, fueled by nationwide antigovernment sentiments and demonstrations. Influential religious leaders near the facility worked all of these groups into frenzies that typically resulted in angry protests and demonstrations. The government posted battle-honed military personnel, just back from duties on the front lines with separatist groups, at the work site. The facility was well fortified, and it certainly had the attention of many who wanted the project to succeed. The ex-officer in charge of security understandably wanted himself and the project to go forward with as little trouble as possible. He sat down with the visiting American security manager, who was in charge of security for those U.S. employees assigned to the project, for a chat in his elaborately appointed office. The tea was served on fine china, and silver tongs and spoons provided the sugar and stirring implements, all served by a staff of immaculately attired local nationals. Men like this are very busy, or so they would like to think, and the talk was quickly directed to the matter at hand. The local national security manager, retired military officer, and apparently part-time dabbler in counterintelligence indicated that in order for him to gather the information necessary to successfully protect the facility and all of the expats and employees coming and going, he would require US$30,000 per month. Many informants, including police officials, had to be paid in order to ensure a steady flow of information and a tamping down of too radical thoughts and tendencies. The proud ex-officer stated he was already paying out a princely sum each month for the same services, but desperate times called for desperate measures. It was a blow to his ego, but a satisfying experience for the American, when the ex-officer was told that the jungle would turn to ice before one cent would be paid to him.

One final case study consists of a situation in Iraq where U.S. expat employees were working on an infrastructure project. The project was surrounded by daily fighting with coalition forces and insurgents. When the insurgents ran out of coalition targets, they would frequently pepper the job site with small arms fire, an occasional mortar, rocket-propelled grenade, or rocket, and would continuously fire upon any supply vehicles entering or leaving the facility. The situation became increasingly tense with the facility security personnel fearing an all-out attack, or that the bad guys would stop the randomness and put forth a concentrated effort to kill Westerners. The security personnel, who had some experience in the region and in the country, devised a plan. They arranged a meeting with local tribal leaders. The sympathetic tribal elders, who wanted the project to continue as well, strategized that the security personnel should meet with the local imam, or spiritual leader, who had a great following. A meeting was set up, and after some tense initial first minutes, the event turned productive. The religious leader was in fact interested in improving the city for his followers, and the project would certainly do this. But, he had been promised some things in the past by other private sector groups that had failed to deliver. When asked what these things were, the imam indicated they did not have reliable transportation for their own supplies and provisions, and something to assist their logistical dilemma was envisioned. The project had a surplus of vehicles, including small pickups ideal for hauling rice, water, and other foodstuffs. It was agreed by the project personnel that one of these pickups would be lent to the religious organization in order to be used for these supplies and community programs. The imam was so pleased he arrived at the facility one day with a round carton under one of his arms. He presented to the security personnel a stack of vehicle decals, each bearing a photograph and blessing of the imam. He instructed the security personnel to paste the decals on the sides of their vehicles and advised them that due to their generosity to the community, no harm would come to them. The attacks upon the facility and the vehicles ceased.

10

Benchmarking International Crisis and Security Management
"Give Me One Good Reason Why Our Company Needs to Do This"

> Learn from yesterday, live for today, hope for tomorrow. The important thing is not to stop questioning.
>
> —Albert Einstein

How does one measure your effectiveness in responding to volatile situations and locations and benchmark with other organizations if your security and crisis management operations meet the grade? One method was discussed in the previous chapter. By interfacing with government and law enforcement agencies, one can determine what your competitors or other Western companies have in place for physical security and protective measures in your country of interest. Hopefully, by now you are a member of the American Society for Industrial Security International (ASIS). In the "members only" sections of the secured website you will find ASIS members listed by country. I have found this an excellent resource to locate colleagues working in the countries you are concerned with, and a telephone call or email to these professionals can provide valuable intelligence and resources. Of course, what goes around comes around, so keep this in mind when a colleague contacts you and take the time to help them out. Sound reasonable? Of course it does, and this is a professional organization that practices what it preaches.

When you are going to be operating in a volatile region, you would want to contact colleagues, hopefully in advance of deploying personnel to these areas. The questions you will want to ask include: What have you experienced as a threat? What incidents/crimes have taken place against your people and assets? What security measures do you have in place? Is there more you wish you could do from a security protective standpoint and are not doing, and why? What type of cooperation are you getting from local governments and law enforcement?

You will take this information and collate it with that which you have obtained from U.S. government agencies, such as OSAC country councils. You will attend these meetings and regional security conferences and take advantage of groups that have formed involving companies operating in difficult regions and countries. You will subscribe to the *New York Times*, the *Christian Science Monitor*, and the *Wall Street Journal*, and listen to the British Broadcasting Corporation radio news programs, such as *World Update*. You will need to speak with your employees when they return from overseas assignments or trips. You should remain on good terms with the employees, who will share information with you about their international journeys and assignments, and have conversations with them whenever possible.

Another great method of encouraging the following of proper practices and procedures when working in volatile areas will be to bring in outside speakers, and sponsor your own conferences. I personally have sponsored groups of companies doing business in the Middle East, for example. At one company, we invited industry, government, and other speakers, and held discussions on topical issues. It was at one such meeting that a diplomatic representative of a Middle Eastern government attended, and he provided a country security update and was gracious enough to answer questions from participants.

Professional certifications not only ensure that employees are obtaining or have obtained the proper training in their respective professions, but with the recertification requirements of programs such as ASIS's Certified Protection Professional (CPP), also ensure that continuing education is taking place. The process of recertification keeps practitioners current with the latest trends, innovations, and issues in the field. ASIS workshops frequently deal with protecting people and assets, and their publications cover international topics and security concerns.

Of course, one of everyone's favorite methods of ensuring your program is robust and efficient is conducting an audit. If you believe that, well … you know the rest. I am fine with audits, if they are in fact used to find weaknesses or inefficiencies that are then improved or repaired. Auditing for auditing's sake will prove one thing only—that you have a security and crisis management program on paper only, and if you have a paper program only, your system may leave you stranded in a true time of need. I am not a big fan of an audit program designed to verify if a facility, office, job site, etc., has conducted a security vulnerability assessment (SVA) or has implemented the results/findings of this SVA. I have found that when you start down this road, or have teams of auditors scouring your facilities and operating from a checklist designed to provide a rating on your security score, you end up with a paint-by-number, ineffective method of inspection. This may be fine for safety programs, but security programs, in my opinion, are more subjective in nature. I do not like checklists for conducting security assessments. I think they can be useful to those who have a limited understanding of physical security programs, and might prompt employees to look at the correct risks and apply the appropriate countermeasures. But, I have found that once you start operating with checklists, and start grading (auditing) based upon these, you end up with a program in paper form only. I don't believe in "cookie-cutter security." Never have, and never will. I call it cookie cutter because we have a tendency to want to place everything into the same mold, the same little muffin tins, and all of our security programs (cookies) turn out the same. Mrs. Fields' makes a lot of money with this concept, but in security you will not like the end product. Some recent (at the time of this publication) government security regulations for domestic American infrastructure, for example, are more smartly crafted in that they might provide a list, not a checklist, of various countermeasures one might consider when crafting a security program. To keep current, to keep a successful security program vibrant and responsive, I totally disagree with the concept of people with clipboards ticking off boxes on whether or not this plant or that office building has done A, B, or C. It is human nature to get nervous, get worked up, maybe even experience outright dread given the approach of the feared "corporate audit team." What can happen, in some programs, is that a facility is "teaching to the audit," much like "teaching to the test" in schools where standardized testing has become the norm. The facility or office knows what the auditors will be looking at or looking for, and they are going to find exactly what they want if the facility employees have anything to do with it. If the audit form, the little boxes to check off or tick, never changes, how can you say you have a vibrant and all-encompassing audit? I don't even use the term *audit* when conducting a security assessment. To me, audit is just that—ticking off the boxes. If you operate in an objective manner with security in hostile environments, you are going to be disappointed, and you are going to miss something critical, or you are going to leave something out. When operating in an emergency situation or in disaster mode, checklists are fine. They can focus the mind when difficult, stressful circumstances might cause a mistake to blossom into an injury, or loss of life. I can train a monkey to walk around with a clipboard, and some scientists or naturalists might be able to train a chimp to try a door to see if it is locked, then check a box stating that it is. I want a security program with some meat on its bones, with room to breathe and take into consideration all of the intricacies of the natural environment, politics, socioeconomics, risk, and human factors.

As has been previously discussed, having internal working groups within your company is a very good way to share the load. I don't feel there is any way for a security manager to properly develop, implement, and maintain a successful security and crisis management system without the assistance of key elements inside the organization. As a big fan of task forces (ones that get things done, I should say) dealing with crisis management/emergency management, emergency action plans/business continuity plans, I feel the same way about security management. When I involve the various cross-functions of a corporation—the legal, human resources, information technology, risk management, communications, finance, corporate (or outside) travel agents, building management, and others—I can guarantee that everyone has their say, and when a crisis happens, all consideration has been given to what a company can and should provide to the facility in need, the business unit that has experienced a problem, or when the corporation as a whole is under duress. I would encourage monthly meetings with these departments to start out; you could use the "security committee" approach, where gathering, receiving, and sharing security information would be the goals. I would make the committee approach more worthwhile by adding a crisis management component for the group. Each of the mentioned departments, and others you might identify, will play a key role in security and crisis management. They can also assist you in providing the help you will need for large-scale programs. The employees who work in these departments will be staffing positions around the world for your corporation, making the international business trips, and hopefully sharing the information you need to have a finger on what is going on with them and your interests around the world.

If I am intending to implement a security program, such as predeployment training for employees prior to departing to assignments or short-term travel to a hostile location, I will only get support and compliance if all business units and departments within the corporation consider this a worthwhile endeavor, and one that they will require their employees to participate in. Training costs time and money. When their employees take time out of their schedules to sit down with you to discuss a security program, or go online to view something that has been predesigned, their department pays them for the minutes or hours they are present.

Employee feedback is critical in keeping your program on the mark and current. If employees are not learning from the program, or do not have the opportunity to ask questions of the presenter (one reason why an in-person briefing should be your preference), even to challenge the assertions being made, you will not see a productive program once employees are deployed or in the field. I have asked employees and their managers to provide feedback for me regarding the program. When possible, I like to implement these suggestions. By including the various corporate groups, as I mentioned before, I can also save time and not bore the employees with information that could have or should have been covered previously. For example, I should not be spending time answering questions about visas for the destination country—corporate or outside travel agents should have done this. I should not be talking about the types of vaccinations required prior to arrival—their health care provider or human resources or other employees should have handled this matter. I really shouldn't become involved in questions about the income tax status of the employee. You should be prepared to answer such questions, or at the very least inform the employee with whom they should speak about this to get an answer.

Here's another way to measure your success—ask yourself: Have any of the employees working for your organization in volatile areas been injured? Have there been major security breaches, incidents of physical assault, kidnapping, or extortion? In my opinion, security has a bit of a hard hill to climb, unless you are involved in retail security. In retail security, one can measure a reduction in loss or shrinkage due to the implementation of a security initiative, such as adding more cameras, radio frequency identification (RFID), or other methods. When dealing with physical security programs in a hostile work environment, how does one prove your methods are deterring, detecting, and delaying that which never comes?

Take a safety program, for example. If your company or a company division had twenty injuries last year that were reportable, lost-time incidents, and this year you had ten, you can say you had a 50% drop or improvement. If your fleet department had forty-five fender benders or more serious automobile accidents last year, conducted a driving safety program, and for 2 years straight accidents among employees driving company vehicles dropped to fifteen or less, all would agree the program had a measurable impact. Security cannot always be quantified in such a manner. It would be difficult to find data to show that improving your lighting at a facility prevented three attacks, or that having a security detail around your principal kept the bad guys from hitting you on five occasions.

Because of the usual "I want to go low-profile" argument, I was once asked by a manager to find data that might prove that having a personal security detail (PSD) actually brought about or caused an attack upon the principals, as opposed to discouraging it. I could not find any, and I actually looked very hard for such information. Quantifying what we do in security is missing the point. I have always operated with the principle that corporate security should almost not be seen and not be heard, that it should cause the least amount of difficulty and discomfort for employees. If security is overt to the extent that it is overbearing, you might be sowing the seeds of your and your security program's demise. By not being seen, I am, of course, not advocating not being seen with a robust security effort in volatile areas, but where possible, the less overbearing one can be, the better off your relations with employees will be.

Having said that, in volatile areas I have had to cancel road trips due to conditions along the way. Maybe rebels or insurgents were active on the roads. The site visits or the project requirements were shut down that day. But, as much as safely possible, to let work continue without beating people about the head, neck, and shoulders with security should be a goal. As I mentioned previously, I know that I can equip and supply employees with adequate security so that they can operate anywhere in the world. To do so in a manner that allows work to actually take place is the challenge.

For the remainder of the chapter, let us turn to hostile area security and crisis management planning, including physical security considerations.

SECURITY AND CRISIS MANAGEMENT PLANNING CONSIDERATIONS

Terrorist acts are planned long in advance, and are utilized to further causes of a political goal or religious extremism, overthrow governments, and other purposes. Facilities belonging to your company or your employees serving around the world may become victims of a terrorist group. One frequent method used by terrorists is bombs, such as the most recent series of improvised explosive devices (IEDs) in vehicles or delivered by other means. Many experts believe that terrorism and terrorist acts can be defeated, deflected, deterred, and prevented by better methods of security. The theory is that the terrorist groups will seek alternative targets that appear to be easier to attack and with a greater chance of success. The information here is intended to give you tools and steps to provide for the proper protection of your people and assets.

By having a successful, well-maintained, and exercised plan in place, your facility or project will have steady footing should an actual terrorist act or other serious man-made or natural disaster take place. Your management and all employees will be required to be involved in this effort, which includes security awareness training so that in the event of serious incidents they will know what they are dealing with, and the proper response for mitigating the effects. It is the responsibility of the corporation and local management and employees to provide the proper planning and preparation, and to work with corporate security in this effort. A properly crafted plan and intense preparation may reduce the risk of success of the groups who might be perpetrating the acts.

The U.S. Department of Defense and the U.S. military have identified threat levels to standardize reporting. They are based on terrorists' existence, capability, intentions, history, targeting, and the security environment. The levels are:

Critical, which means that a terrorist group has entered the country or is able to do so. It has the capability to attack and is engaged in target selection. Its history and intentions may or may not be known.

High indicates that a terrorist group exists that has the capability, history, and intention to attack.

Medium describes the same conditions as high except that intentions are unknown.

Low is a situation in which terrorist groups exist and have a capability to attack. Their history may or may not be known.

Negligible describes a situation in which the existence or capability of terrorist groups may or may not be present.

What You Will Need to Ask Local
Management and Employees to Do

The crisis response group will ensure that the local management and key employees are identified and in place. Although team composition may vary somewhat, the following individuals should be included, as a minimum:

- Senior local project management
- Senior local operational managers
- Local finance and administrative managers
- Human resources, payroll, legal, and other critical managers

Local managers and management will control and resolve all emergent situations supported by the crisis response group in the United States, who in turn reports all actions, recommendations, and outcomes to the company corporate. The crisis response group, with the approval of the company corporate, may elect to send members of the emergency response team to assist the local managers in resolving an incident.

The local management consists of the predesignated senior management representatives closest to the incident. They are responsible for the initial crisis response, carrying out corporate policy and keeping the corporate disaster recovery team advised. The local managers must keep abreast of the in-country developments. Indicators with which they should be particularly concerned include:

- International affairs
- U.S. relations with surrounding countries
- Changes in local sentiment toward foreigners
- Changes in internal affairs—popularity of the current government
- Water, fuel, and food shortages that may result in rioting
- University student protests/demonstrations
- Martial law/curfews
- Armed warfare
- External military threats against the country
- Armed conflict between local tribes/minorities
- Terrorist/guerrilla actions
- Increased press restrictions/blackouts
- Communications disruptions
- Increased travel restrictions
- Currency devaluation and the hording of money
- Increased military activity

- Increase in the departure of other foreign executives and personnel
- Appropriate U.S., UK, or country embassy or consulate change in threat level

States of Readiness and Risk Conditions

1. **State of readiness 4.** This condition applies when there is a general threat of possible terrorist activity against personnel and facilities, the nature and extent of which are unpredictable, and circumstances do not justify full implementation of high-level measures. However, it may be necessary to implement certain measures from higher threat and risk conditions resulting from intelligence received or as a deterrent. The measures in this state of readiness must be capable of being maintained indefinitely.
2. **State of readiness 3.** This condition applies when an increased and more predictable threat of terrorist activity exists. The measures in this state of readiness must be capable of being maintained for weeks without causing undue hardship, affecting operational capability, and aggravating relations with local authorities.
3. **State of readiness 2.** This condition applies when an incident occurs or intelligence is received indicating some form of terrorist action against personnel and facilities is immediate. Implementation of measures in this state of readiness for more than a short period probably will create hardship and affect the peacetime activities of the unit and its personnel.
4. **State of readiness 1.** This condition applies in the immediate area where a terrorist attack has occurred or when intelligence has been received that terrorist action against a specific location or person is likely. Normally, this THREATCON is declared as a localized condition.

Evaluation of the security situation will be an ongoing function of the local managers. They should:

- Listen to area radio programs and read local newspapers to follow the security situation both in the country and in surrounding areas.
- Contact all appropriate embassies. Establish and maintain contact with the regional security officer at the appropriate U.S., UK, or country embassy or consulate. Frequently, the RSOs host conferences with multinational companies to discuss the local secu-

rity situation and the problems faced by expatriates. The local management leader should attend these conferences if they exist.

- Particular attention should be paid to the contacts the company has with the police and military. These contacts may be helpful in the evaluation and collection of information concerning changes in the situation.

Financial Preparations

The local management team should ensure an adequate amount of money is available to cover costs associated with an emergency incident. The manager of payroll or human resources should be prepared to pay cash. He or she should at a minimum:

- Determine if blank airline tickets can be obtained from a travel agent for use in emergencies.
- Prepare an estimate of the amount of money that he or she will need to pay for evacuation, and forward this information to corporate headquarters. The money should be available to the country as soon as an emergency seems likely.
- Issue credit cards to members of the local management for the major carriers in the country.

Consider the range of services that you could provide or arrange for, including:

- Cash advances
- Salary continuation
- Flexible work hours
- Reduced work hours
- Crisis counseling
- Care packages
- Day care

Things to Focus on

- Make every effort to appear too difficult a target in comparison to other potential targets to an adversary.
- The single most useful defensive measure personnel can take is to vary travel routes and times.

- Teach and remind staff to be vigilant and alert to possible surveillance. Terrorist surveillance is often so intensive that an alert person will notice that something is out of the ordinary—something does not seem quite right. To notice anything unusual you must first know what is normal. Look around, introduce yourself to the neighbors, notice the regular shopkeepers.
- Avoid predictable behavior. Vary routes to work, appointments, or other engagements. Terrorists/criminals often survey their targets prior to attack. Being unpredictable is a very effective deterrent.

You must raise your level of awareness to a point where:

- Strange vehicles parked near your residence or place of employment are noticed and promptly reported to the authorities. This must be done immediately. It may be the first time you have seen the vehicle, but it may not be the first time it has been there. You don't know what level of planning the terrorist may be in. Maybe it's only the beginning, but perhaps the planning is in the final stages, giving you little time to act.
- People standing, walking, or sitting in cars near the residence or place of employment must be noticed, especially people loitering.
- You notice someone who always seems to be around you. Another individual can realize when he's being followed.
- If you suspect that you are under surveillance, report it to the police, the appropriate U.S., UK, or country embassy or consulate, and your local management team.
- You practice and teach staff to keep track of any unusual sightings. From notes, a log can be made describing what has been seen.

When recording observations of suspicious vehicles, try to obtain the:

- Make
- Model
- Year
- Color
- License number
- General condition of the vehicle
- Number of people in the vehicle

If possible, get a description of the people involved:

- Male/female.
- Distinguishing marks, beard, mustache, scars, extender.

- Size.
- Features such as hairstyle and color are often unreliable, because they are the result of wigs, dyes, etc. Make note of them anyway. Too much information is better than too little.
- Distinctive features or habits: a limp, a nervous habit such as frequent straightening of a tie, pushing glasses up onto the nose, etc.

Don't do anything to let the surveillants know they have been detected. Do not confront suspected terrorists/criminals and ask them why they're watching. This may initiate an impromptu attack or kidnapping.

If you suspect you are being followed by someone in a vehicle, drive normally and carefully and proceed to a safe location, such as an embassy, police station, or a highly visible or populated area and immediately alert police, embassy staff, or the security network.

Again, do not be predictable.
Be alert for surveillance.
Avoid areas where you could be trapped.
Drive only on a well-traveled streets.
Be alert for blockades or contrived accidents.
Keep staff itineraries and personal details confidential.

PHYSICAL SECURITY CONSIDERATIONS

To follow are some general physical security recommendations. A complete security assessment should be completed for all corporate sites and residences.

Some considerations for exterior protection include:

- Perimeter security.
- Consider using natural barriers, fencing, landscaping, or other physical or psychological boundaries to demonstrate a security presence to all site visitors.
- If the threat is considered to be high at freestanding facilities, there should be a smooth-faced perimeter wall or combination wall-fence, a minimum of 9 feet tall and extending 3 feet below grade. The wall or fence may be constructed of stone, masonry, concrete, chain link, or steel grillwork. However, if area limitations

and local conditions dictate the need, any newly constructed wall should be designed to prevent vehicle penetration, and should use a reinforced concrete foundation wall, 18 inches thick with an additional 1½ inches of concrete covering on the side of the steel reinforcement, and extending 36 inches above the grade. In addition, intrusion alert systems can be used to enhance perimeter security.

- Consider alternative methods if the above are not feasible. Alternate methods can offer comparable protection. These alternatives should maximize the use of locally available materials and conditions to take advantage of existing terrain features or the creative use of earthen berms and landscaping techniques, such as concrete planters.

Inside the perimeter barrier, the building should be set back on the property to provide maximum distance from that portion of the perimeter barrier that is accessible by vehicle. The desirable distance of this setback is at least 100 feet, depending on the bomb resistance provided by the barrier.

Alternative methods for protecting buildings from vehicle attack (for example, car bombs, vehicles laden with explosives) may include installing bollards (a device constructed to protect against a ramming vehicle attack). They are deployed in lines around a perimeter for anti-ram protection or to provide supplemental control of vehicle traffic through permanent checkpoints when other means are not practical or effective. Large cement planters can also be used to strengthen the perimeter boundary. Bollards or planters can effectively increase the setback of buildings. Such devices should be placed in a manner as to allow the maximum distance between the building and a roadway or the equal access area. They should be positioned to impede access to lobbies and other blast areas that can be penetrated by a vehicle, low or no curb, glass wall or door structure between lobby and driveway. Driveways should be designed and constructed to minimize or preclude high-speed vehicular approaches to lobbies and glassed areas.

A positive and concerted effort should be made to contact local host country law enforcement or governmental authorities and request that they prohibit, restrict, or impede motor vehicles from parking, stopping, or loading in front of the facility.

In high-threat locations, if local conditions or government officials prohibit antivehicular perimeter security measures and your business/corporate building is either the sole occupant of the building or located on the first or second floor, you should consider relocating to more secure facilities.

The building exterior should be a sheer/smooth shell, devoid of footholds, decorative latticework, ledges, and balconies. The building's facade should be protected to a height of 16 feet to prevent access by intruders using basic hand tools. The use of glass on the building facade should be kept to an absolute minimum, only being used for standard size or smaller windows and, possibly, main entrance doors. All glass should be protected by plastic film. Consider the use of Lexan or other polycarbonate as an alternative to glass where practical.

Local fire codes may impact on the guidance presented here. As decisions are made on these issues, local fire codes will have to be considered.

Main entrance doors may be either transparent or opaque and constructed of wood, metal, or glass. The main entrance door should be equipped with a double-cylinder dead bolt and additionally secured with a crossbar or slaying dead bolt attached vertically to the top and bottom of each leaf. All doors, including interior doors, should be installed to take advantage of the door frame strength by having the doors open toward the attack side.

All other external doors should be opaque hollow metal fire doors with no external hardware. These external doors should be single doors unless used for delivery and loading purposes.

If double doors are required, they should be equipped with two sliding dead bolts on the active leaf and two sliding dead bolts on the inactive leaf, vertically installed on the top and bottom of the doors. A local alarmed panic bar and a 180-degree peephole viewing device should be installed on the active leaf.

All external doors leading to crawl spaces or basements must be securely locked and regularly inspected for tampering.

The interior side of all glass surfaces should be covered with a protective plastic film that meets or exceeds the manufacturer's specifications for shatter-resistant protective film. A good standard is a 4-millimeter thickness for all protective film applications. This film will keep glass shards to a minimum in the event of an explosion or if objects are thrown through the window.

Grillwork should be installed on all exterior windows and air conditioning units that are within 16 feet of grade or are accessible from roofs, balconies, etc. The rule of thumb found here is to cover all openings in excess of 100 square inches if the smallest dimension is 6 inches or larger.

Grillwork should be constructed of ½-inch-diameter or greater steel rebar, anchored or embedded, not bolted, into the window frame or surrounding masonry to a depth of 3 inches. Grillwork should be installed horizontally and vertically on center at no more than 8-inch intervals. However, grillwork installed in exterior window frames within the secure area should be spaced 5 inches on center, horizontally and vertically, and entered in the manner described previously. Decorative grillwork patterns can be used for aesthetic purposes.

Grillwork that is covering windows designated as necessary for emergency escape should be hinged for easy egress. All hinged grillwork should be secured with a key-operated security padlock. The key should be maintained on a cup hook in close proximity of the hinged grill, but out of reach of an intruder. These emergency escape windows should not be used in planning for fire evacuations.

The roof should be constructed of fire-resistant material. All hatches and doors leading to the roof should be securely locked with dead-bolt locks. Security measures such as barbed, concertina, or tape security wire, broken glass, and walls or fences may be used to prevent access from nearby trees or adjoining roofs.

Vehicular entry-exit points should be kept to a minimum. Ideally, to maximize traffic flow and security, only two regularly used vehicular entry-exit points are necessary. Both should be similarly constructed and monitored. The use of one would be limited to employees' cars, while the other would be used by visitors and delivery vehicles. Depending on the size and nature of the facility, a gate for emergency vehicular and pedestrian egress should be installed at a location that is easily and safely accessible by employees. Emergency gates should be securely locked and periodically checked. All entry-exit points should be secured with a heavy-duty sliding steel, iron, or heavily braced chain-link gate equipped with a heavy locking device.

The primary gate should be electrically operated (with a manual backup by a security officer situated in an adjacent booth). The gate at the vehicle entrance should be positioned to avoid a long straight approach to force approaching vehicles to slow down before reaching the gate. The general technique employed is to require a sharp turn immediately in front of the gate.

In addition to the gate, and whenever justifiable, a vehicular arrest system can be installed. An appropriate vehicle arrest system, whether active (a piece of equipment designed to stop vehicles in their tracks) or passive (a dense mass), will be able to stop or instantly disable a vehicle with a minimum gross weight of 15,000 pounds traveling 50 miles per hour.

All facilities should have some method of vehicle access control. Primary road entrances to all major plant, laboratory, and office locations should have a vehicle control facility capable of remote operation by security personnel with automated systems.

Capabilities include:

- Electrically operated gates to be activated by security personnel at either the booth or security control center or by a badge reader located in a convenient location for a driver.
- At smaller facilities, vehicle access control may be provided by badge-activated gates, manual swing gates, etc.
- CCTV with the capability of displaying full-facial features of a driver and vehicle characteristics on the monitor at security control center.
- Site security should be able to close all secondary road entrances, thereby limiting access to the primary entrance. Lighting and turn area should be provided as appropriate.
- An intercom system located in a convenient location for a driver to communicate with the gatehouse and security control center.
- Bollards or other elements to protect the security booth and gates against car crash.

Some vehicle control issues include:

- Primary perimeter entrances to a facility that have a booth for security personnel during peak traffic periods and automated systems for remote operations during other periods

- Sensors to activate the gate, detect vehicles approaching and departing the gate, activate a CCTV monitor displaying the gate, and sound an audio alert in the security control center
- Lighting to illuminate the gate area and approaches to a higher level than surrounding areas
- Signs to instruct visitors and to post property as required
- Road surfaces to enable queuing, turnaround, and parking
- Vehicle bypass control (i.e., gate extensions), low and dense shrubbery, fences, and walls

As noted previously, at the perimeter vehicular entry-exit a security officer booth should be constructed to control access. (At facilities not having perimeter walls, the security officer booth should be installed immediately inside the facility foyer.)

If justified by the threat level, the security officer booth should be completely protected with reinforced concrete walls, and ballistic doors and windows. The booth should be equipped with a security officer duress alarm and intercom system, annunciating at both the facility receptionist and security officer's office. This security officer would also be responsible for complete operation of the vehicle gate. If necessary, package inspection and visitor screening may be conducted with walk-through and handheld metal detectors just outside of the booth by an unarmed security officer. Provisions for the environmental comfort should be considered when designing the booth.

Security should be considered in the location and arrangement of parking lots. Pedestrians leaving parking lots should be channeled toward a limited number of building entrances.

All parking facilities should have an emergency communication system (intercom, telephones, etc.) installed at strategic locations to provide emergency communications directly to security.

Parking lots should be provided with CCTV cameras capable of displaying and videotaping lot activity on a monitor in the security control center. Lighting must be of adequate level and direction to support cameras while, at the same time, giving consideration to energy efficiency and local environmental concerns.

If possible, parking on streets directly adjacent to the building should be forbidden. Wherever justifiable given the threat profile of your company, there should be no underground parking areas in the building basement, or ground-level parking under building overhangs.

All parking within perimeter walls or fences should be restricted to employees, with areas limited to as far from the building as possible. Parking for patrons and visitors, except for predesignated VIP visitors, should be restricted to outside of the perimeter wall/fences.

For those buildings having an integral parking garage or structure, a complete system for vehicle control should be provided. CCTV surveillance should be provided for employee safety and building security. If the threat of a car bomb exists, consideration must be given to prohibiting parking in the building.

Access from the garage or parking structure into the building should be limited, secure, well lit, and have no places of concealment. Elevators, stairs, and connecting bridges serving the garage or parking structure should discharge into a staffed or fully monitored area. Convex mirrors should be mounted outside the garage elevators to reflect the area adjacent to the door openings.

Exterior lighting should illuminate all facility entrances and exits in addition to parking areas, perimeter walls, gates, courtyards, garden areas, and shrubbery rows.

Lighting of building exterior and walkways should be provided where required for employee safety and security. Regarding building facades, there should be a capability to illuminate them 100% to a height of at least 6 feet.

Although sodium vapor lights are considered optimum for security purposes, the use of incandescent and florescent light fixtures is adequate. Exterior fixtures should be protected with grillwork when theft or vandalism has been identified as a problem.

For leased buildings, landlord approval of exterior lighting design requirements should be included in lease agreements.

The number of building entrances should be minimized, relative to the site, building layout, and functional requirements. A single off-hours entrance near the security control center is desirable. At large sites, additional secured entrances should be considered with provisions for monitoring and control.

All employee entrance doors should permit installation of controlled access system hardware. The doors, jambs, hinges, and locks must be designed to resist forced entry (e.g., spreading of door frames, accessing panic hardware, shimming bolts and latches, fixed hinge pins). Don't forget handicap requirements when applicable.

The minimum requirement for lock cylinders is six-pin tumbler type. Locks with removable core cylinders to permit periodic changing of the locking mechanism should be used.

All exterior doors should have alarm sensors to detect unauthorized openings. Doors designed specifically for emergency exits need to have an alarm that is audible at the door with an additional annunciation at the security control center. These doors should have no exterior hardware on them.

For protection, large showroom-type plate glass and small operable windows on the ground floor should be avoided. If, however, these types of windows are used and the building is located in a high-risk area, special consideration should be given to the use of locking and alarm devices, laminated glass, wire glass, film, or polycarbonate glazing.

For personnel protection, all windows should have shatter-resistant film.

Main entrances to buildings should have an area for a receptionist during the day and a security officer at night. The security control center should be located adjacent to the main entrance lobby and should be surrounded by professionally designed protective materials.

The lobby-reception area should be a single, self-sufficient building entrance. Telephones and restrooms to meet the needs of the public should be provided in this area without requiring entry into interior areas. Restrooms should be kept locked in high-threat environments and access controlled by the receptionist.

Consistent with existing risk level, the receptionist should not be allowed to accept small parcel or courier deliveries routinely unless they are expected by the addressee.

Other less obvious points of building entry, such as grills, grating, manhole covers, areaways, utility tunnels, mechanical walls, and roof penetrations should be protected to impede or prevent entry into the building.

Permanent exterior stairs or ladders from the ground floor to the roof should not be used, nor should the building facade allow a person to climb up unaided. Exterior fire escapes should be retractable and secured in the up position.

Landscaping and other outside architectural or aesthetic features should minimize creating any area that could conceal a person in close proximity to walkways, connecting links, buildings, and recreational areas.

Landscaping design should include CCTV surveillance of building approaches and parking areas.

Landscape plantings around building perimeters need to be located at a minimum of 4 feet from the building wall to prevent concealing of people or objects.

The building area can be divided into three categories: public areas, interior areas, and security or restricted areas requiring special security measures. These areas should be separated from one another within the building with a limited number of controlled passage points between the areas. "Controlled" in this context can allow or deny passage by any means deemed necessary (i.e., locks, security officers, etc.).

Corridors, stairwells, and other accessible areas should be arranged to avoid places for concealment.

Generally, restricted areas should be located above the ground-floor level, away from exterior walls, and away from hazardous operations. Access to restricted areas should be allowed only from interior areas and not from exterior or public areas. Exit routes for normal or emergency egress should not transit a restricted or security area.

Public areas should be separated from interior areas and restricted areas by slab-to-slab partitions. When the area above a hung ceiling is used as a common air return, provide appropriate modifications to walls or install alarm sensors. In shared-occupancy buildings, area should be separated by slab-to-slab construction or as described previously.

Normally, interior doors do not require special features or provisions for locking. In shared-occupancy buildings, every door leading to an interior area should be considered an exterior door and designed with an appropriate degree of security.

Stairway doors located in multitenant buildings must be secured from the stairwell side (local fire regulations permitting) and always operable from the office side. In the event that code prevents these doors from being secured, the floor plan should be altered to provide security to your area.

Emergency exit doors that are designed specifically for that purpose should be equipped with a local audible alarm at the door and a signal at the monitoring location. Doors to restricted access areas should be designed to resist intrusion and accommodate controlled-access hardware and alarms.

Doors on building equipment and utility rooms, electric closets, and telephone rooms should be provided with locks having a removable core, as are provided on exterior doors. As a minimum requirement, provide six-pin tumbler locks. For safety reasons, door hardware on secured interior doors should permit exit by means of a single knob or panic bar.

The design of public areas should prevent concealment of unauthorized personnel or objects. Ceilings in lobbies, restrooms, and similar public areas should be made inaccessible with securely fastened or locked access panels installed where necessary to service equipment. Public restrooms and elevator lobbies in shared-occupancy buildings should have ceilings that satisfy your security requirements.

Building vaults or metal safes may be required to protect cash or negotiable documents, precious metals, classified materials, etc. Vault construction should be of reinforced concrete or masonry and be resistant to fire damage. Steel vault doors are available with various fire-related and security penetration classifications.

All elevators should have emergency communications and emergency lighting. In shared-occupancy buildings, elevators traveling to your interior area should be equipped with badge readers or other controls to prohibit unauthorized persons from direct entry into your interior area. If this is not feasible, a guard, receptionist, or other means of access control may be necessary at each entry point.

All cable termination points, terminal blocks, and junction boxes should be within your area. Where practical, enclose cable runs in steel conduit.

Cables passing through areas that you do not control should be continuous and installed in conduit. You might even want to install an alarm in the conduit. Junction boxes should be minimized and fittings spot-welded when warranted.

If you have a security control center, it should have adequate area for security personnel and their equipment. Additional office area for technicians and managers should be available adjacent to the control center.

Your security control center should provide a fully integrated console designed to optimize the operator's ability to receive and evaluate security information and initiate appropriate response actions for (1) access control, (2) CCTV, (3) life safety, (4) intrusion and panic alarm, (5) communications, and (6) fully zoned public address system control.

The control center should have emergency power and convenient toilet facilities. Lighting should avoid glare on TV monitors and computer terminals. Sound-absorbing materials should be used on floors, walls, and ceilings. All security power should be backed up by an emergency electrical system.

The control center should be protected to the same degree as the most secure area it monitors.

This type of system, if used, should include the computer hardware, monitoring station terminals, sensors, badge readers, door control devices, and the necessary communication links (leased line, digital dialer, or radio transmission) to the computer.

In addition to the normal designated access control system's doors or gates, remote access control points should interface to the following systems: (1) CCTV, (2) intercom, and (3) door or gate release.

Sensors should be resistant to surreptitious bypass. Door contact monitor switches should be recessed wherever possible. Surface-mounted contact switches should have protective covers.

Intrusion and fire alarms for restricted areas should incorporate a backup battery power supply and be on circuits energized by normal and emergency generator power.

Control boxes, external bells, and junction boxes for all alarm systems should be secured with high-quality locks, and electrically wired to cause an alarm if opened.

Alarm systems should be fully multiplexed in large installations. Alarm systems should interface with the computer-based security system and CCTV system.

Security sensors should individually register an audiovisual alarm (annunciator or computer, if provided) located at the security central monitoring location and alert the security officer. A single-CRT display should have a redundant printer or indicator light. A hardwired audible alarm that meets common fire code standards should be activated with distinguishing characteristics for fire, intrusion, emergency exit, etc. All alarms ought to be locked in until reset manually.

CCTV systems should permit the observation of multiple camera transmission images from one or more remote locations. Switching equipment should be installed to permit the display of any camera on any designated monitor.

To ensure total system reliability, only high-quality security hardware should be integrated into the security system.

In multitenant high-rise facilities, stairwell doors present a potential security problem. These doors must be continuously operable from the office side into the stairwells. Reentry should be controlled to permit only authorized access and prevent entrapment in the stairwell.

Reentry problems can be fixed if you provide locks on all stairwell doors except the doors leading to the first floor (lobby level) and approximately every fourth or fifth floor, or as required by local fire code requirements. Doors without these locks should be fitted with sensors to transmit alarms to the central security monitoring location and provide an audible alarm at the door location. Appropriate signs should be placed within the stairwells. Doors leading to roofs should be secured to the extent permitted by local fire code.

Facilities with unique functions may have special security requirements in addition to those stated in this book. These special requirements should be discussed with corporate security personnel or a security consultant. Typical areas with special requirements are product centers, parts distribution centers, sensitive parts storage facilities, customer centers, service exchange centers, etc.

All facilities of any size in threatened locations should have manned 24-hour internal protection. Security officers should be uniformed personnel and, if possible, placed under contract. They should be thoroughly trained, bilingual, and have complete instructions in their native language clearly outlining their duties and responsibilities. These instructions should also be printed in English for the benefit of American supervisory personnel. If permitted by local law/customs, investigations or checks into the backgrounds of security officers should be conducted.

At facilities with a perimeter wall, there should be one 24-hour perimeter security officer post. If the facility maintains a separate vehicular entrance security officer post, such a post should be manned from 1 hour before to 1 hour after normal business hours and during special events. Security officers should be responsible for conducting package inspections, package check-in, and if used, should operate the walk-through and handheld metal detectors. Security officers should also be responsible for inspecting local and international mail delivered to the facility, both visually and with a handheld metal detector before it is distributed. X-ray equipment for package inspection should be employed if the level of risk dictates.

At facilities with a perimeter guardhouse, the walk-through metal detector could be maintained and operated in an unsecured pass-through portion of the guardhouse. In addition, this security officer could also be responsible for conducting package inspections. When there is sufficient room to store packages at the guardhouse, checked packages should be stored here—new guardhouses should provide for such storage. If package storage at the guardhouse is not feasible, then packages should be on shelves in the foyer under the direction of the foyer security officer or receptionist. Generally, security screening and package storage are carried out in the foyer.

Office areas should be equipped with a "reinforcement" to provide physical protection from unregulated public access. Protection should be provided by a forced-entry-resistant reinforcement that meets ballistic protection standards. These standards can be obtained from your corporate security specialist. When a security reinforcement for access control ACM is constructed, the following criteria should apply:

Walls: Walls comprising an ACM should be constructed of no less than 6 inches of reinforced concrete from slab to slab. The reinforcement should be of at least number 5 rebar spaced 5 inches on center, horizontally and vertically, and anchored in both slabs. In existing buildings, the following are acceptable substitutions for 5-inch reinforced concrete reinforcements:
- Solid masonry, 6 inches thick or greater, with reinforcing bars horizontally and vertically installed
- Solid unreinforced masonry or brick, 8 inches thick or greater
- Hollow masonry block, 4 to 8 inches thick with ¼-inch steel backing;
- Solid masonry, at least 6 inches thick, with ¼-inch steel backing
- Fabricated ballistic steel wall, using two ¼-inch layers of sheet steel separated by tubular steel studs
- Reinforced concrete, less than 6 inches thick with ⅛-inch steel backing

Security doors: Either opaque or transparent security doors can be used for access doors. All doors should provide a 15-minute forced-entry penetration delay. In addition, doors should be ballistic resistant. Access doors should be local access control doors, meaning a receptionist or security officer can remotely open the door.

Security windows: Whenever a security window or teller window is installed, it should meet the 15-minute forced-entry and standard ballistic resistance requirements.

No visitor should be allowed to enter through the reinforcement without being visually identified by a security officer, receptionist, or other employee stationed behind the reinforcement. If the identity of the visitor cannot be established, the visitor must be escorted at all times while in the facility.

A telephone intercom between the secure office area, the foyer security officer, and guardhouse should be installed. In facilities where deemed necessary, a central alarm and public address system should be installed to alert staff and patrons of an emergency situation. Where such a system is required, the primary control console should be located in the security control center. Keep in mind that alarms without emergency response plans may be wasted alarms. Design, implement, and practice emergency plans.

Every facility should be equipped with a secure area for immediate use in an emergency situation. This area is not intended to be used for prolonged periods of time. In the event of emergency, employees will vacate the premises as soon as possible. The secure area, therefore, is provided for the immediate congregation of employees, following which time emergency exit plans would be implemented.

The secure area should be contained within the staff office area, behind the established reinforcement segregating offices from public access. An individual office will usually be designated as the secure area. Entrance into the secure area should be protected by a solid-core wood or hollow metal door equipped with two sliding dead bolts.

Emergency egress from the secure area will be through an opaque 15-minute forced-entry-resistant door equipped with an alarmed panic bar or through a grilled window, hinged for emergency egress. The exit preferably will not be visible from the facility's front entrance.

In the event that an emergency or an evacuation is declared, there is a pressing need for a place of refuge for COMPANY professionals and their dependents. These places of refuge are called safe havens, and they may also serve as rallying points prior to evacuation. COMPANY corporate headquarters should consider establishing safe havens for each major concentration of employees and at field sites. The general characteristics of a safe haven are:

1. Location: Away from likely danger areas, but near enough to lines of communication to provide access and egress.
2. Construction: Solid exterior walls that provide privacy and protection. Sturdy gates—solid wooden or metal doors. Metal grills on window.
3. Communications equipment: Communications equipment should be present in the safe havens and ideally should include the following items: telephone, portable radios, transceivers/receivers.
4. Food: At least 7 days' rations of dehydrated and canned supplies, adequate for the number of people programmed to be in the safe haven, should be stored there. Menus should be preplanned. Water should be present in containers or from a reliable source. A water purification kit should also be kept in the safe haven.
5. Medical kits: All-purpose first aid kit. Special medicines required by personnel.
6. Flashlights and extra batteries.
7. Smoke detectors and fire extinguishers.

The administrative management team of the local management has the responsibility to establish the safe havens, to inform COMPANY professionals of their location, to stock the safe havens, and to periodically check them to ensure that the supplies are fresh and adequate.

ADDITIONAL TRAVEL SECURITY SUGGESTIONS

- Discuss travel plans on a need-to-know basis only. Telephone operators and secretaries should not advise callers and visitors when an executive is out of town on a trip.
- Remove company logos from luggage. Luggage identification tags should be of a type that allows the information on the tag to be covered. Use the business address on the tag.
- Do not leave valuables or sensitive documents in the hotel room.
- When sightseeing, observe basic security precautions and refrain from walking alone in known high-crime areas.

- Always have telephone change available and know how to use the phones. Learn key emergency phrases of the country to be able to ask for police, medical, etc.
- Joggers should carry identification.
- Men should carry wallets in either an inside jacket pocket or a front pants pocket—never in a hip pocket. The less money carried, the better. Credit cards can be used for most purchases.
- The telephone numbers of the appropriate U.S., UK, or country embassy or consulate and of company employees should be carried at all times.
- Always carry the appropriate documentation for the country being visited.
- When traveling, ask for a hotel room between the second and seventh floors. Most fire department equipment does not reach higher to effect rescue, and ground floor rooms are more vulnerable to terrorist or criminal activity.
- American-type hotels usually offer a higher level of safety and security inasmuch as they offer smoke alarms, fire extinguishers, safety locks, hotel security, 24-hour operators, English-speaking personnel, and safety deposit boxes, and normally will not divulge a guest's room number.
- Choose taxis carefully and at random. Be sure it is a licensed taxi. Do not use independent nonlicensed operators.
- Be as inconspicuous as possible in dress, social activities, and amount of money spent on food, souvenirs, gifts, etc.
- Stay in or use VIP rooms or security zones when waiting in commercial airports abroad. Minimize the amount of time spent in airports.
- When traveling internationally, keep all medicine in original containers and take a copy of the prescription.

EMPLOYEE PERSONAL SECURITY TIPS AND MEASURES

The safety and security of those affected by security threats is of primary importance whether in a foreign country or in any environment characterized by potential terrorist/criminal threat.

These recommendations may be helpful in reducing risks in these and other scenarios involving risk:

- Avoid predictable behavior. Vary routes to work, appointments, or other engagements. Terrorists/criminals usually survey their targets prior to attack. Being unpredictable is a very effective deterrent.
- You must raise your level of awareness to a point where:
  - Strange vehicles parked near your residence or place of employment are noticed and promptly reported to the authorities. This must be done immediately. It may be the first time you have seen the vehicle, but it may not be the first time it has been there. You don't know what level of planning the terrorist may be in. Maybe it's only the beginning, but perhaps the planning is in the final stages, giving you little time to act.
  - People standing, walking, or sitting in cars near the residence or place of employment must be noticed, especially people loitering.
  - Someone who always seems to be around you is noticed. Another individual can realize when he's being followed.

- Don't do anything to let the surveillants know they have been detected. Do *not* confront suspected terrorists/criminals and ask them why they're watching. This may initiate an impromptu attack or kidnapping.
- If you suspect you are being followed by someone in a vehicle, drive normally and carefully and proceed to a safe location such as an embassy, police station, or a highly visible or populated area and immediately alert police, embassy staff, or the security network.

ROBBERY

In any circumstance, never resist an armed robbery, as resistance usually leads to violence. In fact, it is helpful to consider in advance the possibility of being robbed so that one can think through reactions, and thus be better prepared.

In any conflict with political implications, do not take sides. Plead ignorance of local politics and express only the desire to contact the appropriate

U.S., UK, or country embassy or consulate, for the purpose of being reunited with your family back home.

Do not attempt to gather intelligence. Any individual who attempts to gather information about a situation, particularly by an on-the-scene examination, is in jeopardy from both sides.

If disturbances erupt and prevent evacuation and the outside environment seems dangerous:

- Stay in your hotel or home.
- Try to contact the local management.
- If unsuccessful, try to contact the corporate crisis management team.
- If unsuccessful, contact the IRT.
- If unsuccessful, try to contact appropriate U.S., UK, or country embassy or consulate by telephone.
- If unsuccessful, try to contact other friendly embassies by telephone or note (Canada, Germany, etc.).
- If unsuccessful, try to hire someone to take a note there for you.

If disturbances erupt and prevent evacuation and the outside environment does not seem dangerous:

- Contact the local management for instructions.
- If unsuccessful, try to contact the corporate crisis management team.
- If unsuccessful, contact the IRT.
- If unsuccessful, try to contact appropriate U.S., UK, or country embassy or consulate by telephone.
- If unsuccessful, try to contact other friendly embassies by telephone or note (Britain, Canada, Germany, etc.).
- If unsuccessful, try to hire someone to take a note there for you.
- Do not attempt to circumvent roadblocks or document checkpoints, as you are likely to be shot.
- Stay away from the scene of disturbances. Consider it a life-threatening situation, not an attraction.
- If you hear gunfire or report of hostilities, take shelter inside a neutral building, meaning one that is not a military target. Government facilities of any sort are likely to be military targets, as is television or other communications centers.

- It may be inadvisable to leave a safe harbor, assuming it has sufficient food and water. This would not be prudent, however, if there is immediate danger of it becoming engulfed in hostilities or taken over by a military force. Otherwise, a safe harbor should only be left if evacuation is offered by an embassy or humanitarian organization, or authoritative communication indicates that hostilities have been suspended or terminated.
- If it is necessary to move out of a safe harbor, it is generally best to move in a direction away from hostilities—away from the troops, tanks, or circling helicopters.
- Under most circumstances it is inadvisable to make a run for the airport with hostilities still in progress. The airport probably will be closed. Moreover, it will likely be a magnet for fighting or military positioning, and in any case, your path to it will likely be impeded by military roadblocks.

If stranded in your hotel or home:

- Seek out other guests and organize the group to take care of housekeeping chores and create an emotional support base.
- Do not watch activity from your window, particularly if sniper fire is being directed from your hotel or area.
- Sleep in the area offering the greatest protection against gunfire from the outside.
- Move to a room that is not exposed to the area of gunfire.
- Know your escape routes in case of fire.

If detained by foreign intelligence:

- First, never do anything that would give a hostile intelligence service reason to pick you up.
- However, if you are arrested or detained, ask to contact the American embassy. You are entitled to do so under international diplomatic and consular agreements, to which most countries are signatories.
- Phrase your request appropriately. Your request is more likely to succeed in a communist country if you present it as a demand. In third-world countries, however, making demands could lead to physical abuse.
- Do not admit to wrongdoing or sign anything. Part of the detention ritual in communist countries is a written report, which you

will be asked to sign. Decline to do so and continue demanding to contact the embassy or consulate.

- Do not agree to "help" the hostile service. The hostile service may offer you the opportunity to help them in return for releasing you, or foregoing prosecution. Either refuse outright or delay a firm commitment by saying that you have to think it over. Either action often leads to release.
- Report to the embassy or consulate and the local management as soon as possible after such an incident. You should then request assistance in departing the country. Departure is generally possible with embassy assistance. However, you will risk rearrest on future visits, or may be denied future visas.
- Report to your corporate supervisor immediately upon return to the appropriate U.S., UK, or country embassy or consulate. This is especially important if you were unable to report previously to the embassy, consulate, or in-country manager.

If you are arrested:

- Every year thousands of expats are arrested abroad, many on drug charges. The experience of being arrested overseas is notably different from being arrested in the appropriate U.S., UK, or country embassy or consulate.
- Few countries provide a jury trial.
- Most countries do not accept bail.
- Pretrial detention may last months, often in solitary confinement.
- Prisons may lack even minimal comforts of bed, toilet, and washbasin.
- Diet is often inadequate, requiring supplements from relatives and friends.
- Officials do not speak English.
- Physical abuse, confiscation of physical property, degrading or inhuman treatment, and extortion are possible.

If you are arrested, ask permission to notify the nearest appropriate U.S., UK, or country embassy or consulate. This is particularly important in countries with which the appropriate U.S., UK, or country embassy or consulate has status of forces agreements. Under international agreements and practice, you have a right to get in touch with the appropriate U.S., UK, or country embassy or consulate. If you are turned down, keep asking, politely but persistently. If you are unsuccessful, try to have someone get in touch for you.

Consular officers will do whatever they can to protect your legitimate interests and ensure that you are not discriminated against under local law. Consular officers *can*:

- Provide lists of local attorneys
- Help find adequate legal representation
- Visit you in jail
- Advise you of your rights according to local law
- Contact your company, family, or friends
- Arrange for transfer of money, food, and clothing from your family and friends to prison authorities
- Try to get relief if you are held under inhumane or unhealthy conditions, or if you are treated less favorably than others in the same situation

Unfortunately, what American officials can do for you overseas is limited by foreign laws and geography. The appropriate U.S., UK, or country embassy or consulate *cannot*:

- Get you out of jail by posting bond or bail
- Pay your legal fees or related expenses, serve as attorneys, or give legal advice

KEY POINTS

Keeping your security and crisis management program current, on track, and comprehensive requires constant maintenance and tweaking. Involving cross-sections of your corporate management teams and departments will be essential to ensuring the proper feedback and for sharing the load of gathering the data required for quick and efficient emergency and security program response. Security professionals must keep current in their industry trade groups, keep certifications and education up to date, and attend trade shows and presentations. Interfacing and networking with colleagues and contacts in professional organizations, even competitor companies, as well as with law enforcement and government officials, is a sure-fire way to succeed. It's not easy, but it's worth it.

CASE STUDY

An organization once had looked at its footing from an emergency and crisis management and response nature. It fell upon the security manager to set up the meeting notices, prod people to attend, and coax them into completing a template for calling trees and equipment needs. The security manager was not a very popular hombre during this time, and was quite often seen as a "sky is falling" chap, even though his attitude and demeanor were calm, cooperative, and jovial. Meeting after meeting took place, and eventually, a routine set in. The corporate departments began to realize that how the company would respond should some really bad things happen was not clearly defined. As usual, the IT people had their act together, as nothing makes for a headache more than losing your ability to work with data, emails, and all else that is essential to business lifeblood. On the liaison front, some managers wondered why the security manager traveled across the country or to Washington, DC, for meetings and seminars sponsored by public-private sector groups. There were lunches with local, state, and federal law enforcement and meetings with outside groups, including some companies that were actually in competition for key international contracts! What's up with that?

One morning, a call came in from someone in the federal government, and not the normal agency you would expect to report the following: It seems that an international activist group was upset at a member of corporate management because of a speech given at a global conference. The group had surreptitiously attended the symposium on false pretenses. The person giving the speech was not speaking about the topic that garnered so much animosity by this group, but the mere fact they were present was enough. The caller stated this group was well equipped and prepared to launch a denial-of-service attack against the company and all others who attended the symposium. The caller advised that there was information some companies had already experienced the beginnings of such an action. The security manager thanked the caller, quickly telephoned the IT crisis team contact, and the process of buffering the attack was began. Shortly thereafter, a trickle became a fire hose and the attack had begun in earnest. What little prep time was available was enough to stem the tide and weather the deluge. Survival was achieved.

11

Maximizing Your Security and Crisis Management Efficiency
"How to Be All Things to All People, and Keeping It Real"

In primary freedom, one utilizes all ways and is bound by none, and like-wise uses any techniques or means which serves one's end. Efficiency is anything that scores.

—Bruce Lee

Now that you have established the components necessary to protect your people and assets in difficult places around the world, and have a robust security, emergency, and crisis management response program, what do you do? How do you keep it balanced and together? How do you ensure that you are the go-to resource for everyone within your organization? As has been mentioned in this book, you have to prove your resourcefulness and that you have the attitude that you are willing and able to meet the challenges of a complex organization in a challenging and frequently volatile world. You have to be looked upon as competent, and someone who can handle stress and crisis. You need to make sometimes snap decisions and take action in situations when someone is looking for a leader.

But snap decisions in emergencies are quite different from responses, which can be thought of as always being of a negative nature. If you are seen as always being negative, against this concept, or not for that project, or as only seeing the worst-case scenarios for new contracts, partnerships, building new offices, or any manner of international business opportunities—just because it is in a volatile area—you might quickly be checking to see if your telephone is malfunctioning, or people have just stopped calling. Progress is not painless. Any company worth its salt will strive for new markets and new opportunities. Not every company jumps into volatile regions without doing its homework or not taking the proper precautions, but it does happen. Your job will be to see that this does not happen, that you raise the issues and concerns in a proper, polite, and businesslike manner. Risk for risk's sake gets no one anywhere. But, taking on risk well informed and armed with the proper response planning and security and safety management cushions all against failure.

My recommendations have included the need to stay alert to new trends, new ideas, and new methods for doing things. For example, I have spoken in this book about the security technologies that are out there with respect to travel tracking, or GPS systems that can locate someone in a crisis or that has been abducted. Some security professionals might feel threatened by this new technology. If part of the travel tracking package includes an intelligence component, and employees are given access to this information, will they need you? Could there be a tendency to hoard this intelligence and keep it from those who might begin to think that they no longer need to pay this security professional the enormous salary (author's joke) he or she is making now that the information is readily available? My advice to you is to not feel threatened by information others might have that might support or even contradict your advice.

Here's a little nugget of wisdom I want to pass along to you. If I have learned anything over my career (and this is something that used to cause me heartburn, consternation, and concern, but I can honestly say I laugh at it now), it is that most people—the average person—truly don't know the first thing about security. When people ask you what you do for a living, and you say to them "I am a corporate security manager or director," what is their reaction or assumption? Do they conjure up images of security guards? Do they ask you if you carry a gun? Maybe they ask you how you can stare at closed-circuit television for so long without getting bored. If the people in your organization, and you know they are there, don't understand what you do in your position, how can they comprehend what you can do for their people and their assets in a volatile region or country? Security guards don't have much to do with my traveling to the Kashmir for business meetings! (An actual conversation and situation involving this are presented in the case study at the end of the chapter.)

So, education, training, and awareness are called for. If the employees at your company envision Barney Fife as security manager, because they see security officers when they enter your facilities, you have a lot of work to do. On the other hand, if you have a robust, up-front, forward-thinking, state-of-the-art, well-versed, and professional communications and outreach program, you can do much to disperse these misgivings about corporate security.

It also helps to be challenged in what you are doing. If, for example, you have been recommending the same things to employees traveling to Country Y without really checking to see that these are current and still plausible, then you are doing more harm than good. It might become a running joke if you constantly spout the latest information, book chapter and verse from OSAC or from government websites. Cutting and pasting security summaries can lead to repetition and monotonous briefings that end up in the electronic trash bin. It will help to visit some of the countries your company continues to do business within, but it is not critical. Sometimes having visited Europe you can draw some general comparisons to Great Britain or Germany. Spending some time in Bangkok might give some insight into Singapore or even Vietnam. Some of the best security managers I have ever met had not been to all the countries their companies were based in, and yet, they could spout statistics and give you an on-the-spot assessment of the critical information required to safely operate there and protect your people and assets. As I like to say, I have never been to the moon, but I can tell you that its atmosphere is composed of mostly hydrogen and helium and that the surface consists of a lot of dust and rocks, with a fair amount of silicate and aluminum.

Another, more recent phenomenon, is that of nonsecurity corporate employees being assigned to security roles within organizations. We all have seen it, the safety professional who inherits the security responsibility. In international settings, this might mean the safety manager also manages the security officers at the construction site. Or, the human resource or building managers have these and other security responsibilities. Let me just say, if any organization is turning international security management over to nonsecurity professionals, you are doing your company a great disservice. This concept and practice is partially due to the assertions of many organizations that security cannot be that difficult. It really is just guns, guards, and gates. I covered in a previous chapter how I felt about merging physical and information security to the point where physical security is the responsibility of information technology departments and employees. These areas of emphasis are unique and complicated enough that one cannot be an expert in both, or at least give each area its appropriate due. Conversely, organizations that seek to outsource all of their international security responsibilities to security consultants or firms will find their organization underserved and unprepared. Consultants can supplement such a program, but I feel there must be someone within the organization—a security professional—who understands the concepts, the risk, and the mitigation of such. I don't believe consultants can on their own gauge the true nature and intricacies of the organization as balanced against the type of work, expertise, and capabilities—and appropriately assess the risks to the company.

Security has been stigmatized. The fact that most security officers are paid little better than minimum wage, receive little or no training, and that most states have no minimum standards, is a self-perpetuating situation. We attract those who have difficulty obtaining work anywhere else by paying wages that no one else would accept. The corporate security manager, unless he or she is stepping into an organization where security is ingrained and enmeshed into the corporate culture, will have a hard time initiating a global security program, let alone a domestic one. Many corporations in manufacturing, construction, engineering, petrochemical, and other applications have robust safety programs. Quite often, successful safety programs are top down and senior management driven, to the point where doing the job safely is tightly wound into everything the company does. Security needs to have this type of support and front-and-center appearance. Everything this book has pointed out to you is only valuable with the acceptance and support of all levels of your organization. Given the choice between no security officers and an annual bill that might cause heart palpitations, most managers will choose the former. Given the choice between sitting in a security orientation meeting predeployment or a lecture on overseas tax concerns is a no-brainer. If I can give one more piece of advice, it would be this: keep an open mind. Be accessible and open to new ideas. Be mindful and considerate of those whose opinions differ from yours. Try your best to educate them and impart to them your reasons for thinking the way you do. No doubt, it will be easier if you have the support of senior management behind you. You should look for opportunities to meet with senior management and provide them with your research, benchmarking, and reasons for making the recommendations you are providing to employees.

As I mentioned, training is both required and critical to success. The type of information that will be available to travelers and employees via travel tracking software is limited in nature, and will require analysis.

Travel tracking and intelligence companies will not make pronounce-ments like "Get out of China now!" Your travelers would not be making such decisions, in any event. As indicated in this book, if you have any one single attitude you will face in your professional career dealing with international travel and business, it will be that people will want to go on these trips, unless they are absolutely scared for their own safety. Often, it is when speaking with their family members and others that they can be talked out of assignments or trips. I have encouraged people to be open and honest when speaking with me about trips, to express their concerns, telling them there are no dumb questions.

It is often in a one-on-one situation that people will confide that per-haps they are a little more concerned about their safety than other mem-bers of their team. Or, maybe their manager has been somewhat cavalier in sending people from this location to that one, only seeing the busi-ness need, and not the true risk involved. If this has taken place, if the employee has gotten to this stage in the process and their manager has not been advised of the risk, then I think I have failed as a security manager. There can be a kidnapping a day for 365 days in Town X, and someone will get it into his/her head that he/she absolutely needs to attend that meeting. He will tell you that he has traveled to Town X on a 100 differ-ent occasions, and he will ask if you have ever been there and talk about you to his peers and managers until you seem like either the biggest dope walking or someone who is scared of his own shadow.

You are going to need some successes. You are often going to need to pull a rabbit out of your hat. If you have built and nourished the types of relationships I have recommended in this book, you will have the experi-ence, tools, and comfort in knowing you won't be facing new issues or territories. Look for ways to insert good advice whenever possible. I have found that whether it is in corporate investigations, security awareness training, or providing advice, you are going to need one investigation where you solve the case—catch the culprit, get them to confess, receive restitution. You will need one instance of security awareness training when you have recommended something to a traveler that plays out exactly as you indicated—say, for example, someone tries to steal their laptop right from under their noses at a French train station. You recommend one hotel over another one, and the latter hotel is hit by natural disaster and does not survive, or a bombing takes place. I have had each of these take place, and while it is sometimes difficult to celebrate these events, you need to make your manager aware and keep this information for future use. Maybe you throw it out in a presentation, saying things like, "Our security department can recommend which hotels have better security, such as on one occasion when ..." and you list that circumstance.

I have tried to learn as much as I can about my particular industry, such as chemicals and pharmaceuticals, and try to watch the news for anything I can pick up relating to my employer's interests. When working with petrochemicals, I signed up for receiving studies and maps indicating trends, supply graphics, you name it. Not a time has gone by that I have not found some information that was useful to an engineer or human resources manager, accountant, botanist, or project employees. I tend not to forward the security-related warnings, studies, etc., in their raw form, as this might appear to be overcompensating and trying to give my side of the story an unfair advantage. I will save information such as this to digest, summarize, and use at a later date, such as in project update meetings, even impromptu meetings in the hallway or other locations. Beware of the pitfall of passing along raw intelligence and information. Be sure that anything you send has been well read and crafted so it does not interfere with your message and direction. I have seen security professionals send along stories that might be 85% supportive of their position, such as stating that Country X is experiencing a drastic uptick in terrorist activities or crime, but then go on to illustrate how the author or someone else continues to self-drive around that region, something which you have been preaching not to do.

It will always be difficult to find articles and other information that represent your situation 100%. This is because, if you have not learned by now, there is no such thing as "cookie-cutter security." You will not be able to apply one template to everything you do. I have always made it a practice to have a different security and evacuation plan for each project, not only each country or region. You are always going to need to add this, take away that. You will have different means of evacuation and methods of providing security for your employees on each project. We have discussed these, from the friendly security officer who puts his best foot forward to your visitors and vendors, to the well-armed "shooter" whose message is: "You mess with me, and you will come out on the short end of the stick."

A word or two about dependents, I feel, is required. Dependents are, of course, very important to the employee to whom they are related. Dependents in a volatile region can be a good thing or a very bad thing, depending on how you look at it. I have been in situations where I made recommendations that we not allow dependents to go to new projects or countries, or that they be pulled out of the countries where their employee spouses or parents were already deployed. The latter is most difficult, and I would liken it to attempting to extract impacted molars with a can opener. Many employees will not accept long-term assignments if their spouses and children are not included in the deal. Many corporations pay additional salary for employees who have spouses and dependents overseas. I am not stating that employees consider this a moneymaking proposition, however. Who wouldn't want to give your spouse or children the opportunity to live in, study in, and explore an exotic location? It all sounds well and good, until you begin to factor in the risk involved. I can pretty much determine that I can keep an employee safe on a job site, while on an overseas assignment, even in volatile areas. But, add spouses and children to the mix and you might find your job just got a little more difficult. If an employee's dependents are not happy, or if they feel they are not well protected, the employee might pull up stakes and demand to be sent home. If the dependents at home are hearing news stories about how unsafe the employee's location is, the pressure at home may be too great, and the same outcome might be the result. I have offered and conducted predeployment briefings for employees and their spouses, children, even friends who will be their emergency contacts while they are on overseas assignments. And, as I have mentioned in this book, I have been on call to these same people should they have immediate concerns about their loved ones or friends employed in volatile areas.

Let me say just a word or two about the concept of being "on call." I have been on call in my professional life for over 20 years. I can chart the progression of my being on call through the innovations of the mobile phone industry, beginning with the bag phones I used to carry around to the sleek multifunctional units that now allow me to browse the Internet and send messages and documents from anywhere. If I have learned anything about being on call, it is this: If you answer the phone and act like you are being put out, that this is the greatest inconvenience one can do to you, you are going to make matters worse. People under duress are going to react to you in a more professional manner if you do the same. You can have a calming impact upon the caller, but not if you are acting like an ass. I have had phone calls (pages in past times) or text messages during births, baptisms, bar mitzvahs, birthdays, burials, vacations, sick days, hospital stays, recovery rooms, weddings, anniversaries, you name it. If you can't understand the caller, or they are speaking too fast, ask them to calm down and please repeat themselves. Always repeat what they have told you back to them so that you get it right.

One of the best compliments I have ever received in my security career was that when employees, from senior management to contract employees, called me with emergency situations, they knew that I would react calmly, logically assess the situation, and provide them with some immediate steps to implement. It is the calm response I am most proud of. If you have not already done so, I hope that you can reach this level of confidence in your abilities and maintain this attitude for your organization and employees you are entrusted to help protect.

I hope that something in this book will give you another arrow in your quiver, and that something I have written will be of use to you in your professional career. Keep striving to do better for your companies and their employees. The world is an interesting, fascinating, and beautiful jewel; it is not all gloom and doom. There are many fine people in every country and corner of this planet. Hopefully, you will meet many of them.

FINAL CASE STUDY

The call came in at 5:00 p.m. on a Friday night; the calls on Fridays always come in at 5:00. On the following Tuesday, a group of intrepid employees would be going to the Kashmir region, traveling by road from India, for a very important meeting that might lead to a very large contract for the corporation. The European manager wanted to know what security and safety concerns would be present for such travel—a good sign, however late the call had been made. The security manager promised to make some calls and get back to the manager as soon as possible. Calls were made to colleagues, government contacts, and security personnel. Private intelligence sources were reviewed. A clear picture emerged, with lots of supporting information and data, of how Western companies could deal successfully with a business venture in this area. A strategy was developed and solidified, and emails were exchanged with a security provider in the area. A couple of glitches emerged: The road leading up to the Kashmir border was risky at best, and an armed security escort was going to be the standard operating procedure given the nature of the business, the personnel, and the project. On top of that, any outside security provider would be stopped at the Kashmir border area and would not be allowed to carry weapons from that point forward.

As promised, a call was made back to the European manager. A plan had been developed, and the reasoning behind it was laid out. The manager agreed that it would be prudent to have the armed security detail as part of the operation. Then, the seamless (as far as the manager would see it) solution to the previous dilemma was presented. One armed security company would accompany the employees to the Kashmir border area, where they would be met by and handed off to another similarly equipped and capable armed group. A lot of scrambling and discussions behind the scenes went into this coverage, but to the European manager, it all appeared to be as easy as phoning in a pizza delivery. As logistically challenging and complicated as arranging security coverage for this project was, the team of employees never suspected, nor did the security manager offer, that their arrangements took the better part of the entire weekend to formalize.

ONE FINAL BIT OF TRAVEL SECURITY SUGGESTIONS, FOR SENIOR MANAGEMENT AND EXPATS IN VOLATILE REGIONS

The following are general traveling security suggestions:

- Discuss travel plans on a need-to-know basis only. Telephone operators and secretaries should not advise callers and visitors when an executive is out of town on a trip.
- Remove company logos from luggage. Luggage identification tags should be of a type that allows the information on the tag to be covered. Use the business address on the tag.
- Do not leave valuables or sensitive documents in the hotel room.
- When sightseeing, observe basic security precautions and refrain from walking alone in known high-crime areas.
- Always have telephone change available and know how to use the phones. Learn key emergency phrases of the country to be able to ask for police, medical, etc.
- Joggers should carry identification.
- Men should carry wallets inside either a jacket pocket or a front pants pocket, never in a hip pocket. The less money carried, the better. Credit cards can be used for most purchases.
- The telephone numbers of the appropriate U.S., UK, or country embassy or consulate and company employee contact numbers should be carried with employees at all times.
- Always carry the appropriate documentation for the country being visited.

- When traveling, ask for a hotel room on the third floor. Most fire department equipment does not reach higher to effect rescue, and ground-floor rooms are more vulnerable to terrorist or criminal activity. If none are available on the third floor, don't go above the seventh floor.
- Expat-type hotels usually offer a higher level of safety and security inasmuch as they have smoke alarms, fire extinguishers, safety locks, hotel security, 24-hour operators, English-speaking personnel, safety deposit boxes, and normally will not divulge a guest's room number.
- Choose taxis carefully and at random. Be sure it is a licensed taxi. Do not use independent, nonlicensed operators.
- Be as inconspicuous as possible in dress, social activities, and amount of money spent on food, souvenirs, gifts, etc.
- Stay in or use VIP rooms or security zones when waiting in commercial airports abroad. Minimize the amount of time spent in airports.
- When traveling internationally, keep all medicine in original containers and take a copy of the prescription.

The following are sample emergency contact, policy, and crisis management forms.

COMPANY EXECUTIVE PERSONAL DATA FORM

PHOTO	Name (first/middle/last): _____
	Birth data (month/day/year): _____
	Maiden name: _____
	Passport number/date and place of issue: _____
	Country current citizenship: _____

Social security or ID number: _____

Residences (street/city/county/state/country):

_____

_____

Alternate: _____

_____

Alternate: _____

_____

Height (indicate inches or centimeters): _____

Weight (indicate pounds or kilograms): _____

Hair (color and style): _____

Complexion (ruddy, fair, etc.): _____

Race: _____

Unusual characteristics (glasses, hairpieces, braces, etc.): _____

_____

Spouse (name/age/residence): _____

Children (name/age/residence): _____

_____

_____

Handwriting example:

Copy sample exactly as written.

Four score and seven years ago our fathers brought forth on this continent, a new nation, conceived in Liberty, and dedicated to the proposition that all men are created equal.

Household help (maids, butlers, chauffeurs, etc.)—for each, supply (name/residence/social security number): _____

_____

_____

_____

_____

Close neighbors and associates (name/residence/telephone):

_____

Motor vehicles (used by employee and dependents), company and personal (make/year/model/color/license/vehicle identification number):

_____

_____

Physician(s) and dentist(s) (name/residence/telephone number):

_____

_____

Attorney(s) (name/residence/telephone number):

_____

_____

Required medication(s):

_____

_____

Blood type: _____

Addresses and phone numbers at which you can normally be reached:

_____

_____

_____

_____

Additional pertinent information:

PERSONAL DATA FORM TO BE USED
FOR FAMILY MEMBERS

PHOTO	Name (first/middle/last): _____

Name (first/middle/last): _____

Maiden name: _____

Birth data (month/day/year): _____

Nickname: _____

City/state: _____

Social security or ID number: _____

Relationship to employee: _____

Country of residence (if different from employee): _____

City/street/county/state/country: _____

Telephone number(s): _____

Physical description: _____

Height (indicate inches or centimeters): _____

Weight (indicate pounds or kilograms): _____

Build (slander, stocky, etc.): _____

Hair (color and style): _____

Complexion (ruddy, fair, etc.): _____

Race: _____

School presently attending (name/address/telephone number):

_____

_____

School principal and children's teachers: _____

_____

Current employer, if employed (name/address/telephone number):

_____

_____

If married, name and address of spouse: _____

_____

Required medication: _____

Blood type: _____

Motor vehicles (make/year/model/color/license/vehicle identification number):

_____

_____

Handwriting specimen (copy verbatim):

Our London business is good, but Vienna and Berlin are quiet. Mr. D. Lloyd has gone to Switzerland and I hope for good news. He will be there for a week at 1496 Zermott St. and then goes to Turin and Rome and will join Col. Parry and arrive at Athens, Greece, Nov. 27th or Dec. 2nd. Letters there should be addressed: King James Blvd. 3580. We expect Chas. E. Fuller Tuesday. Dr. L. Mcquaid and Robert. Unger, Esq., left on the Y. X. Express tonight.

Additional comments:

COMPANY—LOCATION

SECURITY AND CRISIS MANAGEMENT PLAN RECEIPT

I have read and understand COMPANY's crisis management plan dated _____ and understand my role in any disaster or crisis response that may be required.

_____   _____   _____

Signature   Printed name   Date

COMPANY–LOCATION

CRISIS TEAM CONTACT SHEET

In an emergency, the Crisis Team Leader will contact the following individuals in the order listed. If an individual listed below is not available or cannot be reached, leave a message on the person's answering machine. In all cases, complete each section of this contact sheet.

Name	Home phone	Office phone	Cellular/ Satellite phone	Time called

COMPANY–LOCATION

INITIAL CRISIS INFORMATION REPORT FORM

No. _____ (in order received)

Name of Reporting Manager _____

Call received at _____ P.M./A.M.   From: _____

Caller's phone number: _____

Address: _____

_____

_____

Nature of inquiry or call:

What action COMPANY has taken?

COMPANY–LOCATION

PRESS CONTACT SHEET

No. _____ (in order received)

Date: _____ Time: _____ P.M./A.M.

Reporting officer: _____

Inquiry received from: _____

Reporter/editor with: _____ (organization)

Question/inquiry:

Response:

COMPANY–LOCATION

AFTER INCIDENT EVALUATION

Please complete this evaluation honestly and thoroughly. If you request, your response will be kept confidential. Be as specific as you can regarding incidents, people, and issues that merit attention. Evaluation is a necessary and important step in planning how to prevent or mitigate future problems.

Your name (optional): _____ Date: _____

Department: _____ Extension: _____

What was your role in the crisis? _____
_____
_____
_____
_____

How did you first learn of the incident? _____
_____
_____
_____
_____

Were you satisfied with how you were notified?   ☐ Yes   ☐ No

Why or why not? _____
_____
_____
_____

Approximately how many hours did you spend exclusively in managing an aspect of this incident? _____

APPENDIX A: EMERGENCY MANAGEMENT PLAN

In close consultation with corporate management, security teams will develop an emergency evacuation plan to cover various contingencies ranging from medical evacuation of one or more casualties out of the country through to complete evacuation of all corporate staff by road or air. Entry into (country) is assumed to be by air via international airport.

SECURITY MANAGEMENT STAFFING

The security operations coverage consists of programs and requirements such as:

- The maintenance of a 24-hour operations and monitoring office/control center
- The production of a daily security and intelligence assessment for management
- Daily meetings with corporate management to plan each subsequent day's activities
- If necessary, providing daily transportation/movement plan, including vehicle, drivers, and protection teams

TRANSPORTATION SECURITY

The security situation across (country) may be such that routine movement in and around the country is dangerous and should only be undertaken when absolutely essential and with sufficient security in place. Security teams will undertake movements several times per day on behalf of a number of clients, and we, and our clients, believe these moves represent manageable and reasonable risks. Movements might include:

- Road moves in and around (country, locations. and the other areas)
- Road moves between the (areas) and international airport
- Road moves into and out of the (areas) and back to facilities, offices, hotels, and secure locations
- Movements from our hotels to government ministries and institutions, such as the university
- Movements from (area) to outlying towns

These moves are undertaken with a minimum of two armored vehicles and probably an additional SUV (Grand Cherokee with the security team). Outside (area): Four vehicles, a mix of sedans, and an SUV.

PHYSICAL SECURITY PROCEDURES

General concepts are:

- Establishment of a secure perimeter with sufficient stand-off distance to living and working accommodation
- Establishment of a main and an emergency access control point with provision for pedestrian and vehicle access
- Search areas for personnel and vehicles entering (and exiting) the site
- A trained and vetted guard force, under the direct control of an expatriate manager, with specific responsibilities for:
  - Access control/ID checking
  - Searching
  - Patrolling
  - Static sentry duties
  - Quick reaction force
- The use of portable technology solutions, including CCTV and lighting where appropriate

These concepts are to assist team leaders in putting together a comprehensive procedure and are not intended to be prescriptive.

A different style of plan, intended for an impending, quickly developing situation: TEMPORARY SECURITY PLAN (to be combined with additional information previously emailed/in process):

Local security vendor contact:
Company name:
Tel: +5555555555
Fax: +5555555555
Mobile: +55555555

U.S. embassy: The telephone number of the US embassy is xxxxxxxxx; emergency after hours, xxxxxxxxxxx. Registering with the U.S. embassy allows the corporate professional to be placed on the warden system and receive warden messages from the embassy.

U.S. embassy locations:	Embassy city
General information:	xxxxxxxx
Street, city:	
	Embassy website
Point of contact:	Name, RSO
Phone numbers:	Main: xxxxxxxxxxxxx
	Police: xxx
	Fire: xxx
	Medical: xxx

U.S. citizens are encouraged to register with the U.S. embassy via this link: https://travelregistration.state.gov/ibrs/home.asp.

British embassy: The telephone number of the British embassy is xxxxxxxxxxxxx.

British embassy locations:	City
Address (street, city):	xxxxxxxxxxxxx
Telephone:	xxxxxxxxxxxxx
Facsimile:	xxxxxxxxxxxxx
Email:	xxxxxxxxxxxxx
Office hours:	GMT:
	Mon–Thurs: 0600–1400
	Fri: 0600–1130
	Local time:
	Mon–Thurs: 0800–1600
	Fri: 0800–1330
Website:	xxxxxxxxxxxxx

British nationals in (country) are strongly advised to register with and to follow local advice issued by the British embassy (country, city) or British consulate general in (city) (see contact details below):

British consulate general address:
Tel: xxxxxxxxx
Email:
Website:

MEDICAL/MEDICAL EVACUATION/CRISIS CONTINGENCY EVACUATION

Quality of health care and dental care in (country) is good. Corporate employees may be provided with a list of doctors by the U.S. embassy. For critical care before an evacuation, you may wish to contact a doctor recommended by International SOS.

International SOS (available 24 hours, 7 days a week)
24-hour emergency numbers (call collect nearest International SOS service center):
Philadelphia, Pennsylvania: (215) 942 8226
Singapore: (65) 6338 7800
London: (44) (20) 8762 8008

Corporate comprehensive worldwide access member number: xxxxxxxxxxxxxxxxxx
International SOS is available for emergency medical evacuation. In addition, International SOS is available for security evacuation depending on situations. See contact information for International SOS above or visit http://www.internationalsos.com.

CORPORATE LIFELINES/EMPLOYEE CONTACT INFORMATION

Individual corporate professionals deployed to (country) will fill in life-line information based on the project they are working on and the corporate department/division associated with that project. Prior to being deployed, corporate professionals should consult project management for exact lifeline information.

If unavailable, contact the security manager or coordinator:

	Security Manager	**Security Coordinator**
Office	xxx-xxx-xxxx	xxx-xxx-xxxx
Cell	xxx-xxx-xxxx	xxx-xxx-xxxx
Home	xxx-xxx-xxxx	xxx-xxx-xxxx
Email	xxx@xxx.com	xxx@xxx.com

Corporate (country) project employee contact information:

• Will update with office and possible addition of satellite telephone numbers

It should be noted that if, at any time, corporate employees feel uncomfortable/unsure about any of their safety/security, they have the ability to halt any process and should contact a lifeline member. This includes evacuation, transportation, lodging, medical, and any other issue.

EVACUATION PHASES/PLAN

So that you are aware of the phases, the plan is described/initiated in phases. Phase I will be termed the *alert stage*. This is a period during which routine collection and assessment of information about local, regional, national, and international events will take place. Staging and debarkation areas for assembling employees and their dependents should be reviewed.

The corporate lead person in-country should consider meeting periodically with the expatriate employees to review current events, intelligence, and trends. It is important to develop a procedure to deal with rumors that have a tendency to emerge with the onset of any crisis situation. Rumors not dealt with can have a demoralizing effect. The best countermeasures are to have an open line of communication designed to address rumors and a set of clear evacuation instructions.

Evacuation priorities should be established and individually assigned. The following categories should be considered:

• First priority—dependents (if applicable)
• Second priority—individuals other than key expatriate employees
• Third priority—key expatriate employees

Alternate routes to international airports, seaports, or land borders should be determined and checked for traversability under emergency conditions.

Note: The RSO has recommended that U.S. citizens maintain a supply of food, water, and cash (local currency) sufficient for remaining in place for 1 week. He further states that he is of the opinion that it would be too dangerous to try to depart by way of road or attempt to fly out of the international airport should a state of general civil disorder occur.

Phase II will be termed the *limited action, increased preparation phase*. This phase should be initiated when, in the judgment of the senior manager, a situation has reached a level of tension or instability that could lead to partial or complete evacuation of expatriate employees and their dependents.

Note: The earlier an evacuation decision can be made (see note above), the more likely it can be affected in a calm and less politically sensitive atmosphere.

The contents of departure kits or "go bags" should be examined and reviewed.

An inventory of household effects should be prepared in duplicate: one to accompany the employee and his or her dependents, and one to be left behind with an appropriate corporate representative. The possibility of having to abandon personal property prior to evacuation should be addressed with each project candidate before he or she ships any goods to (country).

Normal work routines should continue; however, certain preparatory activities, such as obtaining required tickets and clearances, etc., should be undertaken if appropriate.

Phase III will be termed the *evacuation phase*. This phase should be initiated when, in the judgment of the corporate lead person, the situation has deteriorated to the point that the decision to evacuate is imminent or has already been made. At this point, the company home office should arrange for the services of other companies and outside resources necessary to support and coordinate the evacuation process. It is assumed that total withdrawal of personnel will not meet active resistance from the authorities.

The senior manager should determine whether it would be prudent or desirable to relocate evacuees from their quarters to preselected primary or alternate staging area(s) prior to proceeding to the international airport or other departure site(s), for final coordination of procedures for evacuation.

An additional phase should be considered that will be termed *stand fast*. This special phase should be implemented in the event that evacuation is not considered prudent under certain circumstances; for example, if a coup has occurred or if roaming/roving demonstrations, protests, attacks, and vandalism are taking place. Under this phase, operations may slow down or be suspended. Employees and their dependents would remain in their individual apartments or gather in other quarters for an undetermined period of time, awaiting further instructions. Liquids, canned foods, medicines, and staples to support the family/expats for an extended period of time should be kept on hand to support such an eventuality, depending on the local situation.

Instructions to and between families should be transmitted by whatever means available, depending on the circumstances. With the prevalence of mobile phones and landline phones, this should be possible unless a national crisis shuts down the telephone system. However, it is vital that whatever means are employed, the senior manager receive positive feedback to ensure that all expatriate employees are in touch and to confirm their daily whereabouts. An employee warden system should be developed and used in times of increased threat or during actual emergencies.

EVACUATION PROCEDURE

Evacuation Implementation

As stated previously, corporate employees may implement the evacuation plan based upon corporate home office management decision, or by use of information provided by the U.S. embassy.

Evacuation Notification

The corporate lead person will notify each of the expatriate employees. Each expatriate employee will have the responsibility, in turn, to notify support personnel in-country (if needed). The notification information passed on will include as a minimum:

- The cause for the evacuation initiation
- The intended evacuation method
- The assembly location(s)
- The eventual evacuation destination and departure time, if known

If an employee learns of a situation that he feels may warrant evacuation and has not been notified by corporate management, the employee should attempt to contact the corporate lead person or his assistant and other fellow employees. If the employee fails to contact anyone, the employee should contact the U.S. embassy for further information.

Locate all corporate and necessary personnel to advise them of the situation (consider "calling trees" or "cascades" providing designated employees with names/numbers to be called). Check all sources of information.

Evacuation Method(s)

The evacuation method will depend on the threat or crisis. If evacuation of the host country were necessary, the most expeditious means would be determined by the corporate lead person. The corporate lead person will work with whomever or whatever agencies are necessary to determine the best evacuation method available, and the means of transportation (protective detail) to get there.

One means of evacuation/arranging evacuation may be International SOS.

Evacuation Assembly

The corporate lead person will determine the assembly site(s). This decision will depend on the nature, severity, and location of the threat. The assembly site could be someone's house, the project office, or any other predetermined or *ad hoc* location(s). The staging areas will depend upon the safety of the route to the destination and the mode of transportation available.

Evacuation Destination

The corporate lead person, depending on the nature of the emergency, will determine the evacuation destination.

Evacuation Time

This will be determined largely by the nature of the emergency and how it affects the staging sites, evacuation routes, flight schedules, etc. If there is a choice, the time should be mid to late morning, or may be dependent upon arrival times at borders if able to take a land route out.

Personnel Evacuation Accountability

The corporate lead person or his designated representative will maintain a roster to ensure that all personnel and dependents are accounted for and their locations are determined and verified. It will be the responsibility of the lead person or his designated representative to ensure that this roster is kept current and all personnel are accounted for at all times during the declared emergency. Ensure that your designated lifeline or his or her alternate in the home office is kept informed of the current situation and is made aware of any problems or incidents involving your professionals or their family members.

Return

Return to the site/office/area will be determined and approved by the corporate senior management/operational security manager after consultation with all corporate personnel involved, U.S. government officials, or U.S. military and security agencies.

Stand Fast

In some circumstances the security status may go from bad to worse very quickly. In such cases, and due to the history of roving violent gangs, mobs, rallies, and protests, it may be better to remain in the following locations:

Stand fast—hotel/lodging: It may be determined that the best location for safety, given the potential for attack while en route to other destinations, may be the hotel/lodging point.

Stand fast—job site: It may be determined that the safest place to take refuge is the job site.

Stand fast—alternate locations: Alternative locations for safety may be identified, keeping in mind safe transportation means and routes.

DEPARTURE KITS ("GO BAGS")

The departure kit is a collection of items that should always be available for use in an emergency situation. The kit should be in two parts: Part 1 consists of sustenance items and equipment, and Part 2 of a packet of vital personal papers and documents and a departure kit checklist. The kit should be checked periodically for completeness and currentness. It should be properly tagged for identification in a state of complete readiness at the outset of phase II (limited action).

Part 1: Sustenance Items and Equipment

- Without hoarding, maintain a reasonable supply (5–7 days) of food, water, and fuel. If you have a personal or company automobile, be sure it is ready for immediate use. Maintain a full fuel tank and a reasonable supply of spares and other extras as may be necessary. Also, periodically check oil, water, and tires.
- Maintain a family-size (if applicable, otherwise individual) first aid kit and an adequate supply of necessary prescription medicine(s). Have a flashlight with fresh batteries or candles. Keep a supply of matches, preferably waterproof and windproof.
- Keep a small battery-operated shortwave radio with fresh batteries. Monitor the local news media, Voice of America, and the British Broadcasting Company closely, if available, for relevant announcements from the local government or the U.S. embassy. The embassies will be closely monitoring any situation and will provide further information to the liaison contact person.
- Have one blanket and sleeping bag for each family member. Do not carry baggage that exceeds 66 pounds of clothing and personal effects of the individual. (This weight is the absolute maximum that will be permitted on a U.S. government–sponsored evacuation aircraft.)
- Pets are frequently not allowed in the emergency evacuation process. Consequently, owners need to be sure that they make appropriate arrangements.
- Do not include firearms, any other weapons, or liquor in the kit.
- Keep a supply of street and road maps of the metropolitan and rural areas.
- Corporate assigned laptops may be helpful in communication after arrival at the destination.

Note: Laptops are a favorite item for thieves. They will attract robbers. Keep them hidden or locked in a car trunk or out of sight!

Part 2: Vital Personal Papers and Documents

- Current passports for all members of the family.
- Sufficient cash in U.S. dollars, local currency, and traveler's checks should be a regular part of your kit to cover family incidental expenses for at least 3 days of travel (1 week of stand fast). Include sufficient currency in small denominations to take care of incidental expenses while en route to a safe haven.
- Up-to-date international certificates of vaccination.
- Current inventory of household effects.
- All host country identification papers.
- Essential personal papers (birth certificates, marriage license, telephone or address books, etc.).
- Copies of your U.S. federal income tax return, if it has not already been sent to a safe place of record.
- Carry mobile phones if available and system is working.
- Expensive jewelry, if any.
- A blank company expense statement to keep track of expenses.

Note: Have copies of all sensitive documents, such as passports and the back of any credit cards used in the event documents are lost, stolen, or seized. For credit cards, the number to call is located on the back of the card.

APPENDIX B: GENERAL STRIKE/PROTEST OVERVIEW

POSSIBLE PROTEST ACTIVITIES

1. Organizers/representatives will instruct participants on protest conduct.
   - Participants will be "coached" to employees, returning bargaining unit employees, and delivery personnel.
2. Vehicular property damage and obstruction of vehicles should be anticipated.
   - Methods of damage will include roadway nails, welded spike tire shredders, glass and car scratching, spray painting, tire cutting, denting and thrown objects, spitting on vehicles, throwing sugar water on vehicles, and throwing flammable liquids.
   - Participants will attempt to block ingress and egress by walking or standing in front of vehicles entering or exiting facilities.
   - Participants will often feign injuries by brushing against or leaning on vehicles entering or exiting the facilities.
   - Vehicles belonging to unpopular employees and company vehicles will be targeted.
3. Use of intoxicants may occur in the protestors' vehicles and nearby at night. The discharging of firearms during the night may take place. Persons crossing into the property will be targeted for obscenities and challenged to engage in violence.
   - The period of late evening and early morning presents the greatest risk of harassing behavior.
4. Bomb threats may be directed at the company. Suspicious packages must be reported to law enforcement.
5. Management or other employees may receive telephone threats.
6. Security personnel will be harassed.

7. The initial protest activities are similar to a rowdy party. Protestors may exhibit an indestructible attitude, which has been instigated by union representatives.

8. Violence-prone protestors often are able to provoke normally calm employees. These individuals are generally hard-core protestors and are more prone to violence.

9. Activities described as being directed against employees will also be focused upon vendors or contractors attempting ingress or egress.

10. The initial protest euphoria will generally subside in a few weeks.

PROTEST SECURITY MANAGEMENT

Security will coordinate law enforcement liaison, documentation of protest activities and illegal activity, executive protection, incident reporting, and contract security services, and will conduct security awareness training for employees.

PROTEST DOCUMENTATION

1. In order to adequately document violations of local laws, it is imperative that trained personnel capable of using video and still photography be available to respond to locations for the purpose of documenting any violations or destruction of property.
   - Camcorders have proven to be the preferred method of documenting protest activities. This is due to their mobility and flexibility. Camcorders record the language and threats used as well as the act.

2. Objectives of protest documentation:
   - Prosecution of criminal violators.
   - Develop and preserve evidence of ongoing union misconduct, thus enabling the company to obtain legal assistance limiting the activities of protestors.
   - Develop and preserve evidence of protest misconduct.
   - Document activities of company employees and guards. Protestors will often make false claims of assault, harassment, etc., toward company employees, agents, and customers.

- Serve as a preventative tool in that individuals prone to commit illegal acts are more reluctant to do so when they are aware they are being filmed.

SECURITY AWARENESS

1. Management must be informed of anticipated protest activities and advised accordingly of security requirements and operational charges.
2. Employees must be instructed as to their expected conduct, incident reporting, procedures, and documentation measures.
3. Physical security enhancements must be enacted at residences of management members and may include:

  - Improving lighting, including motion lighting
  - Using deadbolt locks on doors with a minimum 1½-inch throw
  - Securing windows by drilling and pinning sashes or installing security locks
  - Using timer lights when away from the residence
  - Parking vehicles inside of garages
  - Testing or installing alarm systems, including alarm contacts on all doors and windows (or motion detectors within windows)
  - Having duress code emergency notification button on alarm panel
  - Having a battery backup of the alarm system
  - Burying or shielding telephone line or installing line loss alarm notification
  - Having caller ID for telephones
  - Using telephone recorder and allowing the recorder to answer the telephone
  - Programming speed dial "911" into telephones
  - Having a cellular telephone for home telephone backup and vehicle assistance
  - Varying routes to work
  - Taking security measures if persons believe they are being followed
  - Advising trusted neighbors to watch residence
  - Requesting law enforcement patrol

- Surveying exterior of the home before exiting vehicle to enter home or entering the vehicle
- Reporting any unusual or suspicious activities to law enforcement and security manager immediately

PROTEST PROCEDURES

Protest Command Center (PCC)

The protest command center will be based at the main office, telephone number 5555555/backup number 5555555, and will be staffed effective p.m./a.m. should a protest take place. The PCC will be staffed 24 hours a day. Security management will be provided by XXX Security, off-duty police officers, and XXXXX.

Chain of Command

During a protest it is critical that serious matters be dealt with effectively and quickly. The PCC should be contacted if a member of management cannot be located. Every officer, department, regional, area, or branch manager must be made available to be reached during this labor situation.

"Stalled" Vehicles, Barricades

In the event that strikers attempt to block ingress/egress from the facility by placing vehicles or objects at entrances, the following measures should be taken:

1. Video documentation.
2. Notification of police department and request that the vehicles, objects be towed/moved.
3. If there is no police response to towing/removal request, and with company management approval, towing companies may be contacted.

Violent or Criminal Acts

1. Every effort will be made to document such activity with camcorders while ensuring the following sequence is initiated:
    a. Removing company employees to area of safety if necessary
    b. Notifying police, fire, and emergency medical response, if
        required, and ensuring that police reports are made of incidents
    c. Preserving evidence (i.e., recovered nails, spikes, statements,
        etc.) and maintaining chain of custody
    d. Obtaining written statements from victims and witnesses
    e. Obtaining a police report
    f. Notifying company management of the incident
    g. Logging the sequence of events/response in daily log book

Key Facility Contacts

Home:
Mobile:
Bus:

ATTACHMENT A

Management and Staff Address and Phone Numbers

Local Maps

PREPARATORY ACTIVITIES

1. Government/law enforcement liaison to determine availability of parking areas; use of off-duty police officers, to advise prosecutors office; emergency responders. Local law enforcement must be continually updated as to developments that may affect the duration, length, or extent of the protest.
2. Mobile lighting unit(s) or ability to obtain units.
3. Property lines must be established and legally defensible (clearly marked with spray paint on paved surfaces and in the presence of law enforcement), and use snow fence on paved and other areas for lines of court-ordered demarcation, if necessary. Place "PRIVATE PROPERTY—NO TRESPASSING" signs along the fence line and front of the building(s).
4. Repairs of fence line by restrapping and replacing three-strand barbed wire.
5. Location of management vehicle parking spot—temporary fencing to "box in" vehicles. This will be a shuttle pickup point.
6. Location of 15-passenger van(s).

ATTACHMENT B

Rentals Available

Vans:

Cots:

---

7. It is recommended that locks to all critical operational and equipment areas be rekeyed with high-security locks, and maintained continuously locked at all times. These areas include telephone rooms, computer rooms, engineering and equipment areas, human resources records, and gate locks. All gates must be secured to eliminate gaps. All exterior doors with key hardware must be rekeyed. If time allows, all exterior doors should be equipped with alarm contacts. Overhead doors must be padlocked when not in use. Keys must be checked out, controlled, and audited.

8. Closed-circuit television cameras and monitors must be maintained or improved for optimum performance. Videotapes of activities prior to and during the strike must be collected and maintained in a secure location by management. Cameras should be added to sensitive areas.

9. Use ¾-inch plywood cutouts for front windows (or Plexiglas) to protect windows from projectiles.

10. Awareness training for management and administrative employees.

11. Add 500- or 1,000-watt lighting near main gate.

12. Determine amount of work in process at deadline.

13. Determine production capacity and schedule with available workforce.

14. Determine alternative producers to assist with production to meet needs of sales.

15. Maintenance concerns.

EMERGENCY PLANNING FOR BOMB THREAT

The following information is designed to indicate the required steps and assistance needed in the event of emergencies taking place at the plant/facility.

- Caller ID for main switchboard if available.
- Telephones used for receiving calls must be equipped with recording equipment. Check on tracing capability with phone provider.

1. Bomb threat called in—business hours:
   - Switchboard operator (or employee taking calls) fills out "Bomb Threat Checklist" form (see Appendix D).
   - Operator activates tape recorder.
   - Call recipient notifies management.

- Operator or recipient notifies security director.
- Security director contacts police department 911 and requests a bomb dog be dispatched and directs responders.
- Security director contacts fire department to stand by.
- Security director contacts FBI/LEGAT/RSO office.
- Security director initiates call trace procedures.
- Security director meets with management in command center.
- Security director collects "Bomb Threat Checklist" form and cassette tape to provide to law enforcement.
- If decision is made to search/evacuate the facility, security personnel assist in process, interior secured.
- Security officers hold all incoming traffic.
- Building exterior is searched and secured.
- Security director coordinates with management and law enforcement on issuing "all clear" and reoccupying facility.
- Security director and management meet in command center upon reoccupying facility.

2. Bomb threat called in—after hours (building occupied):
- Call recipient completes "Bomb Threat Checklist" form and notifies security personnel/director.
- Security director contacts police department 911 and requests a bomb dog be dispatched and directs responders.
- Security director contacts fire department to stand by.
- Security director contacts FBI/LEGAT/RSO office.
- Security director initiates call trace procedures.
- Security director contacts designated member of management (if not on site) and meets with management in command center.
- Security director collects "Bomb Threat Checklist" and cassette in order to provide to law enforcement.
- If decision is made to search/evacuate, security personnel assist and staff command center, interior secured.
- Security officers hold all incoming traffic.
- Security personnel search and secure building exterior.
- Security director coordinates with management and law enforcement on issuing "all clear" and reoccupying facility.
- Security director and management meet in command center.

3. Bomb threat called in—after hours (facility unoccupied):
- Call recipient completes "Bomb Threat Checklist" form and notifies security director.

- Security director/personnel pages facility by dialing _____ and repeats three times, "May I have your attention please, please proceed to _____." Security director and personnel respond to move persons to _____.
- Security director contacts police department 911 and requests a bomb dog be dispatched and directs responders.
- Security director initiates call trace procedures.

PROTEST REQUIREMENTS

1. Travel and outside purchases: General and field travel as well as outside purchases should be eliminated or minimized. Equipment deliveries should be delayed if possible.
2. Vendors/deliveries/pickups: Provision will be made for accessing vendors or deliveries and pickups in the facility. Prior notice must be given to vendors when possible to describe the labor situation and expected conduct of delivery or pickup personnel. Notify trash haulers and delivery services such as UPS and Fed Ex.
3. Construction projects: Provision will be made for accessing construction personnel into the facility only if necessary.
4. The press should be politely directed to contact Mr. Jones, plant/facility manager. If asked for a statement, the standard reply will be, "You will need to speak with Mr. Jones."
5. Mr. Jones, plant/facility manager, must approve all communications.
6. Slow time: Utilize this time for training, catching up on projects, etc.
7. Payroll: Paychecks will be mailed to those not reporting to work due to the protest.
8. End of protest modifications: Only Mr. Jones, plant/facility manager, may give the official notice at the end of the protest or shutdown. Recall procedures will be issued by the appropriate officer.

IMPLEMENTING PROTEST RESPONSE TEAM

1. a. Telephone call to team members to meet at the administration building at 5:00 a.m.
   b. Telephone call to team members to meet at transportation pickup point.

2. Team discusses operations and deployment, equipment disbursed.
3. Security team deploys and takes up positions.
4. Access control and monitoring procedures initiated.
5. Transportation begins.

STRIKE SECURITY

Management: Mr. X, security director, Company, Inc., will provide security management during the protest.

- Business
- Cell

Mr. X will provide for security services in the event of a protest.

Contracted provider during protest: Super Security Services. Estimated cost for contracted security services: $20,000 per week, for a team of five officers and one lead person per 24-hour period (for 7 days).

If one or two off-duty officers could be utilized, this will cut the cost down a little and possibly reduce the number of officers by one per shift.

Once we have injunctive relief we would be able to reduce officers.

Current Security Services

Excellent Security Services are the current providers of security service at this facility. Mr. David Smith is operations manager for Excellent.

- Business
- Cell

SECURITY FUNCTIONS AND REQUIREMENTS

1. **Security management and officers.** Will coordinate their presence with company management. The responsibilities of security officers will include:
   a. Ensuring access control responsibilities are followed and maintained
   b. Protection of employees and assets

   c. Coordinating emergency response and incident response procedures

   d. Recording, documentation, and investigation of incidents and accidents

   e. Law enforcement liaison

   f. Supervision of contract security force

2. **Contract security officer requirements.** The following information describes the coverage required for security personnel at the plant. Super Security will be utilized for main gate coverage and perimeter patrol with:

   - Two officers for the main gate (initially)
   - Three officers for the interior perimeter
   - One officer for shuttle driving and backup
   - One officer for parking pickup location (may use off-duty police)
   - One officer for residence patrol (may be contract security officer)

3. **Safety and security—Mr. X.**

   a. Notify Super Security Company, giving 24 hours advance notice.

   b. Notify local police department: nonemergency number 555555.

   c. Notify local fire department—Mr. Y, at 555555.

   - Contact should be made with these agencies prior to any expected protest. A primary contact should be established with company safety coordinator and Mr. X.
   - Establish a method for quick identification of vehicles and owners through license number verification (security services).

4. **Communications—Ms. Smith.**

   a. Safety coordinator will ensure that any radio or cell phone communications requirements during the protest are met.

   b. He or she will also establish contact with telephone service provider to ensure that our lines are protected and secure, and coordinate with the phone company to provide tracing services for harassing phone calls at plant or managers' homes. Recorders should be placed on those phones through which calls will be routed.

LEGAL

As the need for legal counsel arises, corporate legal, Mr. T, 5555555, would be the plant's resource.

- Company legal counsel will make contact with local prosecutor. If misconduct is evident, it is the management's intent to bring charges.
- Need to develop procedure or policy for disciplinary action against employees engaged in protest misconduct.
- Legal counsel must give opinion on property line boundaries where protestors can form areas of protest lines.

PLANT ACCESS AND CONTROL

Access Control Identification

1. A list must be prepared indicating the names of those persons to be picked up to ride the shuttle vehicle. As each employee enters the shuttle, his or her name must be checked off.
2. Employees will be met at the shuttle vehicle by a security representative, who will request that identification be produced prior to employees boarding. (This may be waived if no replacements are transported.)
3. A security representative will accompany the employees to and from the facility. Boarding procedures will be repeated at the plant prior to reboarding for transport to the pickup locations.
4. Departure and loading schedules must be established and strictly maintained.
5. Carpooling is strongly recommended to off-site parking.

Access Control—Employees

1. Shuttle vehicle will pick up employees at designated site and drive to the facility. Shuttle will enter the main gate. The gate will remain closed until the shuttle approaches. Radio communication from the shuttle will alert security personnel of their arrival. (Depending on the situation, alternative gate may be used.)
2. The gate will remain open only long enough to allow shuttle vehicle ingress and egress.

3. Employees will disembark and load at side entrance away from view of protestors. All employees will enter the facility through the north maintenance door to the training room. The employees will then proceed through training room to the maintenance employee locker room. The employees will exit the maintenance employee locker room into the east hallway. The employees will then proceed to the second floor of the facility by utilizing the central staircase.
4. Employees will be required to wear identification badges while on company property.
5. Access into restricted or rekeyed areas will require issuance of numbered keys to authorized employees. Key audit procedures must be maintained.

Entering and Exiting the Facility/Employment Requirements

1. All vehicles must enter and exit the employee parking lot through the main gate entrance.
2. Employees driving into the lot must keep their windows rolled up and doors locked.
3. Employees must not stop near the protest line while entering or exiting the parking lot.
4. Employees are prohibited from bringing alcoholic beverages or controlled substances onto company property.
5. Employees are prohibited from bringing firearms or other weapons onto company property.
6. Employees must wait inside of their vehicles until the shuttle van picks up employees for transportation, and await transportation from the plant to the parking lot.
7. Employees must not speak to or engage in any harassment directed toward protestors. Such harassment includes:

   - Use of profanity
   - Obscene gestures
   - Threats or taunting of any manner

8. Employees who engage in threatening or taunting or any unacceptable behavior will be subject to termination.
9. Employees must report any harassment or threats they receive.
10. Employees not adhering to any of the above requirements may be subject to termination.

Access Control—Visitors, Vendors, Deliveries

1. Upon arrival at the main gate or designated gate, visitors or vendors will be required to wait while the contact is notified.
2. Once approval is granted, the name, company, time, and vehicle description must be recorded.
3. Prior notice provided to security of the person/visitor arriving will facilitate a quicker entry.
4. Any visitor, vendor, or delivery person granted entry must be met and escorted while on company property.
5. The employee authorizing the visitor must notify security officers when the visitor is exiting the property.
6. The exit time must be recorded.
7. Vendors doing business with the company on a routine basis must be advised of the situation and their expected conduct.

SAFETY TIPS

Unusual activity must be reported to your local police departments. Unusual activity would include:

- Known or strange cars driving past your residence or parking outside your residence
- Known or strange persons walking past or loitering at your residence
- Encounters with strange or known persons at public places, such as grocery stores, malls, etc., where threats are made
- Strange or obscene/threatening/harassing telephone calls to your residence or relatives
- Receiving strange packages or letters/harassing and threatening letters.

Any protestor who engages in any harassing/threatening/abusive/destructive/intimidating behavior perpetrated upon any employee or vendor of the company living in any city is engaging in criminal activity.

After you have notified law enforcement, contact any investigator on duty to report the incident. Do not talk about the protest with persons in public places. Do not talk to protestors.

If you are questioned about your employment with the company or about the protest, consider this an attempt to harass or threaten you and walk away, get out of the situation. Avoid places where protestors are known to congregate or frequent. Do not wear apparel that indicates you are employed with the company.

If your vehicle is followed by persons you believe to be protestors, utilize a cellular telephone to contact the police department. Obtain the license number and vehicle description if you may do so without jeopardizing your safety. Drive to your police department while the vehicle is following you, or drive into a public place such as a fire station, drive-through bank, fast food restaurant, etc., and request that law enforcement be contacted to report the incident.

Keep doors and windows locked.

When you drive into the parking lot at the shuttle pickup location, you will park along the back side of the lot. You will then wait alongside your car while a company shuttle vehicle picks you up to take you to the plant. At the conclusion of your shift you will be picked up and driven back to your car.

When you drive into or out of the lot, you must keep your windows up and your doors locked. Do not stop to talk to any protestors while you are driving into or out of the lot.

You must not engage in any conversation with protestors at any time. You must not make any obscene or threatening gestures toward any protestors at any time.

MISCELLANEOUS

Administration

Arrange for:

- Food supply
- Rental vehicles
- Notification of lessors, vendors, and city and government agencies
- Data security
- Surveillance cameras
- Recorders for switchboards

Sales and Traffic

- Notify regional offices, product managers, and transportation dispatchers that protest is in progress.
- If possibility of protest is evident, promote product deliveries prior to work stoppage.
- Notify common carriers.

Transportation

Carpooling is strongly recommended to off-site parking. Supplies and equipment for providing two meals per shift per employee will be secured. These items will be located in the _____.

Lodging and meals for out-point employees/representatives will be provided if needed. Approximate cost of these items is estimated to be $85.00 per day per person.

Personnel

In the event that a protest is evident, it is necessary to have up-to-date information on all employees. It is also necessary to have employment status for each employee, i.e., on sick leave, occupational injury, etc. The personnel office is responsible for:

- Information dealing with issuance of pay
- Information dealing with benefits, insurance, and other personnel issues

Public Relations

The purpose of such is to present the company's side of the story, to inform the public and our employees of the situation and what the issues are.

- It is necessary to develop a fact sheet—to include plant/facility history and impact on the community.
- Meet with employees prior to protest to make sure they are fully informed about the company's position.
- May consider holding a preprotest meeting with local press. The purpose is to educate and inform them about the company and to explain the company's position.

- A record (copy) will be kept of all interviews, newspaper articles, TV spots, etc., especially those that involve employees or any outside groups.
- All communications will be released through plant/facility manager.

ATTACHMENT C

Date

Vendor XYZ

City

Dear Vendor:

The XXX facility is experiencing a protest and protestors are on site. The facility/plant will/will not remain in operation and will/will not be accepting normal deliveries/services. Normal operations will/will not remain in effect.

Your contact for all orders and deliveries will be _____. This employee should be the only person who requests deliveries and services.

During the protest, it will be necessary to bring your vehicles and employees into the facility using the main vehicle gate located at the northeast corner of the facility, off of _____ Road. We would request that the front door of the facility not be used, and that all pedestrian entry be halted until further notice. All vendors are asked to enter the plant by driving into the facility through the main gate. Parking will be in the rear of the building.

We will be providing security at this gate, and you should advise your employees to not engage in any conversations, arguments, etc., with those protesting. We will process your vehicles and employees into the gate, and will assist them in exiting. It is important that your employees drive up to the main gate when they arrive and remain in their vehicles until they are processed and drive into the area. A uniformed security officer from _____ will be at the gate and will assist you in entering and exiting the facility.

We would ask that whenever possible you contact the plant in advance of your arrival and give an approximate time you will be arriving. We would like to know the name of the driver or employee who will be arriving. Please contact _____ with this information.

If your company or any of your employees experience any problems associated with the protest, please contact _____. Please advise if your company or any employees experience any protests, threats, harassment, vandalism, or damage to company or personal property when entering the facility, your property, or at other locations. Such incidents should also be reported to law enforcement.

We will keep you apprised of any further developments and appreciate your cooperation during this situation. Please contact _____ should you have any further questions.

(Name of company contact)

Telephone

ATTACHMENT D

Determination of Work in Process

1. Approximate amount of widgets on hand:
   a. 70,000 lb whole sprockets
   b. 15,000 lb partial sprockets
   c. 42,000 lb parts
2. Approximate amount of toggles on hand to assemble:
   a. 525,000 lb, or 2 days of assembling

ATTACHMENT E

Operations

Based on one 8- to 10–hour shift:

1. What could be produced?
2. How much could be produced?
3. How many people would it take?
4. Who would do what job?

Management employees available to perform production jobs:

Smith
Jones
Barker
Baker

Types and sizes of products that may be produced:
Projected schedule:

Monday—assemble
Tuesday—build
Wednesday—ship
Thursday—reassemble
Friday–Saturday—shipping parts

Packing schedule:

Wednesday—either 10# and 35# or 12.5# and 28.5#
Saturday—either 10# and 35# or 12.5# and 28.5#

Work positions in assembly:

Injector feeder—
Injector service person—
Tumbler operator—
FP inspection line: #1—
                          #2—

Receiving—
Maintenance—

Production capability if 50 employees show up:

10 people—run the RTE line
20 people—grind and mix and (1) HOT machine
30 people—run the entire plant for one shift except the BIG line, miscellaneous

Additional copies of all operating procedures and guidelines will be available in the work areas.

ATTACHMENT F

Alternate Producers

Sister facility could assume most of our slicing log volume.

Any other business could be assumed by partner companies.

APPENDIX C: BOMB THREAT PROCEDURES

WHEN TELEPHONE CALL IS RECEIVED

1. Keep the caller on the line as long as possible. The bomb threat caller is the best source of information about the bomb. Ask him or her to repeat the message. Write down every word spoken by the caller.
2. If the caller does not indicate the location of the bomb, or the time for detonation of a bomb, ask him or her for this information.
3. Inform the caller that the building is occupied, and that the detonation of a bomb could result in the death or serious injury of innocent persons.
4. Pay particular attention to background noises, such as motors running, music playing, or any other noise that may provide a clue to the location of the caller.
5. Listen closely to the voice (male/female), voice quality (calm/ excited), accents, or speech impediments.
6. Complete the "Bomb Threat Checklist" (see Appendix D) and contact security.
7. Respond as soon as possible to the conference room for interview by _____.

WHEN WRITTEN THREAT IS RECEIVED OR SUSPICIOUS PACKAGE ARRIVES

1. Notify security.
2. Save all materials, including the envelope or container. Further handling must be avoided.

If a suspicious package is observed, it must not be moved or touched.

SWITCHBOARD OPERATOR

1. Telephone call is received.
2. Activates tape recorder.
3. Completes "Bomb Threat Checklist" and calls security.

FIRST RESPONSE

1. Telephone call received.
2. Recipient completes "Bomb Threat Checklist" form and calls security.
3. Security notifies member of management.
4. Make necessary emergency contacts.
5. Management meets call recipient in conference room.
6. Management decides upon actions to be taken.

EVALUATION OF CALL

1. Employee receiving call and member(s) of management will gather immediately in the conference room adjacent to main office.
2. The "Bomb Threat Checklist" will be reviewed.
3. Member of management will determine the appropriate response to the call based upon the following factors:

   - Adult caller (capability)
   - Specific time of detonation stated (time to search or evaluate further)
   - Specific location of bomb stated (caller knows building layout)
   - Reason for call or demand stated (motive)
   - Seriousness of caller when making threat (credibility)
   - Caller identified self or group

   If the caller states that the time to detonation is 30 minutes or less, and has indicated a specific location of the bomb and the reason for placing the device, evacuation must proceed immediately.

   If the answers are no to the factors indicated, the caller's comments must be evaluated and investigation/search must commence.

   In either case, the police must be contacted immediately.

CHAIN OF COMMAND

In the absence of plant manager, a designated member of management will authorize and conduct the evacuation procedure.

Command center: For evaluation of call or threat, conference room next to main office. If a search is initiated, the _____ becomes the command center.

Communication means: During the search, radios must be turned off. Telephones or the paging system must be used.

Evacuation plan and team: As indicated, employees will utilize routes and assemble at designated collection points. Team members assist evacuation.

Search teams: Designated members of management and volunteers.

Areas to be searched: To be designated by search team.

Items required: Flashlights, stickers or electrical tape, blueprints of facility, roster of phone numbers, including home phone numbers.

Evacuation Procedures

Responsibility	Action
Investigators	Investigates and confers regarding threat
	Initiates emergency contacts
Officers	Directs emergency responders
	Holds and stages all vehicle and pedestrian traffic with the exception of emergency responders
Evacuation team	Using voice commands, evacuate all employees to the designated parking area
	Position to ensure a safe exiting and reentering of the facility
	"Sweeps" the area to ensure all are accounted for, "head count" at collection area, and uses phone to advise the command center when evacuation completed
Search team	Conduct search beginning with most accessible areas
	Use phone to communicate and advise when search completed
	Evacuate no later than 15 minutes prior to detonation time
	Assemble in preassigned areas and report to team captain
All employees, visitors, vendors	Leave building through exits as designated by evacuation team
	Wait for further instructions
Incoming visitors, vendors	Held at front gate area
	Wait for further instructions

Maintenance employees	Shut off main gas valve and fuel lines at main valve
	Ensure fire system is operational
	Search areas such as HVAC or other equipment locations
	Shut down appropriate equipment
	Evacuate with search teams
	Do not use radios
Member of management	Makes decision to evacuate
	Remain while building is occupied
	Receives updates on search and evacuation teams

INSTRUCTIONAL CHECKLIST: SEARCH PROCEDURES

The following search technique is based on the use of a two-person searching team. There are many minor variations possible in searching an area. The following contains only the basic techniques.

When the two-person search team enters the area to be searched, they should first move to various parts of the area and stand quietly with their eyes closed and listen for a clockwork device. Frequently, a clockwork mechanism can be quickly detected without the use of special equipment. Even if no clockwork mechanism is detected, the team is now aware of the background noise level within the area itself.

Background noise or transferred sound is always disturbing during a building search. If a ticking sound is heard but cannot be located, one might become unnerved. The ticking sound may come from an unbalanced air conditioner fan several floors away, or from a dripping sink down the hall. Sound will transfer through air conditioning ducts, along water pipes, and through walls. Background noise may also include outside traffic sounds, rain, and wind.

The individual in charge of the area searching team should look around the area and determine how it is to be divided for searching and to what height the first searching sweep should extend. The first searching sweep will cover all items resting on the floor up to the selected height.

The area should be divided into two virtually equal parts. The equal division should be based on the number and type of objects to be searched and not on the size of the area. An imaginary line is then drawn between two objects and understood by both team members.

First Area Searching Sweep

Look at the furniture or objects in the area and determine the average height of the majority of items resting on the floor. In an average room, this height usually includes table or desktops and chair backs. The first searching height usually covers the items in the area up to hip height.

After the area has been divided and a searching height has been selected, both individuals go to one end of the area division line and start from a back-to-back position. This is the starting point, and the same point will be used on each successive searching sweep. Each person now starts searching his or her way around the area, working toward the other person, checking all items resting on the floor around the wall area of a room. When the two individuals meet, they will have completed a perimeter sweep. They should then work together and check all items in the middle of the area up to the selected hip height, including the floor under rugs or mats. This first searching sweep should also include those items that may be mounted on or in walls, such as air conditioning ducts, baseboard heaters, and built-in wall bookcases, if these fixtures are below hip height.

The first searching sweep usually consumes the most time and effort. During all the searching sweeps, electronic or medical stethoscopes might be used on walls, furniture items, and floors.

Second Area Searching Sweep

The individual in charge again looks at the furniture or objects in the area and determines the height of the second searching sweep.

This height is usually from the hip to the chin or top of the head. The two persons return to the starting point and repeat the searching technique at the second selected searching height. This sweep usually covers pictures hanging on the walls, built-in bookcases, and tall table lamps.

Third Area Searching Sweep

When the second searching sweep is completed, the person in charge again determines the next searching height, usually from the chin or top of head up to the ceiling. The third sweep is then made. This sweep usually covers high mounted air conditioning ducts and hanging light fixtures.

Fourth Area Searching Sweep

If the area has a false or suspended ceiling, the fourth sweep involves investigation of this area. Check flush or ceiling-mounted light fixtures, air conditioning or ventilation ducts, sound or speaker systems, electrical wiring, and structural frame members.

Utilize a sign or agreed upon marking (such as a piece of green duct tape) to indicate that a room or area has been searched. A piece of tape should be placed on the floor across the entries to searched areas, or on the doorjamb approximately 2 feet above floor level.

The area searching technique can be expanded. The same basic technique can be applied to search any area.

In conclusion, the following steps should be taken in a search for an explosive device:

1. Divide the area and select a search height.
2. Start from the bottom and work up.
3. Start back-to-back and work toward each other.
4. Go around the walls and proceed toward the center of the area being searched.

ACTION CHECKLIST: SUSPICIOUS OBJECT LOCATED

It is imperative that personnel involved in a search be instructed that their only mission is to search for and report suspicious objects. Under no circumstances should anyone move, jar, or touch a suspicious object or anything attached to it. The removal or disarming of a bomb must be left to the professionals in the bomb and arson squad.

When a suspicious object is discovered, report the location and an accurate description of the object to the search team captain. The team captain should relay this information immediately to the emergency control center, which will notify the police officer in charge. Members of the search teams locating the device should be assigned to meet the bombing and arson squad officers and escort them to the scene.

In the meantime, evacuation team members should create clear zones of at least 300-foot radius around the suspicious object, and on the floors immediately above and below the object.

The decision to evacuate or not should then be made based upon information provided by the police officers on the scene.

ACTION CHECKLIST: DISARMAMENT OR REMOVAL

It is imperative that personnel involved in the search teams be instructed that their only mission is to search for and report suspicious objects. Under no circumstances should anyone move, jar, or touch a suspicious object or anything attached to it. Removal or disarming of a bomb must be left to highly trained professionals in explosive ordinance disposal. When a suspicious object is discovered, the following procedures must be followed:

1. Report the location and an accurate description of the object to the police and fire departments. Responding security officers should be met and escorted to the scene by an assigned search team member.
2. Identify the danger area, and block off a clear zone of at least 300-foot radius around it, including floors above and below the object.
3. Evacuate the building.
4. Do not permit reentry into the building until the device has been removed/disarmed, and the police bomb and arson unit has declared the building safe for reentry.

Report *any* unusual, suspicious packages received via mail or courier to law enforcement.

Reoccupation

Responsibility	Action
Member of management	Makes decision to reoccupy with input from emergency responders
	Enters building first and occupies conference room adjacent to main office
	Receives report from all involved team members
Investigator	Second person to enter the facility to ensure areas are secure and report to conference room
	Reassumes post and ensures area is secure
Evacuation team	Enters facility in preparation of assisting employees entering building
Search team	Enters facility in preparation of assisting employees entering building
All employees, visitors, vendors	Allowed to continue their activities
Maintenance employees	Power up all equipment

THREATENING PHONE CALL FORM

Date threat received: _____

Time: _____

Address threatened: _____

Phone number received from: _____

Phone number received on: _____

Be calm and courteous. Listen carefully. Don't interrupt. Turn on the tape recorder.

Write down exactly what the caller says. Ask the caller to repeat if necessary. Ask the following questions that apply. Use the back if needed.

Caller's name and address? _____

_____

Why is he or she upset? _____

_____

Where is the bomb located? _____

_____

When will the bomb explode? _____

_____

What kind of bomb is it? _____

_____

Why was the bomb placed here? _____

_____

What will cause it to explode? _____

_____

What does it look like? _____

_____

Mark all that apply.

Sex: ☐ M   ☐ F

Approximate age: _____

Race: ☐ B   ☐ W   ☐ O

Attitude:

☐ Angry	☐ Coherent	☐ Crying	☐ Excited
☐ Irrational	☐ Righteous	☐ Calm	☐ Incoherent
☐ Disgusted	☐ Intoxicated	☐ Laughing	

Speech:

- ☐ Accent/foreign ☐ Fast   ☐ Slow   ☐ Distinct
                     ☐ Distorted ☐ Deep breathing
- ☐ Accent/not local ☐ Loud   ☐ Soft   ☐ Familiar
- ☐ Nasal   ☐ Stutter   ☐ Accent/local   ☐ Pitch high
- ☐ Pitch low   ☐ Lisp   ☐ Raspy

Background noises:

- ☐ Airplanes ☐ Car motor ☐ Noisy   ☐ Static
- ☐ Factory   ☐ Animals   ☐ Dishes ☐ PA system
- ☐ Street   ☐ Office   ☐ Booth   ☐ Household
- ☐ Party   ☐ Trains   ☐ Clear   ☐ Music
- ☐ Quiet   ☐ Voices

Language:

☐ Well spoken ☐ Uneducated ☐ Obscene ☐ Reading ☐ Taped

Report call immediately to: Corporate security

Phone number: XXX-XXX-XXXX

Fill out completely, immediately after threat:

Date: _____

Your phone number: _____

Position: _____

Your name: _____

Address: _____

_____

_____

_____

APPENDIX D: SECURITY, SAFETY, AND EVACUATION PLAN

A crisis is defined as *any* incident that can focus negative attention on a company and have an adverse effect on its employees, overall financial condition, relationships with its audiences, and reputation within the marketplace. The purpose of a security and evacuation plan is to provide a systematic approach to managing a security crisis in an organized fashion, without causing a major disruption to normal activities.

This plan is designed to maintain the company's credibility and positive image with all of its identified audiences in the face of adversity.

Our customers, professionals, management, financial supporters, industry peers, and others should all feel we were well organized and handled the emergency in a professional manner. We need to be able to respond very quickly to any type of situation because crises do not pause to allow us to think through the problem.

Documents that are part of the overall plan and must be available for reference include:

- Project/facility-specific data sheet
- Security and evacuation management plan
- Project emergency preparedness plan
- Family emergency notification plan

SECURITY AND EVACUATION PLAN
FIRST-HOUR RESPONSE CHECKLIST

Step 1: Team Leader

☐ Organize your team; establish a command center.

☐ Initiate appropriate countrywide controls if necessary.

☐ Notify the country/senior client representative of the situation.

☐ Make certain that all employees are accounted for.

☐ Ensure telephone and other communications are available and manned throughout the crisis.

☐ Inform local crisis management team to direct requests for information from outside groups to you.

☐ Review crisis support procedures to see if any other crisis plans need to be implemented.

☐ Implement appropriate crisis support procedures
  - Casualty
  - Hostage reporting (kidnapping)
  - Media
  - Other

☐ Determine whether you or other crisis management team members are needed on site.

☐ Advise the team administrator and receptionist how to route calls.

☐ Assess/identify potential spin-off crises.

☐ Notify insurance broker/company.

Step 2: Corporate Security Manager

☐ Contact tactical elements as necessary.

☐ Assess local and country threat conditions.

☐ Ensure evacuation procedures and assets are readily available.

☐ Ensure all communications and vehicles/air transport are available as needed.

DATA SHEET

Team locations

Crisis management command center

 Primary—House/office

 Secondary—House/office

Team leader

 Satellite number:

 Cell phone:

 Alternate

 Satellite number:

 Cell phone:

 or

 Satellite number:

 Cell phone:

 Alternate

 Satellite number:

 Cell phone:

 and

 Satellite number:

 Cell phone:

 Alternate

 Cell phone:

Security manager

 Satellite number:

 Cell phone:

 Alternate

 Satellite number:

 Cell phone:

 Alternate

 Cell phone:

Business management director

 Satellite number:

 Cell phone:

 Alternate

 TBD

CCMT DATA SHEET

SPECIFIC EMERGENCY SERVICES CONTACTS

Hospital: _____

Local ambulance number: _____

U.S. government/private vendor emergency medical evacuation:

  International SOS (www.internationalsos.com)

    Cell phone: 1-215-245-4707

    Account number: _____

    Service member: _____

U.S. government/private vendor government and civilian

  American Red Cross (www.redcross.org)

    1-800-853-2570

GOVERNMENTAL AGENCIES/OFFICES

U.S. regional security office _____ (General number)

U.S. embassy _____ (General number)

U.S. embassy consular section

  Daytime telephone number and extension

  after-hours duty phone

TRANSPORTATION SERVICES—NONMEDICAL

Contact information:

  24-hour crisis hot line

  Airplane charter

CORPORATE SECURITY MANAGER

- Contact tactical elements as necessary.
- Advise security team leader of local and country threat conditions, if any.
- Provide security team leader with recommendation for site/camp evacuation if required.
- Ensure all communications and vehicles/air transport are available as needed.
- Advise security team leader on available support systems, i.e., U.S. government/private vendor.
- Advise other site security managers as necessary.
- Assist with the plan for the recovery of wounded or killed.

SECTION 5: PROJECT EMERGENCY PREPAREDNESS

Emergency Equipment and Supplies

The local crisis management team will verify that these basic supplies are available, as needed, and in proper working order, and mark the locations of emergency equipment on the site map when a map is provided.

From the local crisis management team the project/facility/office manager will identify an emergency supply manager. The emergency supply manager will maintain and control the emergency supplies.

Emergency Equipment and Supplies	Location
20 lb (or two 10 lb) fire extinguisher (A, B, and C classes)	Office and lodging/project
First aid/trauma kits	Office and lodging/project
Personal eye wash	Office
Bloodborne pathogen kit	Office
Emergency food (MREs), water, and fuel to sustain the site/camp for a minimum of 3 days should be stored in a secure location	ESM will control access and maintenance of inventory
Extra fuel—Diesel, benzene	Approved storage area
Flashlights, batteries, maps, compass, etc.	ESM will control access and maintenance of inventory
Additional equipment (specify):	As identified

Basic Guidelines

Keep areas near exits and extinguishers clear.

All trailers/offices must be equipped with smoke detectors and fire extinguishers readily available.

Designate one vehicle as the emergency vehicle; place hospital directions and map inside; keep keys in ignition or readily accessible during field activities.

Inventory and check site emergency equipment and supplies; refer to "Emergency Equipment and Supplies" section.

Ensure every person in the camp/work site has a "bug out" bag packed with essential items, required personal medical items, personal identification documents, and water.

Security managers will establish a warning signal(s) for the site and brief all personnel on the warning signal(s) and actions to take upon hearing the signal.

Security managers will, during periods of heightened threat, brief camp/site personnel on additional security requirements for the site/camp.

Security managers will maintain an up-to-date roster of personnel in the camp/site for use by crisis management team leader in accounting for personnel.

Security managers will establish standard operating procedures for response to different incidents (direct and indirect fire, incidents during travel, actions to take if personnel are away from the camp/site and return to find the camp/site evacuated, etc.) and will brief all newcomers to the site. Additionally, the security manager will, during periods of heightened threat, rebrief the camp/site personnel on responses to incidents, alarms, and warnings, and additional security requirements.

Security managers will establish an evacuation plan for their site. Evacuation plans are a "close hold" item and should not be discussed outside of the local crisis management team, until there is a requirement, based on heightened threat, to do so. Security managers will liaise with adjacent U.S. government/private vendor units for evacuation assistance and Emergency Medical Evacuation assistance, if available. Security managers will be in charge of the evacuation of a site, assisted by other members of local crisis management team.

Post warning/emergency information and other signs in each office and trailer as applicable. Examples include:

"Fire Extinguisher" signs above locations of extinguishers	Emergency contact list (see below)
"No Smoking in Bed" signs	Site/camp maps *Note:* Lodging and office should be clearly marked/numbered.
"Nonpotable Water" signs over sinks	Post the names and locations of the project/office/camp medic and personnel trained in first aid and CPR.

Incident Response

In hostile fire, fires, explosions, or chemical releases, actions to be taken include:

- Shut down COMPANY operations and evacuate the immediate area as directed by COMPANY security and safety personnel.
- Notify appropriate response personnel.
- Account for personnel at the designated assembly area(s).
- Site manager, security, and safety supervisors/managers will assess the need for site evacuation, and evacuate the site as warranted.
- Instead of implementing a work area evacuation, note that small fires or spills posing minimal safety or health hazards may be controlled.
- Response to an incident will use a tiered approach. The security manager will direct the office/facility/site personnel to follow the established procedures for the appropriate tiered response.

Evacuation Procedures

The site security and safety supervisors/managers will designate project/office/site evacuation routes and assembly areas before work/mobilization begins.

Personnel will assemble at the assembly area(s) upon hearing the emergency signal for evacuation. The site security manager, with assistance from the safety supervisor, will account for all personnel at the assembly area.

The local crisis management team will assess the situation and determine the need to conduct an evacuation of the site. Should evacuation of the site be determined as the appropriate response to the threat, the security manager will supervise the evacuation with the assistance of the local crisis management team members. Security managers will notify the functional chain of the decision to evacuate the camp/site. The camp manager will notify the operational chain of the decision to evacuate the camp/site.

The site safety or security managers will prepare an incident/after action report as soon as possible after the incident occurs and submit it to the in-country director of security/safety.

Emergency Medical Treatment

The procedures listed below may be applied to emergency and non-emergency incidents. Injuries and illnesses (including overexposure to contaminants) must be immediately (24 hours) reported to the group safety manager, who will report to the business line director of security and safety.

During nonemergencies, follow these procedures as appropriate:

- Notify appropriate emergency response authorities listed in emergency contacts.
- The site safety supervisor will assume charge during a medical emergency until the ambulance/emergency medical evacuation arrives or until the injured person is admitted to the emergency room.
- Prevent further injury.
- Initiate first aid and CPR where feasible.
- Get medical attention immediately.
- Make certain that the injured person is accompanied to the medical clinic/hospital.
- Report incident as outlined in "Incident Notification and Reporting" section.
- The appropriate medical personnel or safety supervisor will determine mode of transportation and need. Transport for medical evacuation of project site personnel will depend on the number of personnel, urgency of the crisis, and availability of helicopter support, and finally, availability of over-land capability. Rotary lift aircraft could be U.S. government/private vendor or civilian, whichever can be coordinated and in place the soonest. A helicopter landing pad will be prepared at each site as required for medical evacuations. Refer to crisis management plan for more detail.
- If U.S. government/private vendor or coalition emergency medical evacuation support is utilized, the COMPANY site safety and security managers/supervisors will coordinate the preplanned evacuation with the U.S. government/private vendor point of contact.

TASK SPECIFIC EMERGENCY SERVICES CONTACTS

EMERGENCY MEDICAL SERVICES

Emergency surgical hospital	XXX-XXXX
(Emergency medical evacuation/ground ambulance)	
Nearest medical facility	XXX-XXXX
U.S. government/private vendor and civilian	Civilian
Fire department	XXX-XXXX
Poison information center	XXX-XXXX
American Red Cross	XXX-XXXX

GOVERNMENTAL AGENCIES/OFFICES

U.S. or other government agency/client, etc.	XXX-XXXX
U.S. embassy	XXX-XXXX

TRANSPORTATION SERVICES

Airplane charter	Available
Helicopter charter	

UTILITY COMPANIES

Power company	Government Ministry
Gas company	XXX-XXXX
Water company	XXX-XXXX

SECTION 6: SECURITY, EMERGENCY, AND EVACUATION

Security and Evacuation Management Plan

General information

> Plan name and office location
>
> Security and evacuation management plan
>
> COMPANY

Introduction

The security and evacuation management plan (the plan) provides guidelines and direction for actions to be taken in response to various emergency situations, which might impact the safety and security of COMPANY professionals around the world. The plan provides direction to managers who are tasked with emergency planning responsibilities, with the intent being to assist in developing sound processes by which to make decisions during emergency situations. The plan further provides actions to be taken by employees during emergencies. It clarifies the appropriate responses to specific situations and explains the sequential responsibilities as each pertains to the different emergency options available. The plan identifies situations that vary from those confined to specific facilities/sites in a local area, to those that impact on the entire country. Additionally, this plan defines the various interfaces applicable to external organizations.

Emergency situations include but are not limited to:

- Medical emergencies and evacuation
- Nonmedical evacuation
- Natural disasters
- U.S. government/private vendor actions/conflicts
- Civil unrest
- Political instability
- Terrorist activities
- Bomb threats/improvised explosive devices (IEDs)
- Kidnapping

EMERGENCY AND EVACUATION PLAN DEVELOPMENT

This plan has been created for this COMPANY project.
Sources of emergency information:

Television: CNN International
            BBC World News
            Euro News
Radio: Voice of America

Hospital emergency contacts
United Nations regional security office (when established)

Safe Haven

Safe havens are predesignated locations selected as rally points for personnel to meet or where personnel can wait until a period of short-term unrest passes or they are directed to deploy elsewhere. Normally, project sites are considered safe haven locations. There may be periods when employees are directed to relocate to another site or seek refuge at U.S. government or, in some cases, host country government facilities. When UN facilities are established and become available, project employees can seek refuge at any UN location (identified by the white and blue colors on buildings, walls, gates, and signs). Safe havens are:

U.S. consulate/embassy
Any U.S. government compound/facility
Designated project site (currently all sites)

A headcount will be prepared and maintained at the safe haven for force/locator reporting.

The security team leader will determine/designate safe havens to be used in case of an emergency or evacuation. The safe haven selected should be accessible to all personnel, and provide safety, security, and the capability to support personnel for a period of time (personnel may have to wait for the unrest to settle). Depending on the threat and situation, other groups may also be using the same rally point, which could create crowding, confusion, and demand a team approach to problem solving under pressure.

The COMPANY security team leader must be prepared to arrange charter, standby, or reservations promptly if out-of-country evacuation is ordered and commences from the rally point/safe haven.

Transportation/Vehicles

Transportation to and from the support site, work site, and office, as well as any other transport requirement for professionals, may be handled by project drivers, thus normally eliminating a need for other professionals to drive and the need to obtain mandatory documents to drive.

IMPROVISED EXPLOSIVE DEVICE (IED) AND BOMB THREAT PLAN

Scope

The history of IEDs and bomb threats is familiar violence recorded in the Middle East. These activities have created a requirement that practical basic knowledge be made available by the Middle East security manager to expatriate employees, consultants, visitors, and local hires. Knowledge of explosive devices may help employees to better cope with the increase of violent activities by some individuals or groups resorting to the use of IED/bombs to further their own interests.

IED/Bomb Threats

Typically, there are two reasonable explanations for an IED/bomb threat to be transmitted to a specific installation or individual:

- There is real or suspected knowledge that an explosive device will be placed or has been placed in a specific facility or along routes traveled by friendly/contractor personnel, and he or she wants to minimize personal injury or property damage. The informer may be the person who placed the device or someone aware of such information.
- The informer wants to create an atmosphere of anxiety and panic that could result in disruption of normal installation activities.

Objective

The objective of the IED/bomb threat plan is to ensure reasonable actions are taken to protect employees and property if there is an IED/bomb threat incident.

Authority and Responsibility

Professionals working on a project/in an office must be immediately notified when anyone is informed of an IED/bomb threat to the project/office or project site personnel. That person immediately informs the senior project manager and corporate security manager, who in turn:

A. Decides whether or not project personnel should continue work, be immediately evacuated from the project site, or rally at a prearranged point outside of the office or facility. (Senior project managers identify rally points and locations are clearly marked.)
B. Informs on-site security personnel (if any).
C. Informs COMPANY senior management as appropriate (when time allows).

The senior project manager provides updated reports as situations arise, with a complete post-incident report to senior management and corporate security as soon as possible after the event is over.

Receipt of IED/Bomb Threat

- Regardless of who receives the IED/bomb threat or the bomb threat call, the recipient attempts to remain calm and receives and prepares to record as much information as possible (see "Bomb Threat Checklist").
- If possible, the informer or caller is told that the structure is occupied/route is being used and detonation of a bomb could result in death or serious injury to innocent people. This may cause the informer or caller to reconsider actions that may lead to other conversation, which may reveal the location of the IED/bomb.
- When listening to the informer or caller, the recipient tries to detect voice characteristics to help identify the informer. The recipient pays particular attention to the exact words spoken by the informer or caller and documents them immediately on the "Bomb Threat Checklist" form.

- Although the informer or caller should not be interrupted, the recipient determines an appropriate time in the conversation to ask for the informer's name and group affiliation.
- The recipient tries to determine if the informer is familiar with either the facility, the work being conducted at the installation, or someone working there or involved with the project.

In the case of a telephone call, the call recipient must keep the line open (do not hang up) following the call. This may allow authorities to trace the call after the caller hangs up. At all times during the call, the call recipient does everything possible to remain calm and keep the conversation moving, and gathers as much information as possible. As soon as the call recipient can do so, he or she records specific notes of the conversation to aid in post-incident identification of the caller.

Although site security, U.S. government/private vendor, or host country police (if available) efforts and technological capability may be applied differently than in the United States, it is important to keep in mind they are in charge of their task. COMPANY professionals are instructed to cooperate with U.S./host country law enforcement while ensuring their searches of the office/job site for any explosive or incendiary device.

Other Types of Threats

Mail handlers, drivers, couriers, and any office personnel who handle mail need to look for suspicious-looking letters and packages. If a suspicious letter or package is noted, the recipient remains calm and notifies the project/office manager and corporate security manager immediately. Everything pertaining to the letter or package is *not* to be handled and is to be saved to assist in the investigation that will follow.

Post-Incident Action

If suspicious items are determined to be safe by site security, U.S. government/host country government, or law enforcement, the COMPANY team leader makes a determination about whether or not to return professionals to their place of duty. If a suspicious item is found and deemed unsafe (further actions required) and the office/job site has not yet been evacuated, the team leader may order an evacuation based on his assessment of the location and size of the suspicious item. If office/job site professionals discover the suspicious item, they are not to touch, move, or jar it in any way. All suspicious items will be evaluated by site security, U.S. government/host country law enforcement, or U.S. government/private vendor personnel as far as disposition of the items are concerned.

After suspicious items have been cleared, the team leader or corporate security manager makes the decision concerning return to work.

Post-Detonation Action

It is possible that a bomb could be placed in a facility or office space and not be located, or a bomb threat call to announce the threat of the bomb is not received. In an effort to consider all related possibilities surrounding this type of incident, it is valuable to list the basic responsibilities of the project/office management in case a bomb explodes unexpectedly at a project office or job site. Management's first responsibility, in case of a detonation, is to account for all expatriates, other professionals, and visitors as defined under "Applicability and Responsibility." Once this has been done, the following is accomplished as soon as possible:

- Ensure those injured in the blast receive medical treatment as quickly as possible.
- Notify site security, U.S. government/host country law enforcement, or U.S. government/private vendor so that an investigation of the incident can begin quickly.
- Inform corporate senior management and client as soon as possible of the situation, extent of damages, injuries, and casualties.

As the worst-case situation may result in injury or death to the team leader, the project staff must have a clearly defined chain of command so that order can be restored quickly to ensure the welfare of the project expatriate personnel and other employees.

Once site security and U.S. government/host country authorities have finished their investigation and corporate senior management post-detonation requirements have been fulfilled, the team leader in coordination with corporate management must determine the next steps insofar as the project is concerned.

The corporate security manager provides a complete post-detonation incident report to senior management as soon as possible after the incident.

CRIMINAL ACTIVITY

Background

As some expatriates may be working overseas or in the host countries for the first time, it is essential for them to review some of the general differences between living in the United States and living outside of the United States relative to criminal activity exposure.

Criminal activities are often quite different from the problems one would experience in cities in other locations around the world. All project professionals are expected to be cautious and avoid those areas where they would most likely be vulnerable to be selected as a random target of violence. For example, in some countries, it is obviously unwise for project professionals to be walking around alone outside the confines of the project site, in the city, or built-up areas.

Personal/Residence Security

The most important part of personal security is being cautious and following one's intuition. However, it is each expatriate's responsibility to be prudent in his or her actions to remain as safe as possible. To further promote a secure environment, all expatriates are encouraged to share any unfortunate experiences, including cultural nuances, with one another as a learning tool to avoid future confrontations.

Travel Security

Travel to and from locations in host countries must be carefully planned. All project professionals should communicate their travel plans directly with project management or their designee. In some countries, travel outside of secure locations might include escorts.

Terrorist Activity/Threat Reporting

Any person discovering or otherwise acquiring knowledge of actual or potential terrorist activity will report such information immediately to the project manager and corporate security manager. This includes terrorist threats as well as actions impacting professionals and assets.

The project/office management shall assess the actual or potential impact on professionals and assets and shall report its assessment to the home office, corporate security, and the client. The security team leader has full authority, based on current events, to determine actions to be taken at project sites. The security team leader shall take appropriate actions including but not limited to:

- Assigning additional guards to observe fixed assets or to escort professionals as needed
- Implementing adequate security measures to protect project professionals
- Varying routes for movement of professionals and equipment to avoid routines
- Reporting all suspicious activities to appropriate authorities
- Evacuating or relocating professionals as required
- Restricting professionals to designated locations (lockdown)

NONMEDICAL EMERGENCY EVACUATION PLAN

Scope and Purpose

It may become necessary to evacuate nonessential or all project/office professionals from selected or all site locations, depending on safety and security conditions. The security team leader, in coordination with the corporate security manager, will determine initiating the implementation of this plan. When the decision to evacuate project/office professionals for nonmedical reasons is made, the security team leader may direct implementation of parts or all of the plan. The plan provides guidance and responsibilities, options available for in-country and out-of-country relocation and evacuation, COMPANY professional responsibilities, criteria concerning primary and alternate locations, actions to be taken at various levels of the operation, and mode of transport to final locations, as appropriate.

Applicability and Responsibility

This plan applies to all COMPANY expatriates, business travelers, and associated visitors. In some situations, the team leader may deem it appropriate to include foreign expatriate employees in evacuation plans. Appropriate actions in this plan will be directed by the security team leader based on his assessment and evaluation of the situation and local conditions, in consultation with the other members of the management team, client, embassy or consulate general, and the corporate office as necessary.

Travel Documentation

The project manager ensures all personnel possess the necessary official travel documents prior to any site evacuation. Business managers at each site maintain a photocopy of all professionals' visas and passports. Specifically, each individual must have the following documents in hand:

- Passport
- Official IDs
- International certificate of vaccination

Emergency Communication

In an emergency or in standby conditions, the project/office telephones will have a 24-hour watch. The telephone watch will be coordinated and established by the crisis team leader. The fax line will be operational 24 hours. All project locations will initiate and maintain a 24-hour telephone watch until stand-down is directed by the team leader.

If telephone communications are disabled, alternate emergency communication to the appropriate project managers and security manager may be established by telephone communication to the satellite, cellular, and email systems.

COMPANY and Expatriate Professional
Asset (Personal Property) Protection

Under most conditions, it is safe to presume that the COMPANY project/office professionals and staff will not be in any significant position of risk, and they will be able to stay on the site or relocate to a U.S. government/private vendor or host country facility. If leaving the site, transport/convoy should be coordinated/arranged with the corporate security manager. The business manager and the staff under the business manager's supervision will maintain security of all COMPANY physical assets (funds) and COMPANY project documents. All professionals should maintain a current inventory of personal items at site/office/lodging for insurance or possible company reimbursement.

Out-of-Country Evacuation

If it is determined, due to the nature of the threat, that out-of-country evacuation is necessary, the plan will be implemented to evacuate employees from project locations to designated locations to await required air/ ground transport. The security team leader may direct only nonessential professionals be evacuated out-of-country, or he/she may determine all professionals need to be evacuated.

If out-of-country evacuation is not immediately feasible, professionals will seek refuge at a designated site location, U.S. government/private vendor or host country facility, if feasible, or in a United Nations facility nearest to their location (if established).

The security team leader will coordinate in-country relocation and out-of-country evacuation with the corporate security manager to ensure the safest evacuation for COMPANY expatriates.

Based on the nature of the threat, out-of-country evacuation may preclude any stopover in any designated in-country location.

Evacuation out-of-country may involve ground transport to an in-country location where either U.S. government/private vendor or charter air assets will be utilized for further transport out-of-country. Depending on the threat, U.S. government/private vendor air transport could be used to relocate professionals to another in-country location for further transport out-of-country or to relocate professionals out-of-country.

Evacuation Using Air from a Designated Location

If an out-of-country evacuation is planned and air is to be utilized, the primary and alternate in-country destinations will be the international airport, or any other designated U.S./host government facility with capability or a United Nations facility, if established.

If commercial, charter, or U.S. government/private vendor air is utilized from the international airport, the designated manager, when directed by the security team leader, will take those actions necessary to coordinate required evacuation of COMPANY professionals located in the immediate area.

Transportation to a primary or alternate in-country designated location for out-of-country evacuation will normally require ground transport. Often, there are limited transport assets to rapidly relocate all professionals from their normal location at one time. The corporate security manager in coordination with the security team leader will ensure proper escort

305

(which might include private armed/unarmed security) is available for all evacuating professionals to the designated location and air departure location. Depending on transportation availability, close coordination of transport assets and qualified security personnel will be essential.

Out-of-country egress may be established for groups or individuals as short-term or long-term evacuation, based on the nature of the threat and the needs of the project.

- Short-term country evacuation will be to Country A or Country B. Visas may be purchased upon arrival in both countries.
- Long-term out-of-country evacuation will be to the evacuee's home in the United States or country of origin.

Evacuation Using Ground Transportation Only

If out-of-country evacuation cannot be supported by air as a result of security conditions at designated locations or due to lack of air resources, evacuation may be conducted using ground transportation to another host country where air transport can be arranged. In this case, two ground transportation routes are available. Professionals may be directed to rally at a designated location as required prior to convoy movement using these routes. U.S. government/private vendor/host country support for these convoys should be considered and requested. All professionals should carry their evacuation kit.

Evacuation to Country A's Border

The regional crisis team leader in coordination with the COMPANY security manager and site security managers will organize and direct ground convoys to proceed to Highway X and on to Highway Y (stay on the route marked Alpha and Bravo) and move north to Country A's border. The convoys will continue on to a designated location where there is an international airport where air transport can be arranged to final designations.

Previous reconnaissance and use of the route to Country A's border by COMPANY employees indicates that travel time from office/facility to the border is approximately 3.0 hours, with 30–45 minutes travel through the city of XXXXX.

Evacuation to Country B's Border

The senior project manager in coordination with the COMPANY security manager and site security managers will organize and direct ground convoys to proceed to Highway T and on to Highway U and move west to Country B's border and on to XXXX, where air transport will be arranged to designations.

Previous use of this route by COMPANY persons traveling to Country B indicates that from office/facility to Country B's border is approximately 8 hours, and approximately 3 hours from the border to XXXXX. Convoys may experience up to 3.0 hours delay processing through the border point.

The director of business/administration should be fully prepared with funding arranged by the COMPANY senior project manager and will receive instructions to promptly purchase air travel tickets on the most suitable outbound flight to Country C or XXXXXX within 3 hours of notice for either short-term or long-term evacuation.

If ground transport to XXXXX or a destination in Country A is utilized, the director of business/administration should be fully prepared with funding arranged by the COMPANY senior project manager and will receive instructions to promptly purchase air travel tickets from these locations on the most suitable outbound flight if appropriate.

Project Reporting during Evacuation Period

If work continues on the project, the business manager and the staff under the business manager's supervision will provide daily reports on activities and progress to the project office. In a situation where the project is to be permanently shut down, the business manager will make the arrangements for the recovery of COMPANY assets and documents.

Evacuation Procedures

Evacuation operations include personnel notification procedures, assembly of professionals to be evacuated, passing information up and down the organizational chain, and mobilizing personnel and resources.

Evacuation operations will be divided into three stages, which also serve to inform personnel of the status of the operation:

- Warning/level 1: Professionals are ready and transportation and related procedures are in place.

- Assemble/level 2: All professionals to be evacuated move to designated marshaling areas ready to travel.
- Proceed/level 3: Evacuate the area by the prescribed method to designated locations.

Level 1 Threat

General internal social, political, or U.S. government/private vendor instability may be manifested in the occurrence of incidents that may or may not be directed specifically against COMPANY or other U.S. interests in the region. Additionally, regional political tensions or heightened U.S. government/private vendor activity may exist that potentially affects U.S. regional interests. This is a period during which routine collection and assessment of information about local and international events is in progress.

Actions

- Brief all expatriate professionals regarding personal security at their place of work, support location, and in transit to and from work. Emphasize maintaining a low profile, avoiding troubled areas, and avoiding provocative behavior.
- Brief security, guards, and drivers and place on alert.
- Identify and be prepared to evacuate nonessential professionals.
- Implement additional security at the support location, office, and job site (tighter access control, locked-down and additional security staged around the above areas).
- Establish communications with local contacts, to include the U.S. government/private vendor, and monitor the situation.
- Notify the home office.
- Maintain liaison with the U.S. embassy or consulate and the corporate security manager.
- Keep professionals informed. It is important to develop a procedure to deal with rumors that have a tendency to emerge with the onset of any crisis situation. Left unattended, rumors can have a demoralizing effect.
- Identify or set aside documents (company or client sensitive) for possible future destruction. Thought should be given to begin copying of data to disks and "wiping off" all hard drives and systems.
- Check previously established routes to the designated primary and alternate safe locations, as well as the airport, for traversability under emergency conditions.

- Ensure that fuel and gasoline storage levels are adequate or available.
- Review previously established staging areas for assembling employees.

Level 2 Threat

This phase should be initiated when, in the judgment of the security team leader (or directed by embassy/consulate personnel), a situation has reached a level of tension or instability that could lead to partial or complete evacuation of expatriate professionals. The earlier an evacuation decision can be made, the more likely it can be affected in a calm, secure, and less politically sensitive atmosphere.

Activity primarily applies to site and local incidents, but may apply to regional and national incidents. Activities include intensification of regional conflict and U.S. government/private vendor activity and escalated internal social and political instability manifested by frequent incidents, some of which may or may not be directed at the project or other U.S. interests.

Actions

In addition to all activities identified in level 1, the following actions will be implemented:

- Continue normal work routines; however, certain definitive actions, such as obtaining required clearances and conducting programmed document destruction of company or client-sensitive documents, to begin on the order of senior management, should be undertaken as appropriate.
- Copy data to disks and "wipe off" all hard drives and systems, as appropriate.
- Order "stand fast" for all personnel.
- Notify security/guards (if present) to strengthen security (reassign security/guards to office entrances/exits, support site, and job site), as appropriate. Add security if none present.
- Place primary and alternate safe havens on notice.
- If incident endangers professionals, nonessential staff and others may be transported to previously identified safe haven locations.
- Secure personal and company property.
- Notify home office. Provide accurate list of personnel (professionals, visitors, etc.), to include locations and telephone numbers.

- Validate emergency contact list data.
- Address the possibility of having to secure or abandon personal property.

Level 3 Threat

This phase should be initiated when, in the judgment of the security team leader (or directed by embassy/consulate personnel or U.S. government/ private vendor), the situation has deteriorated to the point that the decision to evacuate is imminent or has already been made. Generally, when there is a breakdown in the ability of the local authority to control the frequency and severity of incidents against project work/support sites, the situation has deteriorated to the point where there is imminent danger. It is probable that regional and national incidents have heightened and caused potential antisentiment or regional chaos. It is assumed that total withdrawal of professionals will not meet active resistance from the local authorities.

Actions

In addition to the actions described in level 2, the following will be implemented:

- Coordinate with home office for evacuation assistance as required.
- If incident is national in nature and it is not safe to remain "stand fast," and an evacuation to a designated safe haven location or from the country is required, establish the links for transportation. (If at all possible, notify management in advance and.of the destination.)
- Coordinate payment of foreign expatriates and local staff and agencies for services rendered.
- Coordinate the release of all local hire personnel.
- Coordinate the evacuation of all nonessential personnel.
- Be prepared to evacuate essential professionals.
- Ensure communications to home office, corporate security manager, embassy or consulate, and others as appropriate are completed and, if possible, that authorization for an evacuation has been obtained.
- Advise client of evacuation.
- Initiate shutdown of project, to include secure storage or destruction of sensitive documents and records as required.
- Order evacuation of personnel with armed escorts as required.
- Rally at designated safe haven location or at the airport as directed. Coordinate the release of airline tickets and emergency cash.

- Notify home office and corporate security upon arrival to the safe haven location or airport.

Movement

Site Evacuation

Modes of site evacuation to primary or alternate in-country destinations are ranked by preference.

- By road to international airport and fixed-wing aircraft to Country A or Country B or country of origin
- By rotary lift aircraft to international airport (this movement can commence at the project sites)
- By road to Country A border (continue to designated city for air transport)
- By road to Country B border to XXXXX (for air transport)
- By road to U.S. or coalition facility and U.S. government/private vendor or charter air to out-of-country destination

If over-land evacuation is to be undertaken to international airport or to designated primary or alternate locations, the team leader will ensure all vehicles are fully serviced and fueled and provisions for refueling are established. The security team leader, through the COMPANY business manager, will ensure necessary provisions of food and water are established for all evacuees.

Each evacuee will be permitted one suitcase and one carry-on bag during implementation of this plan.

Coordinating Instructions

Coordinating country egress or evacuation involves proactive planning; therefore, when evacuation becomes a reality, the remaining steps are well in place. Through daily close review and scrutiny of events reflected in credible news sources, as well as continuous close contact with the U.S. government/private vendor, the UN regional security manager (if established), the U.S. embassy/consulate, and other credible sources, the senior project manager and corporate security can stay abreast of unrest, terrorist activities, and political uprising. As a result of this continuous scrutiny, the senior project manager is always prepared to initiate appropriate action at a moment's notice to ensure the safest egress for professionals.

COMPANY Security (Nonmedical) Evacuation Alternative

Although the procedures to support a rapid nonmedical evacuation are best arranged at the local level, should local assets fail to perform to the level expected by the senior project manager, International SOS provides another alternative for the project manager to consider. SOS can support emergency nonmedical cases of civil uprising, insurrection, war, demonstrations/attacks against project personnel, and other civil disturbances and disasters.

International SOS telephone numbers:

Extraction Directed by the U.S. Government/ Private Vendor or U.S. Embassy/Consulate

Under certain circumstances the situation may be of a nature that requires the U.S. government to have command and control. This command and control includes the possibility of a U.S. government/private vendor extraction. In all cases, the senior project manager will follow and fully comply with the directions provided by the U.S. government/private vendor and U.S. embassy/consulate general.

9.1   AREA MAP

9.2   EMERGENCY DATA FORM
COMPANY

Personal Data

Name: _____

Title: _____

Present address: _____

_____

_____

Phone number: _____

Address in-country: _____

_____

_____

Phone number: _____

Date of birth: _____

Place: _____

Marital status: _____

Citizen: _____

Height: _____

Weight: _____

Sex: _____

Name of spouse: _____

Social security number: _____

Passport number: _____

_____

I hereby certify that the above information is true and correct to the best of my knowledge and belief.

Signature _____

Date _____

9.3   Contact List

Refer to project data sheets, Table 1A, or appropriate team tab.

9.4   Evacuation Kit

Individual's Ready Bag

- Currency (U.S. and local, if possible)
- Food/water for approximately 3 days
    1. Canned and nonperishable food
    2. Can opener
    3. Knife
- Nonfood emergency supplies
    1. Blanket/towels/bath cloths
    2. Toilet articles and tissue (to include feminine hygiene products as appropriate)
    3. Extra clothing (appropriate for weather conditions)
    4. First aid kit, prescription and nonprescription medicines, glasses, and contacts, etc.
    5. Maps
    6. Flashlight/batteries
    7. Insect repellent
    8. Canned and nonperishable food
    9. Can opener
    10. Bottled water
- Personal documentation and papers
    1. ID card (forms of personal identification)
    2. Passport (also copy of picture page if possible)
    3. International certificate of vaccination
- Other considerations
    1. Checkbook
    2. Bank book and bank receipts
    3. Credit cards, traveler's checks
    4. Airline ticket

Site management may also identify additional items, depending on space.

9.5 Key Emergency Contacts

When using telephone communication with COMPANY's corporate offices

Electronic communication with COMPANY's corporate offices (use
_____._____@ wgint.com)
Security information services: Access through corporate security at
XXX-XXX-XXXX or email request to XXXXXX.

Refer to project data sheets, Table 1A, or appropriate team tab for other contact information.

SECTION 7: CASUALTY

Casualty Notification Plan in the Event of an Employee Fatality

1. A member of the company's upper-management team, including a human resources representative, makes a "best effort" to inform the spouse/family *in person* of the accident. If it is not possible to make a face-to-face notification, a member of clergy or a police officer may be a possible candidate. The goal is to notify the spouse/family quickly. A phone call is a last resort because of its impersonal nature. (See the following pages for more detail.)
2. The designated company representative remains at the professional's home until other family members arrive or for as long as he or she can.
3. The media may attempt to contact family members. You cannot prevent them from talking to the media. It is their right to speak to the media if they wish.
4. Determine whether the professional's family is in need of money to cover small expenses. If so, it may be appropriate to provide assistance in this area with the VP of human resource's approval. The few dollars spent will come back in goodwill.
5. Maintain contact with a relative or close friend of the spouse or family to ensure that funeral arrangements and related items are being handled.

6. In case of a local national employee, follow the procedure above and any local customs as appropriate.

Note: If the fatality involves a nonemployee, contact the individual's employer for notification procedures. Contact your insurance company and legal counsel as soon as possible.

Fatality Notification

In the event of a professional's fatality, you may be called upon to notify the spouse or family member. This is a traumatic event for both the relative and you. Here are some guidelines to help with this process.

Do your homework. Obtain the full name, address, and social security number of the deceased. Next, get the full name of the next of kin, the relationship (wife, brother, mother, etc.), and determine if the family members are English speaking. Gather all information relative to the case so you can provide an explanation.

Determine where you will meet. Will the contact be at home, work, or school? If it is outside of the home, arrange with the relative's employer or school for a private place to meet. Verify that you are talking to the correct person, i.e., "Are you Sandy Johnson's sister?"

Do not go alone. Take a fellow professional, friend of the deceased, member of the clergy, or police or fire official to support you.

Decide in advance what you will say. There is no easy way to say that someone has died, so do not even try. Speak simply and directly. Using terms like *mortally wounded* only confuses people. While it is not necessary to be blunt or cold, at some point it is necessary to say *dead* or *died*. Example: "Mrs. Jones, there was a very bad accident this morning at the project. Charlie was moving a ladder and fell over a guardrail. The paramedics did everything they could, but he died instantly."

Do not lie. If you tell a mother that her son died with her name on his lips but she later learns his death was immediate, there is a conflict. It may not be necessary to offer all of the details. Example: If the spouse asks, "Did he suffer much?" an appropriate answer might be, "I don't think so."

Be prepared for emotions. There will be shock, denial, grief, numbness, and anger. These emotional reactions will be directed at the deceased, at you, and at the medical staff. Let the relative vent these feelings. Use common sense and do what seems appropriate at this time. Some people will appreciate a touch of a hand; others will not.

Decide what not to say. By not preparing what to say, you may end up saying things that you will later regret. Example: In an effort to offer words of comfort, do not say, "He's with God now" or "You're young and will find someone else." Instead, say, "I'm so sorry this has happened to you" or "What can I do to help you right now?"

Always listen. The formula is 90% listening and 10% talking. If the relative needs to go to the hospital or funeral home, you may offer to drive or get a cab. If there are children involved, help arrange for a sitter or a friend to look after them. When appropriate, offer assistance in getting in touch with the life insurance company, social security, and so forth.

When it is over. You have gone through an extremely stressful event. Take care of yourself now. Use your critical incident stress counselor to review the difficult process you went through. No one ever gets comfortable with this part of the job.

The security team leader will notify the incident response team leader, and the project manager will identify a COMPANY manager who will act as an escort for the remains.

The security team leader will make all other notifications, as listed below.

Notification: (To be immediately notified upon receipt)

Establish family/relative permanent contact: Human resources person assigned to family or designated relative as company's permanent point of contact.

Backup to:

Personal effects:

Personal effects of the individual will be gathered and sent to a location designated by the family.

Backup to:

Personal visit: TBD; company representative will perform a personal visit to the family or relative.

Primary candidates:

Follow-up: The purpose of this task is to double-check that the above assignments are in progress or already completed.

Notification of Various Project Site Locations

Task includes notifying various site locations of the incident, arranging the following:

- Job site observance (type and extent determined by site members)
- Demobilization that may be necessary for close companions or members associated with tragedy
- Counseling for professionals, if required
- Project site employees to call home assuring family of their safety

Benefits Due Beneficiaries

Human resources will gather all company and insurance benefits and present data to the family or designated beneficiary.

Professional Counseling

Arrange professional counseling for the family or individual members of the family if they desire the service.

Casualty Evacuation of Company Employee

A personal security detail (PSD) will, as needed, be responsible to contact the medical or casualty evacuation in case a COMPANY employee or joint venture partner is either wounded or killed in the country. The COMPANY safety or security personnel at the location will notify the medical evacuation as needed. All PSDs are equipped with GPS (grid position station). Other COMPANY employees have a grid locator on their satellite phones.

If proclaimed dead on arrival (DOA), the treating physician will fill out the death certificate and deliver the remains to the appropriate collection points for evacuation to the United States.

Country   City   Phone Number (DSN)   Point of Contact

The COMPANY human resources director will contact the U.S. embassy in the country and will work with the security team leader and corporate security manager for repatriation of the employee's remains using the International SOS response network by calling the operations center at 1-215-245-4707 or emailing www.internationalsos.com. International SOS will not send aircraft to Iraq, but can respond with transportation of the remains to the United States from the country.

After the remains have been transported to the United States, International SOS will transport within the United States to a location agreed upon by the family and COMPANY human resources.

The International SOS contact number for U.S.-based assistance is 1-800-523-6586.

Identification required for transportation of expatriate casualties includes:

- Personal identification
- Passport or copy
- Death certificate

Identification required for transportation of foreign national casualties includes:

- Personal identification
- Passport or copy
- Death certificate

SECTION 8: HOSTAGE REPORTING (KIDNAPPING): KIDNAPPING NOTIFICATION PLAN

1. A member of the company's upper-management team, including a Human Resources Representative, makes a "best effort" to inform the spouse/family *in person* of the kidnapping. If it is not possible to make a face-to-face notification, a member of clergy or a police officer may be a possible candidate. The goal is to notify the spouse/family quickly. A phone call is a last resort because of its impersonal nature. (See the following pages for more detail.)

2. The designated company representative remains at the employee's home until other family members arrive or for as long as he or she can.

3. The media may attempt to contact family members. You cannot prevent them from talking to the media. It is their right to speak to the media if they wish.

4. Determine whether the employee's family is in need of money to cover small expenses. If so, it may be appropriate to provide assistance in this area with the senior VP of human resource's approval. The few dollars spent will come back in goodwill.

5. Maintain contact with a relative or close friend of the spouse or family to ensure that related items are being handled.
6. In case of a local national employee, follow the above procedures and any local customs as appropriate.

Note: Implement the hostage reporting procedures outlined in this section. If the kidnapping involves a nonemployee, contact the individual's employer for notification procedures. Contact your insurance company and legal counsel as soon as possible.

U.S. embassy telephone numbers: XXX-XXX-XXXX
RSO: XXX-XXX-XXXX

Initial information to be provided:

1. Name, phone number, and email of person reporting incident
2. Date of incident
3. Time of incident
4. Location of incident (as specific as possible)
5. Brief description of what happened
6. Description of people involved
7. Description of vehicle involved
8. Hostage name/nationality
9. Employee name
10. Name, phone number, and email address of person who will take follow-up questions from embassy or law enforcement representatives

SECTION 10: OTHER

Crisis Procedures for a Bomb Threat

Note: If you receive a bomb threat and contact your local police department, they will dispatch only one uniformed officer because of the high number of bomb threats received by police departments throughout the United States. The only exception is if you find a suspicious object; then a bomb squad will be dispatched. The officer will not be familiar with your site, so you will be asked to perform a visual search. Use your best judgment on how to implement the following information.

Bomb threats can be made by pranksters, political terrorists, cranks, criminal extortionists, disgruntled employees, or even an employee looking for a few hours off work. The threat can arrive over the telephone, in the mail, or via a written message. *All threats must be taken seriously.* If the threat comes on a piece of paper, do not handle it any more than necessary, and use gloves, a handkerchief, tongs, etc., to avoid ruining fingerprints.

Crisis Procedures in the Event of a Phone Threat

1. Keep the caller on the line for as long as possible. If possible, ask the following questions:
   - When will the bomb go off?
   - Where is the bomb located?
   - What type of bomb is it?
   - How is the bomb activated?
   - Why are you doing this?

2. Take note of the following:
   - Time of call?
   - Exact words of caller?
   - Male or female?
   - Accent?
   - Familiar voice?
   - Background noises?
   - Did the caller seem to be familiar with the building or location?

3. Immediately notify the senior person on site or the team leader who will determine whether or not to evacuate the premises.
4. Immediately notify the local police and cooperate fully with their instructions.
5. Do not allow anyone except authorized personnel to enter the job site. All visitors should be escorted from the job site, but remain available for questioning.
6. The team leader should determine if media attention is likely. If so, the corporate spokesperson should be dispatched to assist in this area.
7. Notify the project owner/developer.

BOMB THREAT CHECKLIST

Date: _____

Time call received: _____

Time call terminated: _____

Telephone number where call was received: _____

Exact words of caller:

Ask Questions   **Do Not Interrupt the Caller**

When is the bomb going to
explode?
Where is the bomb right now?   _____

What does it look like?   _____

Did you place the bomb?   _____

What will cause it to explode?   _____

From where are you calling?   _____

Why did you place the bomb?   _____

What is your name?   _____

Description of Caller's Voice

☐ Male   ☐ Female   ☐ Young   ☐ Middle age   ☐ Old
☐ Accent   ☐ Well spoken ☐ Foul   ☐ Incoherent
☐ Angry   ☐ Irrational ☐ Calm   ☐ Nasal
☐ Stutter   ☐ Whispering ☐ Excited   ☐ Deep breathing
☐ Cracking voice ☐ Raspy ☐ Disguised ☐ Slow
☐ Soft   ☐ Familiar   ☐ Ragged   ☐ Rapid
☐ Loud   ☐ Crying   ☐ Distinct   ☐ Normal
☐ Laughter ☐ Deep   ☐ Slurred   ☐ Clearing throat
☐ Message read by caller   ☐ Message taped/recorded

If voice was familiar, who did it sound like? Local national?

Background Noises

☐ Street noise   ☐ Animal noise   ☐ Voices   ☐ Static
☐ Air   ☐ Voices   ☐ PA system   ☐ House noises
☐ Shopping mall ☐ Cars   ☐ Airplanes   ☐ Office machines
☐ Motors   ☐ Music   ☐ Telephone booth ☐ Local call
☐ Long distance ☐ Other: _____

Name of employee receiving the threat: _____

Office location: _____

Telephone number: _____

Other Information
Comments:

Do Not Interrupt   Keep the Caller on the Line   Do Not Hang Up

Search Procedures

1. Do not turn on the lights, throw any switches, or use the telephone in a search area because a bomb could be attached. Turn off radio transmitters in the area because some bombs can be triggered by radio waves. An ample number of flashlights should be available to aid with the search.

2. The police, fire department, or other officials normally will *not* help search for a bomb on private property. The most senior person on site will determine which personnel will be asked to initiate a search.

3. Visually search a room in sections, starting at floor level and going around the room in one direction. Then search at waist level

323

around the room again, and finally, search the upper walls and ceiling areas around the room. Listen for any unusual noises.

4. If an object is found, have all personnel evacuate the area. *Immediately* notify the authorities, giving the location, size, and shape of the object. Do not touch or move the item. Never place anything directly on the item and do not immerse it in water.

5. The team leader will determine if an evacuation should take place. If an evacuation is ordered, employees should stay a minimum of 300 feet from the building and be prepared to find cover immediately.

APPENDIX E: WORKPLACE VIOLENCE PROCEDURES

Note: A violent workplace incident would be considered a crisis, and the crisis management procedures outlined in this manual should be put in place.

WORKPLACE VIOLENCE THREAT

According to OSHA's 1998 Census of Fatal Injuries, homicide is the nation's second leading cause of occupational fatalities, just behind workplace accidents. While the great majority of these incidents occur in situations where employees have contact with the public, no workplace—including construction sites—is immune to workplace violence. *Take all threats of workplace violence very seriously.*

CRISIS PROCEDURES WHEN WORKPLACE VIOLENCE IS THREATENED

The following checklist has been developed to help you to reduce the risk that a violent incident will occur once a threat has been reported. This is not intended to replace your company policy, but rather to be used as a supplement to help you respond quickly to threats of violence.

STEP 1: VERIFY INFORMATION

☐ Conduct a brief preliminary interview of the employee(s) who reported the allegation to determine as much of the following information as possible:
- What was the threat?
- Who made the threat?
- When was the threat made?
- Could it have been a joke?

- Who or what was the threat directed at?
- Why was the threat made?
- Were there any other witnesses?
- Does the employee want his or her identity known to the person who is accused of making or behaving in a threatening manner?

☐ Verify the information through further interviews with witnesses or a site visit.

STEP 2: ASSESS RISK

☐ Determine whether there is imminent danger to employees or the site.

☐ Determine if the threatening employee is still on site.

STEP 3: CONTAIN SITUATION

☐ If confronted by a potential aggressor, lower your voice, speak slowly and clearly. Minimize your gestures and avoid getting into an argument.

☐ If possible, remove the employee from the workplace until the situation has been resolved. (Company policy will determine the enforcement of punitive employment measures. Some companies may hold hearings to determine the fate of the employee, while others may have a zero tolerance policy, which calls for immediate termination.)

☐ Determine whether to contact local law enforcement authorities.

☐ Decide whether additional security precautions are necessary to protect employees or property.

STEP 4: CONDUCT A THOROUGH INVESTIGATION

☐ Conduct a thorough investigation by reinterviewing all witnesses to the threat.

☐ Make arrangements to interview the alleged threatening employee.

☐ Decide which personnel should be present to interview the alleged threatening employee.

☐ Determine where to hold the interview and whether security precautions should be taken.

☐ Decide whether to reveal the name of the employee who reported the threatening remarks or behavior.

☐ Present allegations to the employee.

STEP 5: MONITOR AND REASSESS SITUATION

☐ Monitor the situation to determine whether there is a continued risk to employees or the site.

☐ Decide whether to continue to maintain extra security precautions.

☐ Decide whether to consult local law enforcement authorities.

☐ Provide counseling support for employees who were impacted by threatening behavior or remarks.

INDEX